Fashion and Motherhood

Fashion and Motherhood

Image, Material, Identity

Edited by
Laura Snelgrove

Foreword by
Christina Moon

BLOOMSBURY VISUAL ARTS
LONDON • NEW YORK • OXFORD • NEW DELHI • SYDNEY

BLOOMSBURY VISUAL ARTS
Bloomsbury Publishing Plc, 50 Bedford Square, London, WC1B 3DP, UK
Bloomsbury Publishing Inc, 1359 Broadway, New York, NY 10018, USA
Bloomsbury Publishing Ireland, 29 Earlsfort Terrace, Dublin 2, D02 AY28, Ireland

BLOOMSBURY, BLOOMSBURY VISUAL ARTS and the Diana logo are trademarks
of Bloomsbury Publishing Plc

First published in Great Britain 2024
Paperback edition published 2025

Cover design by Holly Capper
Cover image © GK Hart/Vicky Hart via Getty Images

Bloomsbury Publishing Plc does not have any control over, or responsibility for, any
third-party websites referred to or in this book. All internet addresses given in this book
were correct at the time of going to press. The author and publisher regret any
inconvenience caused if addresses have changed or sites have ceased to exist, but can
accept no responsibility for any such changes.

A catalogue record for this book is available from the British Library.

A catalog record for this book is available from the Library of Congress.

ISBN: HB: 978-1-3502-7669-7
       PB: 978-1-3502-7673-4
       ePDF: 978-1-3502-7670-3
       eBook: 978-1-3502-7671-0

Typeset by RefineCatch Limited, Bungay, Suffolk

For product safety related questions contact productsafety@bloomsbury.com.

To find out more about our authors and books visit www.bloomsbury.com
and sign up for our newsletters.

Contents

Illustrations

Preface

This collection was conceived in early 2020, just before the Covid-19 pandemic made its way around the world. The book's process of creation has been shaped by this world-historical moment, of course, but also by the more intimate conditions faced by the contributors as academics (and, in many cases, mothers); we've birthed children and dissertations, become grandparents and full-time caretakers, grieved losses, changed jobs and cities, and in some cases left academia altogether. These micro- and macro-realities make their way into the book in both obvious and implicit ways, which I think is entirely appropriate to scholarship on such an intimate range of topics.

When I was pregnant with and then parenting my first baby, I was teaching undergraduate courses in fashion studies and often found myself populating my lectures with examples that related back to the profoundly bodily, maddeningly social, identity-shaking experience I was having outside the classroom. I can't say I found much traction with my students, but I also wasn't finding nearly enough within fashion scholarship that spoke to the maternal. The impetus for this book came from the desire to create, gather, and contribute more motherhood-related research to the fashion studies literature. After all, I knew I wasn't alone as a fashion researcher who, upon having a child, had found it difficult to ignore the influence that parenting had on my dressed body in social space and how I felt about it.

After a decade of curiosity, I realize that a robust conversation was being had in the neighboring field of motherhood studies and that of course there was more motherhood content hiding within fashion and dress history than I initially knew. This book joyfully proposes that the two fields talk to each other to share more of what we've all learned about these two twinned experiences that take place in culture as well as in and on individual bodies. The volume is very much a product of collective imagining and a proposal for where future research on these deeply linked subjects may go, rather than a final word or attempt at a unified theory of the fashioning of motherhood.

As mothers around the world face new and increasing challenges, from reproductive to civil rights, from threats to the safety and freedom of the next generation with which we're tasked, let's use research to keep illuminating the ways in which institutions oppress us, experiences unite us, and our identities empower us.

Foreword

Christina Moon

I search for mothers in writing and clothing.

I search for the ones that resemble my own. All the ones that have raised me. I have many. I search for her in the silhouettes of clothing, in the changing shape of the body, her haircut, the style, the fit. I search for her in the feeling of comfort that is her fashion, my childhood head buried in the pleats of her dress, I cling to her waist, I cling to her legs. I search for her in the bottom of a pocketbook, hers filled with Rolaids and half-used ChapSticks stained with lipstick, the crushed bits of broken blush and eyeshadow scattered everywhere, the free small samples of perfume, the beat-up coupons from Macy's. I search for her each time I put something on and have somewhere to be, would she approve? I search for her in words that describe her habits and gestures, the way she sits or walks, the tone of her voice, the frizzy texture of her hair in the sunlight, the smell of her cream as I lean in to kiss her, the tack of her foundation.

I search for the mother in fashion, not the Madonna in the museum, not the one in any maternal shroud. Just like the authors in this book, who critique the "good mother discourse," the "dutiful selfless mother ideal," I am less interested in the lovable mothers often found. The ones who present themselves as perfectly coiffed and packing the lunches, staunch members of the community or the PTA. I search instead for the ones in rags, crying themselves on the floor; desperate, resigned, a nervous wreck, the mother in descent willing to burn the whole house down. I search for the ones with dandruff on her shoulder, thinning hair, stains of hair dye on the sides of her temple, that widening bald spot, the thick black fuzz growing on her upper lip. I look for the indulgent, excessive, irresponsible ones. The reckless one willing to spend her entire paycheck on a dress. The negligent one who tells her kids to wait in the car, or to wait on that New Jersey boardwalk while she goes and gambles and disappears. In writing and in clothing, I search for the mother before she was a mother, the one seeking recovery of herself. "i remember thinking: what a beautiful lady. she was very deliberately waiting ... maybe for a dream that had promised to come by" (Giovanni 1972).

I was raised by beautiful, fashionable mothers. These beautiful mothers worked in basements, or hardware stores, in laundry mats, selling liquor or candy, they worked in the mechanic's garage and hair salon, they were cutting patterns and sewing clothes, or painting nails, selling wigs, flowers, or oxtail soup. In this country, they donned blown-out hair, wore a full face of makeup, they always had lipstick on. They wore pretty clothes with bright colors and spent time organizing events at the local church. They'd done so well, *they looked amazing.* Who would have ever known that their nice clothes and big hair worked to bury all their stories of teenage pregnancies, all those miscarriages and abortions, the children they had given up or the children that were taken away, the sex they once traded for food or money or marriage into this new country. Here they were, they were present in my childhood, looking for their given-up children, beating the ones they had in front of them, just as their husbands beat them black and blue. These mothers, who weathered all these changes, giving birth to their beautiful children of my generation, they learned to swallow and keep down all the wounds and illnesses that came with war and poverty, all that backbreaking work they found in this new country, and still they put in effort, they labored into their cleaned-up, form-fitting, and moisturized look. They sang in the choir, they cooked Sunday lunch, they worked all day long then drove the kids back and forth to school.

In the beginning there was only my mother, her beauty and womanhood, her naked body and femininity, and none of her anguish. My first memories are of her coming to lift me out of bed, bathing with me in the tub, combing my hair, cleaning my ears, and getting me dressed. And each day, I watched her—watched her get dressed too. I wanted to wear my hair like her. I would try on her clothes, her shoes, feel the molding of her feet in them. I wanted to smell just like her. But as time moved on, I found her irritating—her everyday assertions, so persistent, of what to wear and how to wear it, of what to choose and when to choose it, the weight of her words as a rope tied around me pinning down my arms. With time, I found her fashion—the way she did her hair, her pink frosted nails, that blue eyeshadow—distasteful and outmoded. I felt shame and embarrassment for this vulgar mother, the one who would wear that loud leopard print coat, and that funny, dumpy-looking hat. I felt the problem with this mother of mine was her constantly confused conflation between herself and me. When she spoke, she spoke for me. My body was not mine, but hers.

All those early childhood affections of mine somehow turned into adolescent hostility. I found myself a pair of scissors and used them at every turn, to cut that umbilical cord she had grown outside of my body, which tethered me tightly to her. That red corduroy button-down she bought me, those glass frames, that permed hair—I cut my way through all of it. I shredded my jeans, I cut off all of my hair, I made sure she saw me walk out the door with a bare, unmade face—the one she would never dare leave the house with. I ripped off collars, ripped apart hems. I cut off the sleeves and made as many holes as I could on my ears. If she said dress, then I would wear pants. If she said pants, then I would wear jeans. If she said color, then I wore black. With my scissors, I could make her suffer, cut a pattern that fit completely differently on my body, and assert that my body was not hers but my own.

I have carried these scissors all my life, just to remind her that all the known cords—our profiles, silhouettes, habits, gestures, sense of taste, our codes and lexicons, our thoughts—have been segregated and cut. And each time, she has laughed, laughed in my face. Laughed so hard because she is so proud, that I have traveled even more than a million miles away to shut her out, disparage her, give her the silent treatment, find myself estranged from her, and yet still . . . find my way back again into her feminine beauty, the pleats of her skirt, just as I clung to her as a child. I make my way back to her soupy oatmeal, her frosted pink nails, the crunchy curls of her big hair. I find my way back into her beauty and anguish, the palm of my small childhood hand in hers. She was the mother who insisted on not assisting me—she never did breastfeed me—to make a daughter so strong and so self-sufficient, this daughter would learn to never need her.

At this age, I now find myself among women who've lost their mothers and feel truly free from the authority their mothers exercised over them. And yet here I am, reaching for thick foundation and garish colors, the gaudy jewelry, that leopard print coat. I want to wear my eye liner even thicker. I cannot seem to resist wearing my perfume too strong as I get older. And I now see my mother quite often, she's beside me, and I study her face, the shape of her body, the messy unkempt liquid eyeliner she puts on with a shaky hand. When my mother tells me her hearing is going out in her right ear, it's not to share the ailments of aging, but rather to say, *we are one in the same, of the same body. The ocean that once raged inside of me, now swells in you. Take note. Here it comes for you.* To recognize and accept this, *she's within me, my body is not my own,* is what makes me my mother's daughter.

We never get to choose our mothers. "I've written so much about my mother. I can say that I owe her everything" (Duras 2019). I guarantee you will be searching for her—what she wore, how she looked, what she thought—throughout the pages of this book. Come learn, through these authors in their writing of fashion and motherhood, how to end up loving her.

References

Duras, M. (2019), "Mother Makes You Obscene," in *Me & Other Writing*, trans. O. Baes and E. Ramadan. St. Louis, MO: Dorothy, a publishing project.

Giovanni, N. (1972), "Mothers," Poetry Foundation. Available online: https://www.poetryfoundation.org/poems/48228/mothers (accessed December 5, 2022).

Acknowledgments

I'm grateful to so many people who've shown interest in this project from the beginning and who've engaged with the ideas. Thank you to Mari Tovmasyan for the initial conversation and to the American Everyday conference where it first felt solid and real. I was so excited to be introduced to the Designing Motherhood project there and to have a world of scholarship opened up. Thank you to Michelle Millar Fisher, Amber Winick, and Juliana Barton for their generosity in sharing with FSJ as we put together the Fashion & Motherhood issue that snowballed into this collection.

Thank you to Rebecca Hamilton and Frances Arnold at Bloomsbury for being so receptive, responsive, and knowledgeable.

Immense gratitude to the Pasold Trust for their material support that enabled the use of wonderful images within this volume.

I love and am honored to work with the *Fashion Studies Journal* (FSJ) team, past and present, and I thank them all for their support and understanding, plus for the incredible work they do. Anthony Palliparambil Jr., Lauren Downing Peters, Sara Idacavage, Destinee Forbes, Tessa Maffucci, Natalie Nudell, Olivia Warschaw, and Kelsey Presley: it's a pleasure to Zoom with you all.

The fashion studies community has brought me so much—not just intellectual excitement, but so many wonderful friends I couldn't live without. Thank you so much to Anya Kurennaya (my favorite creative collaborator forever), Kim Jenkins, Alexis Walker, Paula Alaszkiewicz, Carole Schinck, Maria Echeverri, the students and professors of Parsons MA in Fashion Studies (MAFS) 2010–12 (in particular Heike Jenss, Maeve Kelly, and Lauren again), the Canadian Fashion Scholars Network, and everyone who makes this field so much fun to be a part of. Thank you to Christina Moon for demonstrating motherhood amid academic work at a time when I didn't realize I was going to need the example, then for enthusiastically welcoming me into the club, and now for contributing the beautiful foreword to this book.

Thank you to the writers and artists who made the Fashion & Motherhood issue of FSJ so much fun to work on, particularly Aimee Koran, Sam Garritano, Sara Kaufman, and Jennifer Anyan for introducing me to Jane Lazarre's *The Mother Knot* (1976). Thank you to Savona Ling and Martin Iddon for sharing art

---

and knowledge with this publication. Enormous gratitude to all the contributors to this volume. It has been such a pleasure getting to know you all through this often intimate material, and I've loved editing your work. Lauren, I hope you've read this far, because you deserve your third shout-out here. Your belief in me and in the project means so much.

Thank you to the Snelgrove, Gray, and Giroux families for the support of all kinds, especially to my uncle Frank Gray who freely shared his expertise, John Thorpe, a towering intellect and best buddy, my parenting role models Mark and Shannon Snelgrove, my in-laws Peggy and Dan whose example of running a family is second to none, and to my parents Rosemary and Dave for moving to Montreal, among so much else. Mum, I'm so sorry I didn't realize how fashionable you were all along! Special recognition to my sisters-in-law Samantha Giroux and Christina Marinelli for being moms I'm so proud to be raising my kids with, and to Helen and Bonnie Gray—you and your kids were in my mind and heart throughout all the work of creating this book.

Thank you to the Brooklyn Birthing Center, New York, the Maison de Naissance Côte-des-Neiges, Montreal, and the Morgantaler Clinic Montreal for the roles they each played in allowing me to create the family I wanted. And to every éducatrice, teacher, and babysitter who's taken care of my kids since.

Being a mother has been made better from day one by doing it alongside Maura O'Connor, Mary Kate Morookian, and Claire Salloum (even from a distance), and by sharing it with Shannon Webb, Aryana Rousseau, Emma Corosky, Eleanor Rae, Cara Shousterman, Julia O'Byrne, Anne Fuller, Nora Tennessen, Emilie Marzinotto, Jackie Coombs, Sarah Horsley, Tia Marosy, Hannah Rahimi, Clara Halpern, Jackie Soobramanie, and Kath Cullen. Thanks for the thoughtful answers every time I asked for your perspectives on dressing as a mom! Huge love and thanks to my friends who play other caring roles as well, of course, especially for when you've listened to my agonizing over the work of this project.

Love to Jon McPhedran Waitzer, Tara Mandarino, and Jess Lee, my moon systers. This was a seed once upon a time, and now it's grown into a rose!

Marc Giroux has given me more than anyone should dare hope for in this life, and Theo and Lewis are my favorite guys. Thank you, buddies. There's no one I'd rather catch the flu from every few months.

Introduction

Fashion and Motherhood

Laura Snelgrove

This collection brings together work from across disciplines and continents, using a wide range of methods and sources, to offer nuanced insights into the parallels and connections between motherhood and fashion, two inherently gendered practices both intimately personal and subject to public scrutiny. Acknowledging a dearth of existing fashion scholarship that considers the role of motherhood in historical and contemporary dress and media, the book aims to initiate conversations recognizing how both phenomena are determined by structures of power and have the potential to resist the norms of patriarchy. From the birth of commercialized "maternity wear" in the nineteenth century to the avant-garde abstraction of Rei Kawakubo's "lumps and bumps," from Indian films to American tabloids, and from the shallow surfaces of social media to the deep intimacy of family hand-me-downs, these chapters propose ways of thinking about how both motherhood and fashion appear, feel, and determine the experience of one another.

The chapters gathered here ask why motherhood has not been adequately incorporated into serious considerations of fashion. As fashion scholars have fought hard for decades to legitimize the study of a feminized bodily practice dismissed as frivolous and unserious, it may have seemed a bridge too far to attempt to incorporate the similarly maligned experience of motherhood, already forcibly erased from professional spheres. This volume makes clear that the time has come to integrate the histories and theories of these experiences. Both motherhood and fashion are here celebrated as practices with the ability to empower those who engage with them, but also as spaces of social and political relevance not yet adequately recognized for their culturally transformative potential.

Approach

Adrienne Rich's feminist classic *Of Woman Born: Motherhood as Experience and Institution* ([1976] 1995) serves as a foundational text in the field of motherhood studies. The book splits motherhood into two constituent parts: *experience* and *institution*. In its original context, written in 1976, Rich's book was working to theorize and define something that had long been taken for granted as "natural"; it was indeed radical even to propose motherhood as the subject of this kind of critical inquiry, and her perspective was recognized for its intention and potential to "interrupt patriarchal narratives" (O'Reilly 2017). *Fashion and Motherhood* is the beneficiary of the multiple overlapping theoretical traditions that have since come together to create "fashion studies," an interdisciplinary field that respects dress as not only a material object but also a "situated bodily practice," a visual medium, and a cauldron of identity formation (Entwistle 2000a–b). The essays within relish what Heike Jenss has called "the critical unpacking of historical ideas such as essentialist concepts of gender, race, and ethnicity" that defines fashion studies as a field, that allows for the dismantling and remaking of what had previously been handed down as natural, and that owes a debt of gratitude to theorists from Rich's generation who advocated this kind of piercing, deconstructive inquiry (Jenss 2016: 7). It is therefore in tribute to Rich that the book adopts a tripartite structure echoing her own: image, material, and identity are three spheres in which fashion acts upon culture and individuals, and the way they map easily onto Rich's analysis speaks to how closely these two phenomena operate.

Rich made a clear distinction between "motherhood," the institution derived from patriarchy, and "mothering," the potentially empowered act that could itself resist the former (though how exactly to realize this is not outlined in the book) (O'Reilly 2017). In fashion, motherhood is *institutionalized*, reproduced, and idealized through *imagery*—hence this book's first part on "Image"—most of which depicts an exceedingly narrow vision of how a "good" mother can appear, but which is thankfully being expanded as previously marginalized voices have fought to be heard. Mothering is *experienced* first through the body, which is a fashioned body (though not always a dressed body, as anyone cluster-feeding a newborn can attest) and is therefore *material*—the theme of the second part of this volume. This book picks up on another strain in Rich's writing—one regarding the self and how both motherhood and mothering act upon it; Rich uses the term "identity," and to accompany and round out "motherhood" and "mothering," I think of this as "Mama" ([1976] 1995: 22–3, 37). "Mama" is the new name we are not only called but may begin to call ourselves. The *identity* of a mother is indelibly shaped by the *institution* and the *experience*, as her knowledge of the gulf between the idealized *image* and the *material* reality becomes part of her interface with the world as well as her sense of herself.

Despite the pronouns I have just used, the term "mother" should not be assumed to apply only to womb-bearing people who identify as women. Let us adopt an expansive definition of the verb "to mother": "to bring up (a child) with care and affection" (Oxford Languages online). This relational framing recognizes the socially constructed nature of the category of "mother," widens the net as to who can identify as such, and expands the focus from simply bearing children to actually raising them. Anyone can mother, and no uses of "she/her/hers" or "woman/women" in this book are meant to suggest otherwise.[1]

The increasing visibility of trans, non-binary, and other gender-non-conforming parents is incredibly valuable to studies of motherhood for the way it upends long-held assumptions about biology and identity, and this collection wishes to be part of pushing forward that conversation, although openly queer and trans subjects are regrettably absent from the topics handled directly here. Similarly, adoptive and other non-biological mothers are not within the material in these chapters, but their existence must be considered in any conversation about what it means to mother. They may have different considerations than the parent who gestates, births, and nurses a baby, but their experience of the institutionalization of motherhood through image, the way clothes affect their bodies while parenting, and the shifts in their identities when children enter the picture are all profound and worthy of study. It is hoped that future research on fashion and motherhood will pursue these avenues.

Fashion Studies

The scholarship in this book demonstrates what Jenss calls the "dense interdisciplinary entanglements" of fashion studies, a field that draws from art and dress history, material and visual culture, media and film studies, literature, sociology, anthropology, and gender studies, among other established fields with their own research traditions (2016: 11). Fittingly, most of the authors of these chapters do not work or situate their research exclusively in fashion studies but apply fashion and dress as a lens through which to view culture, media, consumption, and the history of gender, among other subjects

Though fashion studies is expansive enough, and "fashion" a big enough tent to encompass everything from fast-fashion production in the global South to historical dress found in costume museums to the most spectacular of avant-garde runway presentations and media depictions, one aspect of fashion studies that draws it particularly close to motherhood is an interest in the everyday. This strain of fashion and dress research resists the conception of fashion as purely surface and transitory, instead embracing and excavating the mundane and the persistent. As Buckley and Clark explain, everyday uses of dress "exemplify continuity and tradition; are responsive to regional and national subtleties, as well as global ones; and are disruptive of fashion's structures and systems, as well as its visual codes and norms of consumption" (2012: 19). And indeed, what could describe motherhood better than that? It is changeable yet rooted in tradition, located in space and place, and culturally separated from ideas of the fashionable and the desirable.

When we begin to look at everything in the human experience through the lens of fashion and dress, motherhood, with its representations in media ("Best and Worst Moms RANKED!" blares the cover of *Star* magazine), negotiations of front- and backstage behaviors (the nursing bra stuffed with absorbent pads under an office-appropriate blouse, for instance), and unavoidably bodily experiences (such as the hips that slowly escape alignment thanks to the constant hoisting of a child onto a preferred side) begins to seem like an obvious yet overlooked site for dress-based exploration.

Motherhood Studies

Though this collection is grounded in the field of fashion studies, it owes much to the similarly multivalent field of motherhood studies. This field has struggled with many of the same prejudices within the academy, forced to justify its interest in a life-defining experience shared by billions of people on this planet. Like fashion studies, motherhood studies is concerned with the cultural contradictions inherent to an institution in which so many people participate, and draws its research methods from across the social sciences and humanities.

After Rich's seminal work in 1976, motherhood found itself woven in with what was then called women's studies for the next two decades of its proliferation. Sharon Hays' *The Cultural Contradictions of Motherhood* in 1996 addressed the history of mothering in the West, identifying the network of beliefs facing mothers at the end of the twentieth century as "the ideology of intensive mothering" (which, the argument can be made, may have only intensified in the decades since). The cover of Hays' book, on which a white mother is split in two, with one side dressed in professional attire, carrying a newspaper, and the other in jeans and a soft sweater, hoisting a toddler, makes dress into a shorthand for the contradictions of which she writes. The book marked an era of prolificacy within the field. But, as Samira Kawash details extensively in a 2011 review, in the years following Hays' breaking of new ground, a poststructuralist turn in studies of gender and power saw motherhood become démodé within feminist academia, perhaps appearing overly traditional, "an embarrassing theoretical relic of an earlier naïve view" in which motherhood was seen as essential to womanhood (Kawash 2011).

Yet, motherhood has risen again in gender and feminist studies, perhaps as the material conditions of mothering in late-stage capitalism have made it hard to ignore as another intersection of identity that either conspires to isolate mothers from one another or draw them together in resistance. Andrea O'Reilly, a leading and prolific scholar in motherhood studies over the last twenty years, has responded to Rich outright by "positing a deliberately constructed, liberatory feminist practice of mothering as an alternative to the oppressive institution of motherhood"— filling in the gap left in *Of Woman Born* (Kawash 2011). O'Reilly, who states plainly that "maternal theory still needs to become more global," has nevertheless been part of a movement making great headway in expanding the scope of motherhood studies away from being exclusive to the experiences of cisgender, middle-class married white women (Mendes, Souto Maior, and de Mendonca 2021) and towards being a site of true empowerment in "theory, activism, and practice," per the subtitle of her book *Matricentric Feminism*, now in its second edition.

The last decade in both motherhood and fashion studies, as in much of cultural theory and the humanities at large, has seen enormous change in the refiguring of what Kawash calls "the relations of body, care, kinship, presence, and desire" and a reorienting towards the voices and experiences of those long pushed to the margins (2011). In this collection, which wishes to begin building a bridge between the two fields but is itself imperfect in terms of representation, the contexts of class, gender identity and expression, racialization, size, sexuality, and economic status, among other intersections of identity, are taken to matter deeply for how mothers experience the institutions of both motherhood and fashion via imagery and material worn on the body, as well as how they internalize those experiences in the creation and re-creation of their selves and subjectivities.

Methods, Materials, and Contributions

Following from the interdisciplinarity of both fields to which this book hopes to contribute, there are a multitude of research methods represented here, utilizing varied materials and sources. As Jenss explains, to adequately explore fashion (and, I add, motherhood, as an equally multifaceted field of study), "research methods are most productive when used in combination" (2016: 137).

The chapters in this volume undertake the exploration using discourse and media analysis, semiotic visual and content analysis, garment histories, literature and wardrobe study, interview, and auto-ethnography, often in combination. They draw material from film costume, historical design patents, news media, social media, museum collections, architecture, advice books, advertisements, medical literature, photography, and used garments bought online. This range is evidence of how far-reaching both fashion and motherhood are into the lives of people and cultures.

Yet, there are absences. Besides the aforementioned gender-diverse, adoptive, and stepparents not explicitly present among the subjects of these chapters, there are other gaps in the material covered here that I hope other researchers will be inspired to fill. While Nash, Gregson and Beale, and Guy and Banim, among others, have performed ethnographies that include pregnant or postpartum people relating to their maternity clothing (trying it on, passing it between friends, discarding it, etc.), I am personally hungry for a similar study that follows mothers beyond the postpartum and infant stage (Nash 2012a, 2012b; Gregson and Beale 2004). Maternity wear is a rich site, but motherhood, mothering, and "Mama" are only just beginning when the nursing bras come off. In a 2021 issue of *Fashion Theory*, Entwistle and Wissinger address the "mumfluencers" of Instagram as a social media archetype and style regime, and I hope more research will follow in that direction.

Further, there are no disabled bodies represented in these pages, which limits how broadly we can understand the material experience of mothering on the physical self. There are geographical and ethnic identity lacks; no South American, Middle Eastern, Australasian, or Indigenous perspectives are heard here, which reflects the biases and exclusions of Anglophone Western academia and should not be excused. We must call for broader inclusion of stories, communities, and experiences not told within this book as the conversation about fashion and motherhood continues.

Still, while imperfectly representative, this book marks the first time fashion and motherhood are being considered under the same umbrella in this way—as coming together to define a type of dressed image, an experience of bodily control, and as a category of lived identity expression. Part of the project of an interdisciplinary field like fashion studies is to continually reach out to other areas of study and find common ground, underscoring the universality of fashion as a determinant of human experience and knitting together a scholarly community; this book extends a hand to motherhood studies and provides evidence of the many ways they can work together.

In considering images of motherhood, both fictionalized and "real," the first chapters of this book extend a conversation about the visual language of fashion. We know this language to be an integral aspect of how fashion operates, but these chapters also consider how it constructs archetypes of motherhood: the authoritarian, the goddess, the commodity; the good, the bad, the ghostly. Where Rich acknowledged that the oppressive institution of motherhood was enshrined through imagery, these chapters examine the contemporary versions of those images in a plurality of cultures and uncover the vital role of dress.

The second part, "Material," considers how life in a dressed body is apt to change when that body undergoes mothering, and particularly how the material of dress itself constructs experience. There is a metaphysical element to this question—what does it mean to *be* a mother, to have *a mother's consciousness* located in the previously non-mothering form?—that I believe is particularly interesting when asked through the lens of fashion history (i.e., how might the experience of mothering have been different when one was expected to do so in a corset?). And of course, asking questions of history always brings us to question how much has even really changed.

I will never choose a favorite between the chapters in this book, all of which have brought into my life ideas and scholars that I cherish. But the third part, "Identity," may be where I see this book's contribution come alive most clearly. First, the argument is made that our identities are the result of a confrontation between that which we see represented in the world of imagery and that which the realities of our human bodies allow. Then, the chapters take a personal turn that epitomizes the potential for bringing studies of fashion and motherhood together: both held at arm's length from the canon for so long, these two subjects and their practitioners should thus feel at liberty to grow wildly and radically feminine, to question and remake the structures that rejected them, and to include the intimate, the vulnerable, and the supposedly small. Who says concepts like fear, meaning, and love don't belong in academic scholarship? Why can't we both think *and* feel? If this book offers one thing above all else, it is resounding certainty that we not only can, but must.

Notes

1 See Millar Fisher and Winick (2021), 18, for more on the guiding approach to gender inclusivity adopted here.

8 *Fashion and Motherhood*

References

Buckley, C. and H. Clark (2012), "Conceptualizing Fashion in Everyday Lives," *Design Issues*, 28 (4): 18–28.

Entwistle, J. (2000a), *The Fashioned Body: Fashion, Dress and Modern Social Theory*. London: Polity.

Entwistle, J. (2000b), "Fashion and the Fleshy Body: Dress as Embodied Practice," *Fashion Theory: The Journal of Dress, Body & Culture*, 4 (3): 323–47. Doi: 10.2752/136270400778995471.

Entwistle, J. and E. Wissinger (2021), "Dress like a Mum/Mom: Instagram Style Mums and the Fashionable Ideal," *Fashion Theory*, 27 (1): 5–42. Doi: 10.1080/1362704X.2021.1934326.

Gregson, N. and V. Beale (2004), "Wardrobe Matter: The Sorting, Displacement and Circulation of Women's Clothing," *Geoforum*, 35 (6): 689–700.

Guy, A. and M. Banim (2000), "Personal Collections: Women's Clothing Use and Identity," *Journal of Gender Studies*, 9 (3): 313–26. Doi: 10.1080/713678000.

Hays, S. (1996), *The Cultural Contradictions of Motherhood*. New Haven, CT: Yale.

Jenss, H. (2016), *Fashion Studies: Research Methods, Sites and Practices*. London: Bloomsbury.

Kawash, S. (2011), "New Directions in Motherhood Studies," *Signs*, 36 (4): 969–1003.

Mendes, M., E. P. Souto Maior, and M. C. de Mendonca (2021), "Interview: Dr. Andrea O'Reilly and the Motherhood Perspective," *Revista Artemis*, 31 (1): 12–22. Doi: 10.22478/ufpb.1807-8214.2021v31n1.60135.

Millar Fisher, M. and A. Winick (2021), *Designing Motherhood: Things that Make and Break Our Births*. Cambridge, MA: MIT Press.

Nash, M. (2012a), *Making "Postmodern" Mothers: Pregnant Embodiment, Baby Bumps and Body Image*. London: Palgrave Macmillan.

Nash, M. (2012b), "Weighty Matters: Negotiating 'Fatness' and 'In-betweenness' in Early Pregnancy," *Feminism & Psychology*, 22 (3): 307–23.

O'Reilly, A. (2017), "Mothering Against Motherhood: The Legacy of Adrienne Rich's *Of Woman Born*," *Women's Studies*, 46 (7): 728–9.

Oxford Languages online (n.d.), "mother," Dictionary. Available online: https://www.google.com/search?q=definition+of+mother&rlz=1C5CHFA_enUS529US529&oq=definition+of+mother&aqs=chrome.0.69i59j69i64j0i512l6.2077j1j7&sourceid=chrome&ie=UTF-8 (accessed October 15, 2022).

Rich, A. ([1976] 1995), *Of Woman Born: Motherhood as Experience and Institution*. New York and London: W. W. Norton & Co.

Section 1

Image: Institution

The essays in this section ask how the mediated world of images serves to create, order, maintain, and perpetuate the *institution* of motherhood, described by Rich as "embodied in the booklet in my obstetrician's waiting room, the novels I had read, my mother-in-law's approval, my memories of my own mother, the Sistine Madonna or she of the Michelangelo Pietà," all of which she says is fundamentally aimed at "ensuring that [the potential relationship of any woman to her powers of reproduction and to children] shall remain under male control" ([1976] 1995: 39, 13). By examining myth-making via fictionalized narratives onscreen and the promotion of individual idealized mothers in the public eye, the following seven authors explore how image renders motherhood a cultural commodity as well as an established series of conventions with enormous power. By defining how the motherly body should be hidden, revealed, celebrated, shamed, and sold, the institution of motherhood has, in Rich's words, "ghettoized and degraded female potentialities" (ibid., 13).

Per Richard Dyer, we take "image" to mean more than the exclusively visual, but "rather a complex configuration of visual, verbal and aural signs [...] manifest in all kinds of media text" ([1979] 1998: 34). Examining films, social media, news media, onstage performance, and more sources of imagery, these chapters address how spectacle helps to telegraph meaning searingly, hauntingly, and too often reproachfully, to all mothers. The part is divided in two, separating images of real-world mothers in the public eye from those of characters in narrative fiction, to encourage reflection on how differently these forms of mediated storytelling convey moral imperatives and otherwise construct the social category of "mother." Importantly, they also take steps towards seeing things another way.

References

Dyer, R. ([1979] 1998), *Stars*. London: BFI (British Film Institute).
Rich, A. ([1976] 1995), *Of Woman Born: Motherhood as Experience and Institution*. New York and London: W. W. Norton & Co.

Part 1

Mediated Role Models

The essays in this part explore how themes of power, morality, privacy, and progress are projected by and onto images of real individual mothers in the public eye. These mothers, Carrie Lam, Beyoncé Knowles-Carter, and Kylie Jenner, the subjects of the chapters by Pui-sze Leung and Kin-long Tong, Danell-Jamal Lisby, Maureen Lehto Brewster, are deeply aware of their places in the world of images and, in many instances, able to use it as a site of control. These authors ask: With knowledge of the image as commodity, how do these mothers strategically deploy it? Harnessing their cultures' beliefs about motherhood, how do they uphold or contest expectations of what a mother can or should be?

Although evaluating real people, this group of chapters is concerned with an idealized motherhood, as opposed to real mothering, given that the act of observing these celebrity mothers *do* mothering flattens that which is being observed into an image. Said image then enters a communication system—whether television or online news, tabloids, social media, etc.—described by Christopher Breward as "a mirage of desires where all human values are commodified" (2003: 103). So indeed, whatever experience of mothering (radical, resistant, or empowering as it may be for them) these women have is not accessible to the majority of those who perceive them and thus they remain emblems of the institution.

The subjects here are all contemporary, though references to art and dress history are important to their signification (particularly in the case of Carrie Lam and her cheongsam and Beyoncé's polymathic image collaging). The focus on contemporary images means that this analysis is limited to photographic and video sources, with their attendant dynamics of proliferation, dissemination, and reception, as opposed to historical sources of maternal imagery such as painted portraits. It is interesting to think about how these contemporary media compare to their predecessors in determining how we receive images of mothers.

As Karen Hearn, curator of the 2020 exhibition, *Portraying Pregnancy: From Holbein to Social Media* and author of its catalog, says, "At many periods, [...]

images of pregnancy have been seen as transgressive, provoking embarrassment at, and even hostility to, such visible signs of female sexual activity," and that "[i]t was not until the later 20th century that pregnancy stopped being 'airbrushed out' of portraits. [. . .] In a painted portrait, [. . .] it was easy for an artist simply to depict the sitter without her baby bump, but with the advent of photography— where the camera records everything that is in front of it—greater ingenuity was called for" (ibid., 12, 113). Not coincidentally, since this shift in sensibilities in the later twentieth century in the West, there has been little cultural imperative to hide pregnancy in imagery (for which Annie Liebowitz's photo of Demi Moore naked on the cover of *Vanity Fair* in 1991 is given much credit by Hearn and others), but "airbrushing" in general has only increased. Airbrushing remains a tool for controlling the visual narrative, and therefore of institutionalization, but rather than obscuring maternity itself, airbrushing now tends to be wielded to obscure any traces of its less picturesque realities. The chapters in this part contend with the negotiation of reality versus symbolism, and they find that the consequences for the institution of motherhood are enormous.

References

Breward, C. (2003), *Fashion*. Oxford: Oxford University Press.
Hearn, K. (2020), *Portraying Pregnancy: From Holbein to Social Medi*. London: Paul Holberton Publishing.

1

Dress to Repress

Fashioning Motherhood in Semi-Authoritarian Hong Kong

Pui-sze Leung and Kin-long Tong

In 2019, the Hong Kong Special Administrative Region government pushed forward a controversial bill that would have allowed it to extradite Hong Kong citizens to Mainland China. This led to the largest political crisis in Hong Kong's postcolonial history, the Anti-ELAB (Extradition Law Amendment Bill) Movement. People were worried that the Chinese government could make use of the bill to arrest political dissidents in Hong Kong, so millions took to the streets in protest on June 9 and June 16. The movement only ended in mid-2020, when the Covid-19 pandemic hit the city and the government promulgated a national security law capable of sentencing political dissidents to life imprisonment.

As the Chief Executive of Hong Kong—the political figure with the highest executive power in government—Carrie Lam played a critical role in the introduction of the extradition bill. She appeared in press conferences and legislative council meetings to promote the bill despite immense opposition from civil society. The most striking example of this may have been when she gave a personal interview broadcast by pro-government media Television Broadcasts Limited (TVB) on June 12, the day many young protesters violently clashed with police outside the Government Headquarters in a bid to stop the second reading of the extradition bill at the Legislative Council. In the interview, Lam reminded readers that she was a mother of two children and stated she has also been "married to Hong Kong." She used this motherhood analogy to justify her hardline policy against the protesters, claiming that if she did not indulge the irresponsible behavior of her children, it was for their own sake.

Throughout her political career, Carrie Lam has repeatedly emphasized her role as a mother of two children and used the motherhood analogy for political communication. In fact, the family-state analogy is deeply rooted in Confucian philosophy, making parenthood a site of political contestation. However, while the politicization of parenthood is widely discussed by political philosophers, only a small amount of literature explores how parenthood is performed by politicians through daily practice, including fashion. This chapter investigates the fashion choices of Carrie Lam, particularly her notable use of cheongsam, to explore where and how motherhood, fashion, and politics intersect. It combines two qualitative research approaches: first, a semiotic analysis of Carrie Lam's dress is conducted to decode the underpinning visual symbols. Then, a historical analysis is performed to contextualize the cultural meaning of cheongsam in Hong Kong. From the case of Carrie Lam, this chapter demonstrates that fashion (as well as motherhood status) can be a political tool for authoritarian leaders to project their governing discourses and build up their public images.

Politics of Fashion and Politicized Motherhood

Informed by post-modernism and the notion of body politics, many scholars argue that fashion is a contested ground upon which social hierarchy and state power are articulated. In the most totalitarian form of authoritarianism, states would even retain control over fashion choices just as they might dominate other aspects of everyday life (Stitzel 2005); for instance, North Korea's female fashion is used to construct an "ideal female body" that served both socialist revolution and national tradition in the second half of the twentieth century (Kim 2011). Similar examples could be found in Fascist Italy, where fashion was a tool for discipling the female body and presenting a radical form of modernity (Paulicelli 2004); in Communist China, women were motivated to reconstruct their bodily identity in accordance with a Maoist critique of patriarchy, even though the new imagination of female bodies was also driven by a masculinized political party, the Chinese Communist Party (Finnane 2008).

While the mainstream literature has offered a lens for understanding the functionality of civilian fashion under authoritarianism, this chapter aims to contribute by focusing on the fashion choices of an authoritarian leader—Carrie Lam, Chief Executive of Hong Kong. In Hong Kong, the logic of authoritarianism largely departs from the aforementioned examples that are totalitarian in nature. The semi-autonomous territory is often classified as a liberal autocracy, in which people enjoy socio-economic freedom and civil society is vigorous despite being without an electoral democracy (Kuan and Lau 2002). Cultural diversity and economic liberty are the key governing discourses of the Hong Kong government, while Hong Kong has a thriving fashion industry. Still, fashion can be politicized in such a semi-authoritarian context, particularly when the ruling elites encounter political crises such as the Anti-ELAB Movement.

This chapter introduces a political culture approach to enrich the extant literature as the authors have observed that Carrie Lam's fashion choices have become an important component of her paternalistic discourse. Rooted in Confucian philosophy, Chinese society has a long tradition of family-state equivalence, in which people regard the ideal state as a harmonious family (Kim 2011). The family-state analogy is more than a cultural metaphor, as the parent-child relationship structures political-social relations in Chinese society. In Parsons' words, China is a "familistic society" and the traditional virtue of *xiao* (filial piety) is at the center of social existence (1991). Political relations are perceived as the extension of familial relations; the leaders should love their subjects as if they are their own children, while people should be loyal to their leaders as if they were their own parents (King 2018). Thus, in the Chinese context, motherhood has occupied a strategic place in the discursive domain; the local officials consider themselves *fumu guan* ("father and mother" officials) while the empress should *mu yi tian xia* ("be the mother of the world"). Such kinds of familial metaphors are still actively employed by the government; for example, President Xi Jinping is portrayed as "Grandpa Xi" in some primary school textbooks (Chen and Lau 2021). Hong Kong, on the one hand, is a former British colony and a "capitalist utopia" that champions neo-liberal values (Tremlett 2015). On the other hand, the city is a Chinese-dominated society with a culture of "utilitarianistic familism" that prioritizes familial interests that are sometimes defined in economic terms (Lau 1981). The influence of utilitarianistic familism can be found in the political vocabulary of the Hong Kong people. Since Hong Kong was handed over to China and became its special administrative region in 1997, the Chinese Central Government, which retained supreme power over the city state, has been called *ah ye* ("Grandpa") by people in Hong Kong. In the existing constitutional framework, the Chief Executives of Hong Kong supposedly represent Hong Kong's interests. Still, in practice, they are selected by the central government through an election that is only voted in by 1,500 pro-government elites. This chapter will combine fashion politics and Chinese familistic politics to investigate how Carrie Lam integrates motherhood into her governing discourse.

Carrie Lam's Motherhood Discourse and Cheongsam-philia

The mother of two children, Carrie Lam is the first female Chief Executive of Hong Kong. She was appointed as Secretary for Development in 2007 and later elected as the Chief Secretary of Hong Kong, the most senior principal official, in 2012. In the earlier stages of her political career, she was known for her combative approach to controversial issues and was nicknamed "tough fighter" (Lim 2018). At that time, she often dressed in a unisex style with a short pixie haircut (Figure 1.1). One of the most iconic examples was what is known as the Queen's Pier incident. In July 2007, the government announced its plan to demolish Queen's Pier, a historic landmark in the Central District. A group of protesters, arguing that Queen's Pier symbolized the collective memories of Hong Kong citizens, occupied the pier and called for the withdrawal of the demolition plan. As the Secretary for Development, Lam attended a public forum held by the activists in the hopes of persuading the protesters to back down. That day, she wore a pink polo shirt and long trousers with her signature haircut, and firmly reiterated the government's position. Carrie Lam's masculine image as the "tough fighter" became one of her greatest political assets in her political career. However, her hawkish image attracted widespread doubt and

Figure 1.1 Carrie Lam attending a forum at Queen's Pier in 2007 in the uniform of her early political career. © [Gavin Bobo] [2007]. Reproduced under a Creative Commons Attribution-ShareAlike 2.0 Generic License (CC BY-SA 2.0).

criticism when she ran for Chief Executive in 2017. Political scientist Ivan Choy (cited in Cheung 2017) commented that "people feel that she is very combative. I fear even if she wins the top job, it will be difficult for her to lead society in reconciliation, especially between the government and the pan-democrats."

Perhaps with this critique in mind, Carrie Lam gradually revamped her public image, taking a feminine turn to cast off her very stern bureaucrat image. She invited her low-profile husband and older son, whose safety she guarded cautiously, to join the electoral campaign team, and she frequently appeared in media interviews, sharing her family matters and parenting methods (Ko 2017). She emphasized that she is a responsible mother who took care of the children by herself when they were young. She particularly highlighted her intimate relationship with her older son, Jeremy Lam, who also became a keynote speaker sharing their mother-son moments in her electoral campaign. She even made youth issues one of her key visions in her manifesto, seeking to build connections with the younger generation, claiming she would "walk with the youth" (Manifesto 2017). Throughout the later stage of her political career, Lam frequently stated that she is a mother who can always show empathy to others. For example, when three student activists, including Joshua Wong, were sentenced to jail in 2017 for participating in the Umbrella Movement, Carrie Lam claimed that she could understand the feelings of their mothers ("Carrie Lam" 2017).

Lam began to strategically use cheongsam, a traditional Chinese dress, to complement her motherhood discourse (Figure 1.2). As she revealed in her official social media, she prepared more than 30 sets of cheongsam for her electoral campaigns and showcased her collection at one of her political rallies (Lau 2017). For instance, she wore an Oxford-blue cheongsam with a white floral pattern in the Chief Executive Election forum on March 19, 2017. On July 1 of that year, to celebrate Hong Kong Special Administrative Region Establishment Day as well as her inauguration, Lam dressed in a candy-red cheongsam with a flowery pattern. Peng Li-yuan, the wife of President Xi, who also often appears in cheongsam during diplomatic trips, wore a comparatively reserved brown embroidered cheongsam when visiting Hong Kong with Xi at Lam's ceremony. Since then, the cheongsam has become Lam's signature style. In another video on her Facebook page, she explained her various cheongsam choices at the Chief Executive inauguration ceremony and showed a series of photo montages of her in cheongsam with Xi Jinping, claiming that "as the first female Chief Executive, I want to display the features of East Asian women" (Facebook 2017). In her own words, she believes that cheongsam is the best vehicle to demonstrate not only

Figure 1.2 Carrie Lam wearing cheongsam for a speech. © [Iris Tong] [2016] Voice of America, Wikimedia Commons.

the charisma of Asian women, but also of Hong Kong's first female politician able to exercise the highest power. Her cheongsam images have also been widely popularized by pro-Beijing media, such as the newspaper *Tai Kung Pao* (2017), which acclaimed Lam's style for coupling strength and gentleness.

Carrie Lam's motherhood discourse converged with her cheongsam image in a very symbolic moment for the Anti-ELAB Movement on June 12, 2019. The controversial extradition bill that seemed to critics to provide a plausible excuse to arrest local political dissidents led to millions of citizens protesting. On June 12, thousands of young protesters clashed with police forces outside the Government Headquarters in a bid to stop the second reading of the extradition bill at the Legislative Council. The police fired around 240 canisters of tear gas, as well as dozens of sponge grenades and rubber bullets at the unarmed protesters. It was the first time the police had fired rubber bullets in Hong Kong's postcolonial history; some protesters were shot in the head and suffered severe injuries. The violence was unprecedented, exceeding the level experienced during the 2014 Umbrella Movement, one of the largest democratic movements in Hong Kong, which disrupted established understandings of local identity. This heated debate remains relevant. While some proclaim the legitimacy of and support the current one-China rhetoric, many actively denounce intrusive Chinese patriotism or anything representing it.

During the June 12 protest, Carrie Lam attended a personal interview broadcast by pro-government media Television Broadcasts Limited (TVB) with the hope of de-escalating the situation and pushing forward with the bill. In the interview, she dressed in a cadet-blue cheongsam with a U-neck knitted cardigan. The cheongsam would depict her refined maturity properly, present a distinctive form of Chinese femininity, and visualize her motherhood discourse, which was the central theme of the interview. She mentioned again that she is a mother of two children and has been "married to Hong Kong." She embraced this motherhood analogy to justify her hardline policy against the protesters, claiming that she would not indulge the irresponsible behaviors of her children for their own sake. She shared her "parenting secrets," saying if she were to satisfy every demand from her son, he would be spoiled and would regret having everything he desired and blame her for not teaching him how to distinguish right from wrong (Tam 2019). She burst into tears when she said she has never betrayed Hong Kong's people, given her love for the city.

The paternalistic speech Lam gave was crafted not only by her words of motherly discipline but also the carefully exhibited orthodox Chinese family-style interior decor (orchids, embroidered furniture) and by her distinctly strategic use of a traditional cheongsam—all these elements merged into an immaculate mise-en-scène repudiated by many for its pro-China associations. Carrie Lam's stylistic transformation from the Margaret Thatcher-like, combative look of a loyal civil servant to a Chinese mother of the nation was key to materializing her Chinese motherhood discourse. Despite cheongsam's recent fashionable resurgence, these "national/ethnic" dresses have become iconography on souvenirs, dress codes at formal ceremonies, festive occasions, and are seldom worn daily in cosmopolitan Hong Kong, favored by transnational fashion corporations targeting affluent consumers with global aesthetics. The cheongsam has been replaced with Western fashion for the younger generations. Carrie Lam's conscious decision to present herself in heritage fashion would thus seem to suggest an effort to revitalize a historical moment or evoke a particular cultural imagination. How did cheongsam eventually come to symbolize Chineseness, a Chinese mother, and an authoritarian figure?

Cultural Symbolism of Cheongsam

Carrie Lam's cheongsam-philia can be made sense of from a historical-cultural perspective. In fact, cheongsam is a highly condensed symbol as, in multifarious designs at different times and as an ever-changing visual signifier, it has actually embodied distinct—even divergent—identities and discourses of gender, modernity, and Chinese nationalism (Ng 2018).

Despite a rich profusion of debates on the origins of the cheongsam, scholarly evidence indicates a close affiliation and resemblance between the Manchurian menswear of the Qing Dynasty changpao and the cheongsam (Ling 2017). The early cheongsam had a wide and angular cut close to changpao's baggy and loose silhouette. The initial endeavor was to advocate gender equality by donning the male-dominated attire in imperial China when anti-Manchu sentiment was heated. Some Manchu women even wore cheongsam to disguise their ethnic roots. Subsequent to the fall of the Qing Dynasty in 1911, the popularity of the subversive cheongsam surged and gained extensive endorsement from female activists, educated, intellectual women, students returning from overseas, and women who accepted new ideas and wished to display their individuality and desire to dress for participation in social reforms during the peak of women's emancipation, particularly in affluent cities like Shanghai (Clark 2000). The cheongsam emerged at the right time to tackle the bodily transformation Chinese women experienced following the abolition of foot-binding and breast-binding in Early Republican China (Ling 2017). Cheongsam also replaced the scholarly male gown at schools and gradually became a uniform for female teachers and students to signify modern womanhood.

Decades after the fall of the Qing Dynasty, the modern cheongsam was in full vogue during the early 1920s and 1930s. The cheongsam became a symbol of urban modernity while the Manchu reference diminished (Ng 2018). The popularity of cheongsam was then fueled by prevailing capitalist consumerism, refined Western aesthetics, and was in high demand by the urban bourgeoisie, socialites, the middle classes, and fashion-conscious ladies seeking the latest trend. Infused with Western cuts and embellished with high heels and clutches, the modern cheongsam then evolved and flourished into a form-hugging, waist-and-buttock-emphasizing silhouette by popular demand. However, the omnipresence of women in cheongsam featured in consumer and foreign product advertisements raised questions of female objectification and commodification, complicating women's emancipation and revealing the still-stringent social constraints on women under patriarchy (Finnane 2008; Edwards 2000). It wasn't until the May Thirtieth Movement in 1925 that the popular consensus turned cheongsam into a nationalist token when anti-Western-imperialist protests flared, despite its Westernized designs. Cheongsam then became the dominant female daily wear up until the establishment of the People's

Republic of China, when cheongsam was pronounced dead for its "capitalistic and consumeristic" associations.

Cheongsam continued to thrive in Hong Kong's culturally hybrid environment under British colonial rule. The interplay of multiple forces made Hong Kong an unrestricted breeding ground for cheongsam: talented Shanghai tailors who migrated to Hong Kong because of the Chinese Civil War provided the creative software, the colonial government's non-interventionist take on local customs and relaxed rules on dressing choice the strong drive of modernity, and waves of commercialization boosted demand and encouraged innovative designs beloved by many. Beyond these factors, the two Hollywood movies *Love is A Many-Splendored Thing* (1952) and *The World of Suzie Wong* (1960) showcased cheongsam on the international stage. Central to the films is cheongsam as the prominent marker of Chineseness apart from the filmic negotiation of the dual heritage and identity struggles of the colonized collective; however, cheongsam as the Chinese symbol in these films is "interwoven with constructs of race, class and gender" (Ng 2018). Both female protagonists in cheongsam are portrayed as subservient, docile, and humble in the face of a white American love interest. The Eurasian female doctor in *Love is A Many-Splendored Thing* dresses in cheongsams of plain colors and traditional accessories to remind herself of Chinese virtues and heritage, while the protagonist in *The World of Suzie Wong* is a Eurasian stripper who wears snug cheongsams of bold colors and high slits up to the thighs. This polarized depiction of women in cheongsam shares one common point: female entrapment in stereotypes through the Orientalist gaze (Ng 2018). Despite the stereotypes, the two films consolidated the connection between cheongsam and Oriental sensuality in popular cultural imagination inside and out of Hong Kong (Ling 2017), morphing cheongsam into a symbol of Chineseness.

Cheongsam in Hong Kong eventually moved into quotidian life and was widely adopted by schools as uniforms for teachers and students—a custom that still stands today. This practice was a tradition inherited from Republican China where cheongsam was able to bear associations with both scholarship and desirable femininity (Clark 2000). Gradually replaced by Westernized clothing, cheongsam diminished to either hospitality uniforms in Chinese restaurants or ceremonial or pageant show attire, balancing between kitsch costumes and representation of virtue. Of all Chinese traditional outfits, the versatile cheongsam best manifested and concretized these many cultural and moral statements, and the dress has been in constant evolution throughout its history. Now, one finds many creative cheongsam designs with high slits, short length, no sleeves, and many other variations, but what never changes is the cultural association with Chineseness.

A small resurgence happened in the 1990s with Hong Kong's retrocession to China, when cheongsam was deployed to mix Chinese virtues with political statements by female politicians including Former Chief Secretary of Hong Kong Anson Chan, as well as Carrie Lam. They both favored cheongsam and their style evoked respectable and educated women from the Republican era, or school teachers in Hong Kong who encapsulated Chinese feminine virtues, elegance, and power (Ng 2018). One relevant example would be the notable Republican-era female politician Soong May-ling, who married the Nationalist Party leader Chiang Kai-shek in 1927 and wore luxurious cheongsam to intentionally craft a dignified, well-contained Chinese feminine outlook during overseas trips and political meetings to win sympathetic aid from the USA against Japanese aggression (Wilson 2002). She started The New Life Movement in 1934 with Chiang to seek to revive Confucian morality for national unity. Soong stressed the modesty of the cheongsam with her far more humble collection of cheongsam at home, playing the humble mother of the nation (Ng 2018). Cheongsam became an iconic trademark of hers in her image as a Chinese cultural ambassador, which helps to explain the efforts by Carrie Lam to infuse the Chinese cultural element into her political discourse.

Conclusion

The case of Carrie Lam can contribute to the extant literature on fashion politics and how it relates to authoritarian leadership. From the unisex "tough fighter" in the earlier stage of her political career to the "model mother" before and after the electoral campaign, Carrie Lam made strategic use of fashion to accumulate political capital and visualize her motherhood discourse rooted in Confucian paternalism. Given its well-fitted cut, tailored to refine professional postures and mannerisms, and Lam's go-to choices of floral patterns and modest colors often giving a soft edge, her cheongsam constructs a distinctive form of female maturity that fits with her political image as virtuous, educated, and maternalistic.

While her motherhood discourse and Confucian-paternalistic style might appeal to the political elites as well as the conservative bloc of the Hong Kong population, it backfired on her after the June 12 protest, drawing widespread criticism from the general public. Soon after the broadcast of the interview, a group of "Hong Kong mothers" initiated petitions, and 6,000 of them joined a sit-in protest in a Hong Kong park on June 14. They dressed in black T-shirts and trousers, holding signs reading "DON'T SHOOT OUR KIDS" in support of the black bloc protesters of June 12. The "Mother Protest" poses a direct challenge to Carrie Lam's motherhood discourse by suggesting that a responsible mother should in fact stand *with* their children and keep open the lines of communication (Yam 2019). Political cartoonists have created parodies of Carrie Lam's cheongsam image, becoming part of Hong Kong's visual subculture. The cartoonists criticized the hypocrisy of Carrie Lam's motherhood discourse; in one image, Lam, on one hand, is wiping her tears on camera, while off-camera she holds a gun (Figure 1.3). Motherhood will continue to be highly contested political terrain, given the long-established Confucian-paternalistic culture as well as the escalation of socio-political tension. Fashion and body politics in general will remain an important domain of political struggle, in Hong Kong as elsewhere.

Coda

In April 2022, Carrie Lam announced her intention not to seek her second term as Chief Executive. At the time, her HKSAR Government had a -42 percent net satisfaction rate, according to the Hong Kong Public Opinion Research Institute (2022). Lam's stepping down has been described by commentators as a strategy on the part of Beijing to select a new figurehead to continue its repressive policies (Siu 2022); indeed, Lam was eventually replaced by the former police chief, John Lee, seen by many as a pro-Beijing hardliner. As journalist Jessie Lau (2022) noted, with this new leader, the future for progressive politics in Hong Kong faces many challenges. For feminists, she writes, the outlook was already bleak. Lam's gender alone did not make her a force for women's advancement, nor did her manipulation of her image to underscore her "mother of the nation" credentials; as local feminist scholar Petula Ho is quoted in Lau's article, "She used her image to justify certain actions and present herself as a good mother, as if by virtue of being a mother that [a positive] implication is there. But [...] people really don't think she's motherly at all, she is somebody who we think is against ethics of care" (Lau 2022). The following chapters in this book will take up the question of what makes a "good" mother in public and what positive implications are assumed to accompany her. For now, Ho leaves us much to consider with respect to privileging the "ethics of care" above the biological fact of motherhood when determining what defines the "motherly."

Figure 1.3 "Mother" by Savona Ling, created at the time of the 2019 protests. ©
Courtesy of Savona Ling.

References

"Carrie Lam: As A Mother, I Can Understand the Feelings of Their Mothers (林鄭： 作為人母 理解幾位母親心情 Lam Cheng: Chok Wai Yanmo, Likai Geiwai Mocan Sumching)" (2017), *Stand News*, August 21. No longer available online: https://bit.ly/31qzgQJ (accessed June 28, 2020).

Carrie Lam (2017), "Facebook Watch Video," Facebook, July 2, 2017. Video no longer available: https://www.facebook.com/watch/?v=752294804950088 (accessed April 15, 2021).

Chen, S.-W. S. and S. W. Lau. (2021), "Little Red Children and 'Grandpa Xi': China's School Textbooks Reflect the Rise of Xi Jinping's Personality Cult," *The Conversation*, November 22. Available online: https://theconversation.com/little-red-children-and-grandpa-xi-chinas-school-textbooks-reflect-the-rise-of-xi-jinpings-personality-cult-168482 (accessed December 15, 2021).

Cheung, T. (2017), "Hong Kong's Ice Cool Iron Lady with a Will of Steel," *South China Morning Post*, January 12. Available online: https://www.scmp.com/news/hong-kong/politics/article/2061660/hong-kongs-ice-cool-iron-lady-will-steel (accessed June 28, 2020).

Clark, H. (2000), *The Cheongsam*. Oxford: Oxford University Press.

Edwards, L. (2000), "Policing the Modern Woman in Republican China," *Modern China*, 26 (2): 115–47.

Finnane, A. (2008), *Changing Clothes in China: Fashion, History, Nation*. New York: Columbia University Press.

Hong Kong Public Opinion Research Institute (2022). PORI Releases Popularity Figures of SAR Government, PSI and People's Appraisal of Policy Areas of the Government, Press Release, April 26. Available online: https://www.pori.hk/wp-content/uploads/2022/04/pr_2022apr26.pdf⊠ge=7 (accessed April 20, 2021).

Kim, S.-Y. (2011), "Dressed to Kill: Women's Fashion and Body Politics in North Korean Visual Media," *Positions: East Asia Cultures Critique*, 19 (1): 159–91.

King, A. Y. C. (2018), *China's Great Transformation: Selected Essays on Confucianism, Modernization, and Democracy*. Hong Kong: Chinese University of Hong Kong Press.

Ko, F. (2017), "Carrie Lam: A Good Wife and Mother after Work (林鄭月娥：公職之外也做好妻子與母親 Lam Cheng Yuct-ngor: Kungjik Yingoi Ya Zouho Caizi Yu Mocan)," *Wenweipo*, 2 July. Available online: http://news.wenweipo.com/2017/07/02/IN1707020018.htm (accessed June 28, 2020).

Kuan, H.-C. and S.-K. Lau (2002), "Between Liberal Autocracy and Democracy: Democratic Legitimacy in Hong Kong," *Democratization*, 9 (4): 58–76.

Lau, J. (2022), "With New Leader, the Future for Progressive Politics Looks More Challenging—for Feminists in Hong Kong, It was Already Bleak," CNN, May 5. Available online: https://edition.cnn.com/2022/05/05/asia/john-lee-hong-kong-gender-feminist-movement-as-equals-intl-cmd/index.html (accessed March 31, 2023).

Lau, S. (2017), "Hong Kong's Ice Queen Carrie Lam Melts Hearts at Maiden Political Rally," *South China Morning Post*, February 3. Available online: https://www.scmp.com/news/hong-kong/politics/article/2067946/hong-kongs-ice-queen-carrie-lam-melts-hearts-maiden (accessed June 28, 2021).

Lau, S.-K. (1981), "Chinese Familism in an Urban-Industrial Setting: The Case of Hong Kong," *Journal of Marriage and Family*, 43 (4): 977–92.

Ling, W. (2017), "Nationalism, Women and Their China: What More the Chinese Talk about When They Talk about the Qipao?," in J. Jefferies (ed.), *TECHSTYLE Series 1.0: Ariadne's Thread*, 91–101. Hong Kong: Mill6 Foundation.

Manifesto of Carrie Lam Chief Executive Election (2017), *The Government of the Hong Kong Special Administrative Region of the People's Republic of China*. Available online: https://www.ceo.gov.hk/archive/5-term/eng/pdf/Manifesto_words_E_revised.pdf (accessed November 15, 2022).

Ng, S. (2018), "Clothes Make the Woman: Cheongsam and Chinese Identity in Hong Kong," in K. Pyun and A. Y. Wong (eds.), *Fashion, Identity, and Power in Modern Asia*, 357–78. Shanghai: Palgrave Macmillan.

Parsons, T. (1991), *The Social System*. London: Routledge.

Paulicelli, E. (2004), *Fashion under Fascism: Beyond the Black Shirt*. New York: Bloomsbury.

Siu, J. (2022), "Carrie Lam's Departure Signals a Further Crackdown in Hong Kong," *The Diplomat*, April 11. Available online: https://thediplomat.com/2022/04/carrie-lams-departure-signals-a-further-crackdown-in-hong-kong/ (accessed March 31, 2023).

Stitzel, J. (2005), *Fashioning Socialism: Clothing, Politics and Consumer Culture in East Germany*. New York: Berg.

Tam, L. (2019), "Carrie Lam's Clumsy Parenting Analogy was Designed to Take Sting Out of Extradition Bill Protests, But Only Burns Relations with Hong Kong Mothers," *South China Morning Post*, June 17. Available online: https://www.scmp.com/news/hong-kong/society/article/3014863/carrie-lams-clumsy-parenting-analogy-was-designed-take-sting (accessed June 28, 2020).

Tremlett, P.-F. (2015), "Affective Dissent in the Heart of the Capitalist Utopia: Occupy Hong Kong and the Sacred," *Sociology*, 50 (6): 1156–69.

Wilson, V. (2002), "Dressing for Leadership in China: Wives and Husbands in an Age of Revolutions (1911–1976)," *Gender and History*, 14 (3): 614.

2

Beyoncé

Mistress of Slaying Oshun

Darnell-Jamal Lisby

In her 2019 song, "Mood 4 Eva," globally renowned artist and entertainer Beyoncé Knowles-Carter sings, "Why would you try me? Why would you bother? I am Beyoncé Giselle Knowles-Carter. I am the Nala, sister of Naruba; Oshun, Queen Sheba, I am the mother." Oshun, to whom this lyric refers, is a central motherhood figure of the West African Yoruba religion. In the Yoruba Orisha belief system, similarly to that of Christianity, the divine creator has multiple aspects—401 to Christianity's Holy Trinity (WGBH 2015). Each spirit, or orisha, has an association, and Oshun is one of the more notable orishas whose domain extends over femininity, beauty, rivers, love, and fertility (Mesa 2018). Expressing the intersection of her Blackness and her perspectives on motherhood, in recent years, Beyoncé has incorporated imagery often associated with Oshun into her onstage costumes, fashions, and public persona. Examples include a golden chiffon Balmain halter dress and a yellow Madame Adama bodice, skirt, and *gele* crown-like headdress (a traditional headdress worn predominately in West Africa), both worn in the 2020 *Black is King* visual album (2020). Motherhood has become a cornerstone of Beyoncé's artistry, drawing from a myriad of art historical and Black cultural references that speak to her celebration of family, marriage, and motherhood. Throughout her career, Beyoncé has used fashion as an integral tool in connecting with audiences, increasingly channeling the social messages in her music through evolvingly avant-garde visual imagery. This chapter will explore how Beyoncé communicates her reverence for motherhood (and Black motherhood in particular) through her onstage style. This chapter aims to analyze the art-historical nuances Beyoncé weaves throughout her costumes and fashions, from the orisha Oshun to the Virgin Mary, that amplify her message of motherhood as empowerment.

It is easy to identify the first time in Beyoncé's career that motherhood was referenced explicitly in relation to herself: her iconic performance at the 2011 MTV Video Music Awards, when, while singing her hit song "Love on Top," she unbuttoned her Dolce and Gabbana sequined tuxedo jacket to reveal a nascent baby bump (she was pregnant with her first child, Blue Ivy) (Figure 2.1). However, there are plenty of instances in her earlier career, from before she became a mother herself, where a vision of motherhood as aspirational power can be interpreted, including in her time as the lead of the girl group Destiny's Child. In the song "Survivor," she sings, "You know I'm not gon' diss you on the internet, cause my mama taught me better than that!" (Destiny's Child 2001). In context, the lyric was intended to silence public discourse on how the members of Destiny's Child were evolving as a group and as young Black adult women. Wearing battle dress uniform-inspired ensembles in the music video underlined the group's convictions, and this lyric demonstrates

Figure 2.1 Beyoncé reveals her "baby bump" onstage at the 2011 MTV Video Music Awards. Kristian Dowling / Getty Images.

how their belief system was built in part by the group's collective mother figure, and Beyoncé's biological mom, Tina Knowles. The lyric also demonstrates a belief that mothers act as the moral barometers in the lives of their families. Additionally, it highlights how Beyoncé and her Destiny's Child bandmates connected with their audiences by sharing their valuing of traditional maternal and familial relationships.

Even before Beyoncé's solo career turned toward the incorporation of more literal displays of celebrating motherhood through costumes and overall visuals (as in the previously mentioned 2011 MTV VMA performance), there were instances where her costumes more abstractly exuded this heralding of motherhood. From Destiny's Child's through the first half of Beyoncé's solo career and up to approximately 2012, Tina Knowles was Beyoncé's primary costume designer ("Behind the Seams" 2013). Acclaimed stylist Ty Hunter was also brought on during these years; he remained as Beyoncé's stylist until 2015. Many of the most notable ensembles of Beyoncé's career were conceptualized by her mother. As Richard Dyer explains, we only ever "know" a star "as they are to be found in media texts"; for Beyoncé and other star musicians, those texts include both the auditory (i.e., their music) and the visual, which need to work seamlessly together to produce a persona (Dyer 2019: 2). To have her mother woven so indelibly into the essential visual component of Beyoncé's work illustrates the significance of motherhood in the construction of her persona right from its very foundation.

Tina Knowles was integral in partnering with Beyoncé on their first fashion label, House of Deréon, named for Tina Knowles's mother, Agnèz Deréon, evidencing the importance of the matrilineal in their self-creation (Tietjen 2016) (Figure 2.2). The mission was to create an accessible range of sportswear and eveningwear in a wide size range, giving curvy and non-curvy women an opportunity to participate equally in the landscape of style. Tina Knowles would use House of Deréon fashions as costumes for Beyoncé's music videos and live performances; one notable instance is the House of Deréon designs that Beyoncé and her backup dancers wore throughout the 2006 music video for "Freakum Dress," a song with a critical female-empowerment message (2006). In the video, Beyoncé and dancers of all sizes wore House of Deréon cocktail dresses, again illuminating the mission of the fashion label. This video, emblematic as it is of Beyoncé's early solo career, shows the literal importance of her mother and how maternal legacy has always played an essential role in Beyoncé's self-presentation.

Motherhood took on a much more immediate role in Beyoncé's visual presentation when she became pregnant with her first child, Blue. In an interview

Figure 2.2 The matriarchal House of Deréon: Beyoncé, Blue Ivy Carter, and Tina Knowles attend the 67th NBA All-Star Game, 2018. Kevin Mazur/WireImage.

in the January 2020 issue of *Elle*, she opened up about suffering miscarriages before her first child's birth. She said, "Having miscarriages taught me that I had to mother myself before I could be a mother to someone else. Then I had Blue, and the quest for my purpose became so much deeper" ("For Beyoncé" 2019). This transition to motherhood and a deeper purpose is prevalent in the lyrics of this period of Beyoncé's output, but it also is easily seen in the evolution of her onstage costumes and fashions. Several performances in particular exemplify how pregnancy and later motherhood shaped her overall artistry. The first of note is her performance at the 2011 Glastonbury Festival, where she was the first Black woman solo artist to perform on the famous stage. In her self-produced 2013 *Life is But a Dream* documentary, we learn that she was in the early stages of her pregnancy during this performance (Knowles-Carter 2013b). She wore a radiant, gold sequined jacket from the Alexandre Vauthier Fall 2010 collection to hide her early pregnancy from audiences and thus control the media narrative around it. Upon the suggestion of her mother, she wrapped a wide belt to cloak the appearance of her pregnancy further. Without missing a beat, she gave a critically acclaimed performance without mention of her pregnancy. A review of the performance by Running Lip said, "Beyoncé at Glastonbury 2011 was the epitome of everything a good performance should be. Up-beat, Edgy, Diverse, and above all Entertaining. No "wardrobe malfunctions," falls, lip-syncing, or other distractions [...] Just good music, good choreography, and one fantastic performance to bring the most prominent music festival in the world to a fitting close" (2011). Several weeks later, she performed several nights in New York City at the Roseland Ballroom, wearing a sequined custom two-piece bralette and briefs ensemble, with an additional flap covering most of her stomach region. Even then, no one knew about the pregnancy. Given Beyoncé's traditionally guarded public image, one can only speculate that hiding the early stages of her pregnancy was a way to protect her space because of her previous miscarriages. Beyoncé's reasoning for hiding her pregnancy is not something she's ever been obligated to share, but it could have stemmed from wishing to defy the fallacy that women are prohibited from certain strenuous activities, like performing, when they are pregnant. Regardless of the reason, fashion was used strategically to hide her condition, controlling the narrative around her pregnancy.

A month after Glastonbury, we saw the famous baby bump reveal at the MTV Video Music Awards (Kaufman 2011). On the surface, the message of this revelation was that if a woman has the desire and ability to work during her pregnancy, she should be celebrated and supported in doing so. Beyoncé, known to be a tireless worker, performing while pregnant suggested a degree of relatability to the laborious motherhood journeys of so many. Additionally, her persistence, not allowing her physical condition to stop her from delivering high-level performances, speaks to a perspective on feminism she advocates. As Emily J. Lordi wrote in her chapter, "Surviving the Hustle: Beyoncé's Performance of Work," in the publication *Beyoncé: At Work, On Screen, and Online*, "Although she notes the emotional and economic injustices of [the] system [in which women "have to work much harder"], Beyoncé proceeds to present her own 'lean in'-style philosophy of female empowerment through personal perseverance" (2020: 28). For those watching the performance, especially with the very gleeful tone and lyrics of "Love on Top," and her interjection to the audience that "I want you to feel the love that's growing inside of me" (Kaufman 2011), the performance was upbeat and positive, but also meant to empower them. After revealing her baby bump, it could be understood that she was foreshadowing this moment in the performance and through the costumes from the previous series of live performances in which her midsection was obscured, to celebrate motherhood as first a private sanctity and then a triumphant component of women's work.

The ensemble she wore for this performance was a perfect encapsulation of the historical symbolism she wanted to channel. The Dolce and Gabbana sequined blazer, in conjunction with the happy-go-lucky, rhythmic, Motown-esque "Love on Top" song immediately signaled the golden age of soul when entertainers like James Brown, Diana Ross, Little Richard, and the Jackson 5 performed in embellished tailored suits and costumes, bolstering larger-than-life personalities. Lordi even writes that Beyoncé has "regendered James Brown's soul-era self-designation as the 'hardest working man in show business'", a process at least partly achieved with this costuming and further underscoring the association of her pregnant performance with hard work. Beyoncé wanted the reveal of her pregnancy to shine bright, so bringing in visual reference to those inspirational performers was fitting.

The next phase of her career, the first phase of her motherhood, was relentlessly productive, from the 2013 Superbowl Halftime show to her residency at the Revel Casino. In December 2013, she quietly released her eponymous visual album[1] *Beyoncé* without any advance press (Henry 2018). Fans immediately flooded the internet to buy the album and its video component. The album was monumental not only because it was a successful promotional experiment, but it also contextualized her journey as a mother and a wife. Many of the songs conveyed an unabashed sensuality, as in "Drunk in Love" and "Partition," that women, especially new mothers, are often ridiculed or shunned for expressing. A Black woman embracing her sexuality and taking agency over her body has always been judged harshly by mainstream society, e.g., the demeaning of Janet Jackson after her own 2004 Superbowl Halftime performance in which her breast was exposed. For Beyoncé, unashamed of who she was and showing that her sexuality did not diminish after motherhood, this album was a symbol of the power she had to transform cultural narratives. A 2014 *Guardian* review reads, "With its frank lyrics about female power, desire, libido, envy and sex, Beyoncé's self-titled studio album, surprise-released last December, has been received as a kind of mission statement about empowerment and third-wave feminism" (Michaels 2014). This album and its visuals were a snapshot of her journey and, together with the music and lyrics, her onstage and video costumes exuded this mantra of empowerment.

The narrative of "Partition" involves Beyoncé asserting her own sexual desire within her marriage. In the video, from the crystal-embroidered corset from the Christian Lacroix Spring 1996 collection to the crystal-encrusted lingerie sets, the sensual message was clear. The Lacroix corset refers back to the S-bend corset that dominated fashionable silhouettes during the Edwardian period at the turn of the twentieth century (Johnston n.d.). To contemporary eyes, corsetry of any type is often read as a signifier of sex, specifically subcultural (i.e., BDSM, etc.) sex (see Steele 1996, for more on the multifaceted meanings of the contemporary corset). Therefore, Beyoncé subverted the original episteme of this corset meant to reference fashion in the late-nineteenth and early-twentieth century by leaning into the more contemporary eroticization of the garment. There is also a scene where she dances in a crystal lingerie and cap ensemble in an ode to Josephine Baker, an artist seen to have "paved [the] way to stardom" for many contemporary Black women artists, specifically as pertaining to embracing one's sexuality in public (Kooijman 2020: 117). Adding more evidence to the intentionality of the visual relationship to Baker, Beyoncé recorded the video at the famous Parisian Crazy Horse cabaret establishment, of which Baker is considered an icon in France. Regardless of all the innuendos and visual spectacle, Beyoncé was taking control of how people wanted to see her; in spite of the stereotypes associated with mothers becoming more matronly after having children, she maintained a high level of visual sensuality.

A significant moment honoring her motherhood journey on the self-titled album also appears in the song "Mine," featuring rapper Drake. The lyrics say: "I've been watching for the signs / Took a trip to clear my mind, oh / Now I'm even more lost / And you're still so fine, oh my, oh my / Been having conversations about breakups and separations / I'm not feeling like myself since the baby / Are we gonna even make it?" (2013). The lyrics seem to hint at postpartum depression, as she questions her state of mind since having her child, but she still wants to keep her relationship with her partner strong. According to postpartum statistics, about 70 to 80 percent of birthing mothers experience the "baby blues," while a large portion will experience the more severe condition of postpartum depression (Langdon n.d.). As dark as it may be, postpartum depression is a unifying human experience, and one that even mega-celebrities endure. Beyoncé using her lyrical platform to build relatability with her audiences has pushed her from just a pop icon into a cultural one, inspiring a parasocial relationship with her fans (and "stans") the intensity of which eclipses that of most contemporary stars (Termini 2015: 23).

In the music video's opening song where she sings the previously mentioned lyrics, she sits on a pedestal wearing a gray corseted bodice and skirt by designer Gareth Pugh and a veil. Around her are dancers framing the scene with large swaths of fabric, and a woman lies in Beyoncé's arms in a lifeless dramatic pose. The image is inspired by Michelangelo's 1499 masterwork, *The Pietà* (Columbia University 2019), a sculpture of Mary holding her son, Jesus, after he was taken down from the cross. In the Christian story, Mary was essentially a vessel for Jesus to enter the physical world from the spiritual one, yet she was left to mourn his death. The *Pietà* depicts a moment of humanity where the spiritual significance of Jesus giving his life on the cross coincides with the human prerogative of a mother to grieve her dead son. The grief over a child, which Beyoncé has endured through her miscarriages and the depression that followed her child's birth, is used to shape the bounds of her art. The lyrics and visuals, including the assemblage of fashion, together offer a chance to express and confront this pain in a way that connects and elevates the suffering of mothers across time and space. As referred to in the introduction to this book's part on the "Image," Adrienne Rich saw the *Pietà* as among the images that have embodied and entrenched the institution of motherhood; here, Beyoncé perpetuates the sculpture's place in that history.

Building on the "Mine" video's imagery, she extended the reference to the *Pietà* for the 2014 MTV VMAs, where she won the Video Vanguard Award (Alexis 2014). She opened her performance with "Mine," sitting in a similar pose to the one in the video with dancers surrounding her. There was a dancer also between her legs in the same lifeless, dramatic pose. There she wore a crystal bodice by Tom Ford, a reworked design from the Fall 2014 collection, which allowed her to execute the intense choreography needed for the performance. Behind Beyoncé in the opening scene was a projection of the Rose stained glass windows of Notre Dame, underlining the art-historical and Christian inspiration of this song and performance.

Following the eponymous album, a new era of Beyoncé's work began. In this phase, Beyoncé used her music to discuss her Blackness unabashedly and to transparently promote Black empowerment. This is not to say that she did not celebrate Blackness in previous chapters of her career, but these recent works, including *Lemonade* (2016), *Everything is Love* (2018), and *The Lion King: The Gift* (2019) / *Black is King* (2020), directly revolve around celebrating the richness of the Afro-Diaspora and using the various subcommunities as inspiration. A primary inspiration for this period has been the orisha Oshun, and through the appearance of this figure, motherhood has been imbued in much of her art and onstage imagery. As the orisha of femininity, beauty, rivers, love, and rebirth, motherhood is intrinsic to Oshun's persona. Oshun is often depicted radiantly and associated with the colors gold and yellow.

Many of the visuals from the 2016–20 period contain a consistent interpretation of Oshun's essence as a mother figure, used to convey messages of personal rebirth and to encourage a renewal of Black empowerment. One of the first instances we see is in the "Hold Up" scene of the *Lemonade* visual album (Knowles-Carter 2016). The album recounts a specific narrative of the main character, presumably Beyoncé (her husband Jay-Z confirmed in his 2017 *New York Times* interview that the story was based on their real-life marriage, yet Beyoncé has been coy about discussing it), discovering that her partner has been unfaithful (Baquet 2017). Each song represents the stages of emotion that the main character endures before reconciling with her partner. In the second song, "Hold Up," the character experiences anger after discovering infidelity. The song's lyrics admonish the partner, reminding him that he is only where he is in life because of her sacrifices. Beyoncé wears a marigold-colored Cavalli Fall 2016 sheer ruffled off-the-shoulder dress. Before the song begins, she swings open the doors of a bank-like building as a rush of water flows out of the facility past her—this immediately sets up and makes clear the Oshun reference. Even though Oshun's character seems very calm, she also contains rage. Indeed, this aspect of Oshun was clearly being channeled as Beyoncé, in character, walked through the video with her baseball bat, swinging cathartically at parked cars. *Lemonade* played with a significant dual meaning, conveying the anger within the collective Black experience due to historical oppression and ongoing, unjust violence and lack of protection from law enforcement and the overall justice and political systems, in addition to the personal narrative about marriage and motherhood. Therefore, the righteous anger of "Hold Up" and the yellow dress represent Beyoncé using the motherly essence of this deity to activate a spirit of power within Black audiences, encouraging them to use anger for positive action that advances the Black community.

Oshun has continued to appear within Beyoncé's onstage costumes and fashions as a way of layering motherhood with social activism. Her 2017 Grammy Awards performance, for which she sang two ballads from *Lemonade*, "Love Drought" and "Sandcastles," while heavily pregnant with her twins, Rumi and Sir, was the epitome of the two (Figure 2.3). With only light choreography included in the performance to accommodate her advanced pregnancy stage, Beyoncé wore a custom Peter Dundas gold netted gown and House of Malakai crown, emitting an undeniable radiance as well as explicit reference to the "Black Madonna" art historical tradition in which the Virgin Mary and Jesus are both depicted as Black ("Hollywood Reacts" 2017).[2] Before the performance began, a video montage played of Beyoncé in various scenes with dancers or by herself, gracefully moving her body with a voiceover of a monologue. The moment had religious overtones, not least due to the House of Malakai crown's resemblance to a halo. Yet, the Western Christian tradition was not the only bank of religious

Figure 2.3 Beyoncé performs, pregnant with twins, during the 59th Grammy Awards, 2017, employing the visual symbolism of the orisha Oshun and the Virgin Mary. Larry Busacca / Getty Images.

symbolism from which this performance drew visuals to underscore the power of motherhood.

In one scene, Beyoncé wears the crown and a silk bikini-like suit with long strips, the strips of which dancers flared the ends around her. This visually calls upon Durga, the Hindu supreme motherhood goddess. Bringing motherhood into central focus, she says in the voice-over monologue, reading the poetry of Warsan Shire as she does in the voiceover of *Lemonade*:

> Do you remember being born? Are you thankful for the hips that cracked? The deep velvet of your mother and her mother, and her mother? You look nothing like your mother, everything like your mother. You desperately want to look like her. How to wear your mother's lipstick. You must wear it like she wears disappointment on her face. Your mother is a woman, and women like her cannot be contained.

Then, a video played of Beyoncé's mother, Tina Knowles, and her daughter Blue Ivy as the monologue finished. With Beyoncé so visibly pregnant at the time, celebrating motherhood and the matrilineal line of her family was the theme of the night. When the live performance began, the netted gown gloriously clung to and emphasized her baby bump. The stage was adorned with flowers and vegetation, and her dancers in lightweight sheer dresses embodied nymphs surrounding Beyoncé as if she was Oshun come to physical manifestation. The dancers also wore halos and danced around a table, which could have been a subtle nod to Da Vinci's *The Last Supper*, equating Christ's sacrifice to the sacrifice of motherhood. Following the two ballads she sang, the voiceover returned, and the last words spoken were, "Now that reconciliation is possible, now that we're going to heal, let it be glorious." Again, a second meaning is contained within the lyrics. On one hand, the character is speaking to her partner about reconciliation, yet these words could also be interpreted as a rallying cry for Black audiences to actively participate in efforts to make the United States reconcile with its history and work for a better future.

As Beyoncé moved into her next album and the accompanying film *Black is King*, various odes to Oshun continued to be made. The film was developed in conjunction with her 2019 *Lion King: The Gift* album that was created to accompany Disney's 2019 *Lion King* live-action remake of the 1994 film. The album is a compilation of songs meant to sonically narrate the emotions of each of the major scenes from the *Lion King* film. In addition to this direct intention, the lyrics also operate as calls for Black empowerment. *Black is King*'s production was global and incorporated a myriad of inspirations from the Afro-diaspora in the settings and costumes. From the *gele* headdress meant to celebrate West African peoples to the cowhide ensembles by Ricardo Tisci for Burberry meant to commemorate the Zulu and Xhosa people of South Africa, the film was a celebration of Blackness. There were instances of Oshun seen throughout the film, like the pleated yellow silk chiffon dress designed by longtime collaborator Olivier Rousteing of Balmain or the radiant yellow satin dress, *gele*, and briefs ensemble by Adama Paris.

Oshun aside, there were additional examples of Beyoncé celebrating motherhood through fashion in *Black is King*, including two that directly involved her daughter Blue Ivy. In the song and accompanying video for "Spirit," a song with a motivational message about fighting through oppression (Knowles-Carter 2020), she walks in a desert in a lavender ruffled gown by Pierpaolo Piccoli of Valentino that he designed for the Spring 2019 Couture collection. Blue Ivy also appears in the scene dressed in a smaller, child's version of the gown, sitting right under her mother. Incorporating both the royal theme of the Lion King story (itself loosely based on *Hamlet*) and the media characterization of herself as "Queen Bey," Beyoncé used this imagery to elevate her daughter and position her own family as being of a regal bloodline and lineage. In embracing the queenly persona and giving her daughter a similar place, the visuals also echo royal and aristocratic portraits throughout art history that depict multiple generations of family members as subjects. Positioning such a visual specifically in the African context enshrines both Beyoncé and Blue in the pantheon of African-diasporic icons and asserts that, per what Patricia Hill Collins calls "an Afrocentric ideology of motherhood" that sees motherhood as a symbol of power deeply connected to the continuity of bloodlines and communities, that the love and respect Beyoncé has earned from her global fandom should be extended to her entire network of kin (Collins 1987).

Once again uplifting her daughter in the context of Black womanhood, she featured her in a later song entitled "Brown Skin Girl," which became an anthem for Black women and girls worldwide (Knowles-Carter 2020). The song's lyrics celebrate the beauty in the spectrum of Blackness and darker skin hues; the song is meant to offer an empowering counterpoint to society's frequent dismissal of Black women and their physical beauty. Blue Ivy in fact won a Grammy for the song alongside her mother in 2021. It is important to note that as a Black girl, Blue Ivy has experienced vitriolic hatred, especially regarding her hair, since she was a toddler. When commenting about a satirical social media petition to change Blue Ivy's hair, Sonita R. Moss said in her chapter, "Beyoncé and Blue:

Black Motherhood and the Binds of Racialized Sexism," that "within a racist and sexist social system, Black women often propagate and instantiate extent hatred of Black womanhood. Black females are expected to meet a standard of beauty, regardless of their age. Blue Ivy was two years old when this petition circulated, revealing the unscrupulousness of racialized sexism" (2016: 156). The "Brown Skin Girl" song and visuals were ways that Beyoncé provided a path for her daughter to reclaim her power as a developing Black young woman, much as her mother Tina had previously done for her. As Gloria I. Joseph wrote in 1981, quoted in *Of Woman Born*, "there is a tremendous amount of teaching transmitted by Black mothers to their daughters that enables them to survive, exist, succeed, and be important to and for the Black communities throughout America. These attitudes become internalized and transmitted to future generations" (1981; quoted in Rich [1976] 1995: xxvii). Furthermore, as Hill Collins emphasizes, this transmission also occurs in role modeling. By including women like Kelly Rowland, Naomi Campbell, and others in the video, Beyoncé evidences Hill Collins' point that: "Black women-centered extended family networks foster an early identification with a much wider range of models of Black womanhood which can lead to a greater sense of empowerment in young Black girls" (Collins 1987: 7). This vision of a mother-daughter relationship that includes non-biological "othermothers" is very much in line with the traditions of West African societies for whom motherhood is "symbolic of creativity and continuity"—traditions to which Beyoncé's costuming continually refers.

The setting for the "Brown Skin Girl" video is a cotillion with charmingly dressed young Black men and women dancing and acting out various social graces. In one scene, Beyoncé wears a black layered tulle gown by Timothy White and a braided hairstyle reminiscent of the Mangbetu Edamburu hairstyle technique. The Mangbetu people are native to the Congo region, where a traditional practice for women of the aristocratic class was head elongation. After elongating the head, the wearer would have a series of braids held together by pins to create a circular, crown-like finish. Surely, Beyoncé did not endure the elongation process, but her team recreated the essence of the Mangbetu style using contemporary hair technology. This is not the first time we have seen this Mangbetu reference in Beyoncé's career—we see it in *Lemonade* in the video/scene for the song "Sorry" (Knowles-Carter 2016). In both instances, she uses the style alongside references to motherhood. In conjunction with the lyrics of "Sorry," in which she speaks of taking her child away from her cheating partner, she wears a similar hairstyle. As mentioned, the Mangbetu hairstyle has royal connotations, meant to emanate a sense of regalness that's not only physical but also emotional. Thus, in the vein of the "Sorry" video and song, she holds herself in high regard, above the drama her husband created through infidelity. The use of the Mangbetu-esque hairstyle represents the strength and poise she must possess to make such a decision as a mother to pack her bags and her children and leave her husband. In *Black is King*, the style has similar connotations, being used to highlight the beauty of Mangbetu women and the diversity yet interconnection of Black mothers around the world.

Conclusion

Even more than the assemblage of ensembles that continue to inspire contemporary fashion, Beyoncé's onstage style uses a diverse range of art- and fashion-historical references that celebrates Blackness, enumerates her spirituality, and advocates feminism. More precisely, in Beyoncé's onstage style, we also begin to understand how she reveres maternity as a source of internal power. When answering fan questions in 2013, Beyoncé said that she felt that motherhood had liberated her artistry. As shown throughout that year's visual album, she does not shy away from the provocative, sensual imagery traditionally associated with her pre-motherhood onstage persona. In that album and afterward, Beyoncé embraces her sexuality in ways hegemonic protocol traditionally prevents mothers, let alone many communities of women, from doing due to the misogynistic fallacy that sex and motherhood are somehow separate and should not be openly embraced. Beyoncé uses her onstage costumes and fashions to dismantle social constructs built around motherhood, specifically regarding the Black experience, and to reject and counter the idea of motherhood as a monolith. Instead, she boldly claims through her visuals as much as her lyrics that motherhood can be freeing for anyone who chooses it.

Notes

1   For her 2006 *B'Day* album, Beyoncé created individual videos for each song that wove a narrative across the album, similar to a film—hence the term "visual album." She has reused the format multiple times.
2   Also see Cheryl Thompson (2020) for more on how Beyoncé has embraced the recontextualization of Western art symbols to center Black women.

References

Alexis, N. (2014), "Beyoncé's 2014 VMAs Performance: Fearless, Feminists, Flawless, Family Time," MTV, August 25. Available online: http://www.mtv.com/news/1910270/beyonce-2014-vma-perfomance/ (accessed November 1, 2021).

Baquet, D. (2017), "Jay-Z & Dean Baquet: On Therapy, Politics, Marriage, the State of Rap, and Being a Black Man in Trump's America", *New York Times*, November 29. Available online: https://www.nytimes.com/interactive/2017/11/29/t-magazine/jay-z-dean-baquet-interview.html (accessed November 30, 2021).

"Behind the Seams: Beyoncé's Stylist Ty Hunter" (2013), *Billboard*, July 12. Available online: http://www.billboard.com/video/behind-the-seams-beyonce-stylist-ty-hunter-1665036 (accessed November 11, 2021).

"Beyoncé at Glastonbury 2011 Review" (2011), *Running Lip*, June 26. Available online: http://runninglip.com/music/live-music/beyonce-at-glastonbury-2011-review/ (accessed October 23, 2021).

Beyoncé Doing Tingz (2019), "Beyoncé live performance at the 2017 Grammys (Love Drought + Sandcastles)," YouTube, August 3. Available online: https://www.youtube.com/watch?v=ZhdTAwkDu1Q (accessed Novemer 1, 2021).

Collins, P. H. (1987), "The Meaning of Motherhood in Black Culture and Black Mother/Daughter Relationships," *SAGE: A Scholarly Journal on Black Women*, 4 (2): 3–10.

Destiny's Child (2001), "Survivor," music video. New York: Columbia Records.

Dyer, R. (2019), *Stars*, 2nd ed. London: Bloomsbury.

"For Beyoncé, Creativity is the Ultimate Power" (2019), *Elle*, December 9. Available online: https://www.elle.com/culture/celebrities/a29999871/beyonce-ivy-park-adidas-interview/ (accessed November 11, 2021).

Henry, P. (2018), "Five Years Later, Beyoncé's Surprise Album is Still One of the Most Important Moments in Music," *Teen Vogue*, December 13. Available online: https://www.teenvogue.com/story/beyonce-surprise-album-five-year-anniversary (accessed October 23, 2021).

"Hollywood Reacts to Beyoncé's Grammys Performance: 'She is Magic'" (2017), *Hollywood Reporter*, February 12. Available online: https://www.hollywoodreporter.com/movies/movie-news/hollywood-reacts-beyonces-grammys-2017-performance-975252/ (accessed November 6, 2021).

Johnston, L. (n.d.), "Corsets in the Early 20th Century," V&A Museum. Available online: http://www.vam.ac.uk/content/articles/c/corsets-early-20th-century/ (accessed November 6, 2021).

Kaufman, G. (2011), "Beyoncé Put Love on Top at VMAs: Reveals Pregnancy," MTV, August 28. Available online: https://www.mtv.com/news/1669858/beyonce-vma-performance/ (accessed October 23, 2021).

Knowles-Carter, B. (2006), "Freakum Dress," *B'Day*, album. New York: Columbia Records.

Knowles-Carter, B. (2013a), *Beyoncé*, album. New York: Parkwood Entertainment.

Knowles-Carter, B. (2013b), *Life is But a Dream*, film. New York: Parkwood Entertainment.

Knowles-Carter, B. (2013c), "Partition," music video, *Beyoncé*, New York: Parkwood Entertainment.

Knowles-Carter, B. (2016), *Lemonade*, film. New York: Parkwood Entertainment.

Knowles-Carter, B. (2019), "Mood 4 Eva," *Lion King: The Gift*, album. New York: Parkwood Entertainment.

Knowles-Carter, B. (2020), *Black is King*, film. New York: Parkwood Entertainment, and Burbank: Walt Disney Pictures.

Kooijman, J. (2020), "'At Last a Dream That I Can Call My Own': Beyoncé and the Performance of Stardom in Dreamgirls and Cadillac Records", in M. Iddon and M. Marshall (eds), *Beyoncé: At Work, On screen, and Online*, 114–135. Bloomington, IN: Indiana University Press.

Langdon, K. M. D., ed. (n.d.), "Postpartum Depression Statistics," *Postpartum Depression*. Available online: https://www.postpartumdepression.org/resources/statistics/ (accessed October 23, 2021).

Lordi, E. (2020), "Surviving the Hustle: Beyoncé's Performance of Work," in M. Iddon and M. Marshall (eds.), *Beyoncé: At Work, On Screen, and Online*, 23–39. Bloomington, IN: Indiana University Press.

Mesa, V. (2018), "How to Invoke Oshun, the Yoruba Goddess of Sensuality and Prosperity," *Vice*, April 20. Available online: https://www.vice.com/en/article/3kjepv/how-to-invoke-oshun-yoruba-goddess-orisha (accessed November 1, 2021).

Michaels, S. (2014), "Beyoncé: 'Men are Free and Women are Not,'" *The Guardian*, April 9. Available online: https://www.theguardian.com/music/2014/apr/09/beyonce-double-standard-contemporary-sex uality-equality (accessed November 20, 2021).

Moss, S. R. (2016), "Beyoncé and Blue: Black Motherhood and the Binds of Racialized Sexism," in A. Trier-Bieniek (ed.), *The Beyoncé Effect: Essays on Sexuality, Race and Feminism*, 155–76. Jefferson, NC: McFarland Books.

Rich, A. ([1976] 1995), *Of Woman Born: Motherhood as Experience and Institution*. New York: Norton.

Steele, V. (1996), *Fetish: Fashion, Sex and Power*. Oxford: Oxford University Press.

Termini, A. (2015), "Crazy in Love with a Smooth Criminal: An In-Depth Look at Parasocial Relationships and How Celebrities Affect the Relationship," *Academic Symposium of Undergraduate Scholarship*, 31. Available online: https://scholarsarchive.jwu.edu/ac_symposium/31 (accessed November 1, 2021).

"*The Pietà* by Michelangelo Buonarrot" (2019), *The Core Curriculum*. New York: Columbia University, September 26. Available online: https://core100.columbia.edu/article/pieta-michelangelo-buonarrot (accessed November 1, 2021).

Thompson, C. (2020), "From Venus to 'Black Venus'": Beyoncé's *I Have Three Hearts*, Fashion, and the Limits of Visual Culture," *Fashion Studies*, 3 (1). Available online: https://www.fashionstudies.ca/from-venus-to-black-venus (accessed November 10, 2021).

Tietjen, A. (2016), "Remember House of Dereon, Beyoncé and Tina Knowles' Fly AF Fashion Line," *VH1*, March 23. Available online: http://www.vh1.com/news/251636/house-of-dereon-throwback/ (accessed November 15, 2021).

WGBH Educational Foundation (2015), "Yoruba Religion of Southwestern Nigeria: Initiation of a Yoruban Priestess," *PBS*. Available online: https://ideastream.pbslearningmedia.org/resource/sj14-soc-yorubarel/yoruba-religion-of-south western-nigeria/ (accessed November 20, 2021).

3

The Hidden Life of Kylie

Fashioning a Private (and Privatized) Celebrity Pregnancy

Maureen Lehto Brewster

Once hidden under layers of fabric, moral tensions, and media anxiety, pregnancy has become highly visible with the advent of social media. Several decades of celebrity pregnancies, from Lucille Ball to Rihanna, have also made pregnancy more public. Publicly witnessed pregnancies are now not just acceptable, but fashionable: countless online guides instruct parents on how to share their pregnancy "with the virtual world" (Cichowski 2017). Despite these new norms, some expecting parents are opting to keep their pregnancies and bodies offline (Russo 2018). Among them was reality television star and beauty mogul Kylie Jenner, who released a mini documentary of her pregnancy "journey" with fans only after the birth of her first child, Stormi Webster, in February 2018. Jenner stated that she "kept [fans] in the dark" during this pregnancy because she "needed to prepare for this role of a lifetime in the most positive, stress free, and healthy way I knew how" (@kyliejenner 2018a). However, on February 22, 2018, she announced the "Weather Collection" for Kylie Cosmetics, inspired by her newborn daughter. The collection's development and release timeline illustrate that while Jenner was working to maintain the privacy of her pregnancy, she was also working to privately profit from it: after all, she claimed to have spent "pretty much her entire pregnancy" working on the collection (Muller 2018).

This chapter analyzes the development of the Weather Collection and frames it as an example of celebrity pregnancy in postfeminist (social) media culture, which has transformed celebrity pregnancy from an embodied experience to a fashionable product that can be branded and sold (Gill 2007; Lagerwey 2016). The Weather Collection is but the latest example of celebrity marketing ventures linked to pregnancy and parenthood, epitomizing the celebration of "brandable" parenthood in contemporary brand culture (Banet-Weiser 2012; Lagerwey 2016). However, the timing and development of the Weather Collection makes it a particularly intriguing case study to explore how celebrity pregnancy has shifted from private, to public, and increasingly *privatized*—that is, refashioned as a private rather than public commodity.

In this chapter, I will consider how media discourse on the pregnant celebrity body, particularly of young parents, influenced Jenner's decision to keep her first pregnancy private. I use archival coverage from *People* magazine to further contextualize the tabloid and entertainment media landscape in 2017, around the time that Jenner became pregnant. Next, I turn to Jenner's pregnancy announcement as well as the promotion of the Weather Collection on her social media accounts to reflect on the medium, rollout, and reception of these posts. Pregnancy announcements, particularly the elaborate audiovisual versions produced by Jenner, Beyoncé, and other celebrities, are a means of not only publicizing but narrativizing pregnancy (Winter 2018). I use content analysis of Jenner's posts to frame them as a form of self writing (Foucault 1997) which enabled her to (re)shape her star image (Dyer 1998) and branding as an entrepreneurial mother, both on and offline (Weisgerber and Butler 2016). I also use product images and e-commerce listings for items from the Weather Collection to analyze their packaging and formulation, to show how the line commodifies Jenner's new motherhood through references to her daughter Stormi.

While Jenner's decision to keep her pregnancy private was partly personal, this chapter ultimately argues that it was also a strategic decision that enabled her to monetize her pregnancy. Jenner's media and branding practices reframed her pregnancy, and by extension her daughter, Stormi, as private business assets rather than public content (Wubbena 2016). This reflects a broader economic and political shift toward neoliberal market economies, which champion individual choice, self-regulation, and the accumulation of capital (Gill and Scharff 2013; Harvey 2007). Under this system, and further aided by social media and information technologies, parenthood has become a commodity (Lagerwey 2016). Privatizing her pregnancy allows Jenner to maximize her material profit, demonstrating the continued power of the pregnancy industrial complex. More importantly, it also enables her to extend her self-brand and (re)articulate herself as a loving, entrepreneurial power mom, thereby extending the methodology and mythology of the Kardashian Industrial Komplex—itself a matriarchal brand par excellence (Figure 3.1).

Figure 3.1 Kylie Jenner shielding daughter Stormi from photographers, 2019. Robert Kamau / GC Images.

Keeping up with Kylie

Jenner was a highly visible figure in media and popular culture at the time of her first pregnancy. She is the youngest daughter of "momager" Kris Jenner and former Olympian Caitlyn Jenner. Kylie quite literally grew up on the screen, first appearing at age 9 on her family's reality television show *Keeping Up with the Kardashians* (KUWTK 2007–2021), and later headlining a spin-off called *Life of Kylie* (2017). She also has a very large following on social media, which she first used to promote various endorsements and later leveraged to found her own brand, Kylie Cosmetics. Jenner's star image, i.e., the multiplicity of meanings and affects produced by various media texts (Dyer 1998), is related to her "it girl" persona as cultivated via social media and her association with the Kardashian-Jenner transmedia empire prior to her first pregnancy (Edwards 2012). Although her 2019 appointment as the youngest self-made billionaire has been rightfully questioned—first informally, via critiques of her significant wealth and notoriety prior to founding Kylie Cosmetics in 2015, and later by *Forbes*, which demoted her billionaire status after concluding she had falsely inflated her financial records (Peterson-Withorn and Berg 2020)—Kylie Jenner is nevertheless a highly successful example of the hyper-entrepreneurial, self-commodifying, niche marketing celebrity in the early twenty-first-century media economy (Marshall 2021).

Her family also epitomizes this mode of celebrity. The rise of the Kardashian-Jenners is considered emblematic of the demotic turn in late twentieth-century celebrity culture, in which the growth of tabloid and social media democratized access to fame as well as to celebrities themselves (Turner 2016). The family's fame has been endlessly contested and theorized: it has been variously attributed to their "entrepreneurial" social media use (Ingleton and York 2019); their performance and monetization of glamour labor (Monteverde 2016; Wissinger 2016); their use of transmedia storytelling (Edwards 2012), and their appropriation of Black culture (Cherid 2021), among other factors. Kylie herself has frequently used Blackfishing to "wear Black women's features like a costume" for cultural and financial gain while retaining her racial privilege (Thompson 2018). She quite literally built her brand upon Black aesthetics: early in her career, she monetized her penchant for wigs and extensions via brand endorsements, and her famously plump lips, first attributed to cosmetics and later revealed as surgically enhanced, served as the inspiration for Kylie Cosmetics' inaugural Lip Kits.

The brand represents Jenner's first foray as an entrepreneur and the first instance of using her body—albeit enhanced by both surgery and Black cool (Tulloch 2016)—as the anchor for her brand. Following Barron (2007: 454) and Craik (1994), Kylie Jenner is "both transmitter [and] subject" of the Kylie Cosmetics fashion habitus, which promotes cosmetics as a tool of bodily management and identity construction. Until Stormi was born, Kylie Cosmetics glamorized and sexualized Jenner's body, highlighting her famous curves in sensual editorial and social media campaigns. However, it was always firmly anchored to Jenner's personality, family, and body through product packaging, marketing, and fulfillment, suggesting a desire to maximize a sense of authentic connection to Kylie Jenner herself. This is characteristic of celebrity branding, which relies on the perception of an authentic connection to the founder's persona and lifestyle (Moulard, Garrity, and Rice 2015). The Kardashian-Jenner family of brands, from Skims to Poosh to Good American, has perfected and profited from this model. Social media has enabled them to perform and monetize authenticity work for fans, further enhancing their self-brands (Banet-Weiser 2021). Meanwhile, their reality shows have allowed them significant control over their images, allowing them to reshape scandalous narratives in their favor, and also provided an anchor for their brands' transmedia storytelling (Edwards 2012; Woodward 2020). In the Kardashian-Jenner world, cameras control the narrative: rather than leave her pregnancy narrative to the tabloids, Jenner restricted access to her pregnancy from any cameras other than those she was able to control, allowing her to produce her ideal pregnancy for maximum (branding) impact. The result, *To Our Daughter* (2018), is a publicity "master class" that is perfectly calibrated to perform not just privacy but family and togetherness (Freeman 2018). I will analyze this film and its role in the privatization of Jenner's pregnancy in later sections. First, it is important to offer further context into Jenner's decision to keep her pregnancy private. Regardless of the potential branding opportunities, the media landscape at the time of Jenner's first pregnancy certainly offered other incentives for a young celebrity mother to keep her body under wraps.

Celebrity Pregnancy, Public and Private

Previous research explores the surveillance of women's bodies in entertainment and tabloid media, and how this often intensifies during and after pregnancy (Brewster 2014; Cramer 2015). Celebrities are scrutinized for the presence of a "baby bump" at all times; in the case of Jennifer Aniston, even the absence of a bump is newsworthy (Kirkpatrick 2021). This reflects the disciplinary function of celebrity culture, which has historically used the media to cultivate reflexive bodily surveillance (Bartky 1990; Gill 2007; McRobbie 2007). The instability and transgression of the maternal body, constantly becoming and resisting containment, contradicts the slender, normative ideal of feminine embodiment (Granata 2017; Nead 1992). However, celebrity pregnancy coverage glorifies the pregnancy, representing the pregnant body as desirable and aspirational (Tyler 2011), and the baby bump as a coveted accessory to be styled and flaunted (Cramer 2012). Pregnant people who do not comply with established norms of self-fashioning and embodiment during pregnancy are subject to shaming and harassment (Lehto Brewster 2020; Petersen 2017). Those who do perform pregnancy in the public eye are also subject to media critique of their diet, fashion, and behavior, which is increasingly punitive for young people as well as people of color (Butler Breese 2010; Cramer 2012).

Archival research of *People* magazine's coverage of celebrity pregnancy from 2013–18 shows that Jenner would have likely seen many examples of mediated pregnancy that may have informed her decision to remain private. The most covered pregnancies during that period in the magazine were, in order: Kate Middleton, the Duchess of Cambridge; Kim Kardashian; and Meghan Markle, Duchess of Sussex. Coverage of their pregnancies mainly focused on their health (particularly for Middleton, who struggled with hyperemesis gravidarum, and Kardashian, who developed preeclampsia and placenta accreta); their bodily appearance and style; and their relationships with their partners and families. Unsurprisingly, much of this coverage was punitive, and directly compared the style, weight, and lifestyles of these women. Middleton was praised for her "perfect little bump" on her otherwise thin figure; though Markle's pregnant body also followed this idealized form, her status as a Black biracial woman made her a frequent target in the British press (LaConte 2020). Kardashian was also targeted for "excessive" weight gain and form-fitting attire during her first pregnancy, which emphasized her body's diversion from the slender, contained model of pregnant beauty (Brewster 2014; Tyler 2011).

Most of the other pregnancies depicted in the magazine were highly publicized. There is also, however, evidence of a more private model of celebrity pregnancy (re)emerging in media coverage throughout this period. Celebrities such as Mindy Kaling, who has kept both the births and paternity of her two children a secret, seem concerned about revealing children's birth stories or parentage publicly (Juneau 2017); others, such as Alexis Bledel, whose pregnancy was revealed months after her son was born, are simply portrayed as extremely private people ("Alexis Bledel is a Mom!" 2020). Some are less public or well known, which might make it easier to stay private. Kaling's most recent pregnancy is intriguing because she continued posting new images of herself to social media throughout her pregnancy, making her announcement of her son's birth that much more surprising to fans (LaConte 2020). Though she was photographed by the paparazzi, and the images were published, the website did not claim that she was pregnant, which she suggests was due to her fuller figure (LaConte 2020). It's also worth mentioning that Beyoncé's first pregnancy, despite vast amounts of photographic evidence, was the subject of conspiracy by people who thought it was contrived because her performance of pregnancy did not align with established norms (Kornhaber 2017; Lehto Brewster 2020). This demonstrates how hegemonic gender and racial ideologies influence representations of celebrity pregnancy, deeming some bodies untrustworthy and rendering others invisible (Cramer 2015).

Kaling, Beyoncé, and Jenner's narratives also offer insight into how self-representations are related to media discourses about celebrity pregnancy. Beyoncé's first pregnancy was performed in more formal, traditional media settings, which contributed to accusations that it was fake; when she documented her second pregnancy more cohesively on social media, conforming to the norms of "bump culture," it was perceived as more authentic, which is explored in more depth in the adjoining chapter by Darnell Jamal Lisby (Lehto Brewster 2020). Kaling and Jenner used social media to obscure their pregnancies. Kaling hid her pregnancy using clothing and posture as an optical illusion, hiding her belly in plain sight. Jenner mainly relied on a mixture of "throwback" photos and photos she had taken in advance, but also posted a few new photos in which she used props or strategic cropping to hide her belly. These celebrities used their social media accounts as a form of self-writing to reveal and reflexively perform their pregnancies (Foucault 1997). Writing has been used for centuries to shape and communicate the self, and to define one's relations and reality; it is therefore considered a "technique of the self" (ibid.). New technologies, particularly social media, provide new ways for people to curate their lives, relate to themselves and others, and thereby practice self-governance (Sauter 2014; Weisgerber and Butler 2016). The latter component is significant here: self-writing does not merely describe an act of self-expression, but one of internalization and subjectivation, in which the writer collects and annotates discourses to transform their very soul (Foucault 1997). I will argue that Jenner's use of social media during and after her pregnancy is a form of self-writing that (re)writes her pregnancy narrative, and thus transforms her from reality star to matriarchal mogul.

Digital self-writing has transformed pregnancy from an embodied experience into a spectacular performance (Brewster 2014). Pregnancy appears smooth, neat, and stylish in the pages of magazines, on webpages, and on Instagram, structured into a predictable narrative like Jenner's announcement video: each trimester is prepackaged, marked by photos of announcements, gender reveals, baby showers, and finally, birth. When that performance is disrupted, or delayed as was the case with Jenner, it reveals the seams in the construction of celebrity pregnancy. This is not necessarily by showing something more "real": rather, the very lack of reality emphasizes just how artificial the narrative we're accustomed to has become. These representations of pregnancy are firmly rooted in postfeminist and neoliberal discourses, which have very real cultural consequences, as I will discuss in the following section.

Celebrity Pregnancy, Neoliberalism, and Postfeminism

Jenner therefore had not only the means but also the motive to keep her pregnancy private until she was able to shape her own narrative. However, tabloid and entertainment media covered Jenner throughout her pregnancy as if it had been confirmed, and she was hounded by paparazzi desperate to capture a photo of her pregnant body. Celebrities are often viewed as public property and are expected to disclose these sorts of experiences and life events, even those of their children; this is especially true when they identify as women. This obsessive surveillance of the pregnant body (re)enforces regimes of self-care, personal choice, and stylized femininity (Nash 2012; Negra 2008; Tyler 2011). These regimes are notably reflexive and are increasingly taken up by celebrity and non-celebrity parents alike—especially on social media. Much research has focused on the neoliberal and postfeminist discourses that underpin these representations, and how these have (re)shaped feminine subjectivity (Gill 2007; McRobbie 2007; Negra 2008).

Postfeminist values and practices are influenced by neoliberalism, which arose in the 1980s. Neoliberalism is a mode of political economic practices characterized by deregulation and privatization, that is, a shift of assets from public to private ownership (Gill and Scharff 2013; Harvey 2007). It champions individual freedom and choice, property rights, the accumulation of information and capital, and the free market as key to the advancement of human wellbeing (Harvey 2007). The mode of subjectivity advanced by neoliberal policy—individuated, autonomous, and self-disciplined—can also be found in postfeminist media culture. Postfeminism has been described as a sensibility (Gill 2007) characterized by choice, freedom, and empowerment (McRobbie 2007). Postfeminism is also characterized by consumerism as a form of self-production (Tasker and Negra 2007). Postfeminist subjects selectively take up and reject feminist principles, and often reject feminism in favor of celebrating a universal and "emphatic individualism" that ignores ongoing intersectional and systemic exclusions (ibid., 2007).

Previous literature has explored how neoliberal and postfeminist sensibilities have influenced the performance (Nash 2012; Negra 2008; Tyler 2011) and representation (Cramer 2015; Lehto Brewster 2020) of celebrity pregnancy. Others have noted how these frameworks have branded and commodified motherhood itself, leading to a proliferation of lifestyle brands and products by (micro)celebrity moms (Lagerwey 2016). This can also be linked to the rise of brand culture, and the concurrent rise of celebrities as brands (Banet-Weiser

2012; Barron 2015). In this context, celebrity and influencer mothers are encouraged to become entrepreneurial subjects to enhance their cultural value and attain material profit (Lagerwey 2016). These mothers bare their pregnancies and parenting experiences, using publicity as a shorthand for transparency, authenticity, and connection. Their highly public pregnancies tend to glamorize and sanitize the grotesque, embodied nature of pregnancy, reinforcing the hegemonic ideal of pregnant beauty (Tyler 2011; Russo 1995). They also reinforce the cultural imagination of celebrity pregnancy as a commodity for public consumption, quite literally in the case of those who use it as a branding opportunity.

While some celebrities, such as Mindy Kaling and Beyoncé, have negotiated more private pregnancies and thereby (partially) disrupted this model, Jenner's immediate commodification of her previously private pregnancy invites a slightly different reading. I argue that Jenner's development of the Weather Collection just weeks after her daughter's birth is a means for her to privatize her pregnancy, that is, to (re)frame it as a private rather than public good for greater material profit (Goodman and Loveman 1991). Privatization is typically used in economic and political contexts to refer to state deregulation and divestment (Savas 2000), or the transfer of enterprises from the public to private sector (Parker and Saal 2003). Proponents argue that it increases organizational efficiency and maximizes profitability (Radić, Ravasi, and Munir 2021). Applying the framework of privatization helps illuminate the links to neoliberalism and postfeminist media culture (Gill 2007), while also illustrating the industrialization of celebrity pregnancy. I do not argue that Jenner is the first to privatize her pregnancy; previous studies have analyzed celebrity and influencer parents who have similarly used (social) media to bring their parenting narratives under private control for financial gain (Lagerwey 2016; Jezer-Morton 2021). Jenner's pregnancy narrative—and, in particular, the timing and rollout of her branded initiative—shows the seams in this process by demonstrating how greater control over media representations might make a branded pregnancy more efficient and profitable for celebrity parents.

Producing a Private(ized) Pregnancy

Jenner's various media and social media activities enabled her to produce a strategically permeable boundary around her private life and created an idealized vision of her pregnancy and motherhood in order to package and sell it to fans.

However, Jenner's privacy during her pregnancy, as well as her privatization of it, also helped her establish a sense of agency and perhaps refashion her established star image (Dyer 1998). The following section will analyze Jenner's pregnancy announcement on Instagram and YouTube, as well as the announcement and rollout posts from the Weather Collection, in order to parse these seemingly contradictory goals.

"There was No Gotcha Moment"

Kylie Jenner posted the short film titled *To Our Daughter* (2018) to her social media accounts on February 4, 2018, days after the birth of her first child. The film was ostensibly made by Jenner and partner Travis Scott for baby Stormi, as the title suggests: Stormi is also directly addressed by several subjects throughout the film, who tell stories of her parents' relationship, share how they found out about the pregnancy, and emphasize her mother's desire to become a parent. These intimate, faux-nostalgic scenes of Jenner and Scott, as well as their friends and families, are scattered throughout the film to emphasize their love and connection with each other. The film is careful to emphasize that despite her age, she is mature and prepared for motherhood: multiple people in the film mention her long-standing desire to become a mother, which seems like a calculated retort to those who might balk at her age or relationship status. As friend Jordyn Woods puts it in the video, "When you're 20 years old—you're just figuring out your life. You don't know what you want, you're an indecisive teenager and you're just becoming a young adult, and—there was one thing that your mom knew for sure, and that was you" (3:28). Jenner and Scott are constantly seen together, at doctor's appointments and family events: they are loving, involved, and present in each others' lives, as well as their future daughter's. The film therefore (re)casts Jenner as a caring and careful young mother, adding layers of complexity and agency to her existing star image (Dyer 1998).

The dark, rough, and jumpy editing style, as well as the melodic piano that scores the film, help build a narrative that is cohesive but feels more intimate, as if it were produced retroactively from found footage by two new parents as opposed to meticulously framed and captured by a documentary crew. Handheld cameras follow Jenner to her doctor's appointments and baby shower; Jenner also films herself, capturing her pregnant body in various outfits as it changes size and shape. The film essentially portrays many of the milestones and moments that other celebrities—and indeed many (if not most) pregnant people more generally—otherwise share publicly on social media. Here, however, they are captured and stored, to be edited and packaged neatly only after the pregnancy is actually over. The film's aesthetic and tonal composition therefore echoes similar celebrity documentary projects, such as Beyoncé's *Life is But a Dream* (2013), Taylor Swift's *Miss Americana* (2020), and Lady Gaga's *Gaga: Five Foot Two* (2017), among others. This formula, as Tolson (2001) notes, aims to construct a persona that merges the celebrity's public identity with their authentic, "authored 'ordinary' self." Grainy and shaky footage, bare faces, personal confessions, and intimate settings have become tropes in this genre, producing "infomercials" for these celebrities' authenticity (Stanley 2013). Any and all rough edges are all but eliminated; such films are coded to present their subjects as genuine, earnest, and endearing, creating narratives that anticipate and evade an oppositional gaze (Hall [1973] 1991; hooks 1992). *To Our Daughter* thus serves as a form of self-writing (Foucault 1997) that enables Jenner to curate her pregnancy by limiting real-time access to her pregnant body and narrative, allowing her to (re)shape her star image (Dyer 1998).

This film was released the same day that Jenner posted a statement acknowledging her pregnancy and the birth of her daughter. The post consisted of just two short paragraphs in black text on a white background and was captioned with a small black heart (@kyliejenner 2018). She first apologizes to fans, who Jenner acknowledges are "used to me bringing you along on all my journeys": that unlike most of her young adult life, most of which has been broadcast on *Keeping Up With the Kardashians* or social media, "my pregnancy was one I chose not to do in front of the world." She alternately describes her pregnancy as a "beautiful, empowering, and life changing experience," a "special moment," and a "blessing," and thanks her friends and "especially my family" for their help in insulating her from the media. She confirms that she has had a "beautiful and healthy baby girl," who was born several days prior—but that she "just couldn't wait to share" with her fans and the media because she "has never felt love and happiness like this [I] could burst!" She closes the statement by thanking those reading, presumably her fans, "for understanding."

Jenner's shift from apology to justification and then emotional appeal throughout the post is masterful. The simple layout and casual language make the post feel personal, as if Jenner herself wrote it. The tone of the message alternates between formal announcement and informal gushing, working to justify Jenner's privacy during her pregnancy through references to her physical and mental health. The text style of the post is also interesting and recalls similar celebrity usage of the Apple Notes app to write "off the cuff social media responses," which leverage the informal nature of the app to appear less constructed and more genuine to fans (Feldman 2016). This doesn't appear to be from the Notes app: the post's formatting, i.e., centered text in a sleek, condensed font, suggests careful planning, even as the lowercase letters scattered throughout evoke immediacy and intimacy. The simple heart caption is also effective at making the post seem more authentic and spontaneous: Jenner often uses emoji captions in her Instagram posts. In other words, it may be a glorified press release, but it's thoughtfully produced to appear like a personal, heartfelt message. The coordinated release of the announcement post and film notably follow the Kardashian-Jenner playbook: always release your own media on your own terms, so that you retain control of the narrative. The post ultimately justifies Jenner's privacy through references to her physical and mental health, underscoring the thoughtful and maternal vision of Kylie as seen in *To Our Daughter* (2018).

While it's easy to dismiss this as an elaborate public relations strategy, Jenner's deliberately constructed and opaque statement helps her to establish a boundary between her public persona and private life as a young, new mother—both of which are on display no matter what she does. After witnessing some of the stressful, punitive coverage of pregnant celebrities such as that of her older half-sister, Kim Kardashian, it is reasonable that Kylie would leverage her wealth and power to shield her body from the media gaze—that she would try to protect "her little life and our happiness" rather than performing her pregnancy "in front of the world." Delaying and curating this performance also allowed her to (re)write her pregnancy into a warm and sweet yet aspirational, contained model of pregnant beauty (Tyler 2011). However, it's also worth noting that there is, in fact, a "gotcha moment" in this process: the release of the Weather Collection.

The Eye of the Storm

Kylie Cosmetics has perfected the art of "dropping" products and collections as limited releases, which can sell out in a matter of minutes. The Kylie Cosmetics Weather Collection was marketed as such and "dropped" on February 28, 2018, at 3 p.m. PST, after six days of promotional Instagram posts, Stories, and wider media coverage. The collection, released February 28, 2018, included thirteen limited-edition products: a highlighter palette, two eyeshadow palettes, three matte lipsticks, two pairs of liquid eyeshadows, a glitter lip gloss, a cream eyeliner, and a loose highlighting powder. Each of these products was sold individually or available as a bundle for $280. True to form, the collection sold out "within minutes," and was restocked on March 9, 2018—and also later sold out. The majority of content on the Kylie Cosmetics Instagram feed for the next two weeks is dedicated to the collection. However, by March 14, 2018, both Jenner and Kylie Cosmetics are promoting a new range of glitter lip glosses, and the Weather Collection is but a distant memory. The sheer proliferation of limited-release Kylie Cosmetics products makes it difficult to trace individual collections, especially when they are several years old (Figure 3.2). While I found several products available on resale sites such as eBay and Poshmark, in the interest of time and money I have mainly based my analysis on social media content from Jenner, Kylie Cosmetics, and mass media coverage. I used these sources to analyze the Weather Collection itself, in order to consider how the products privatized Jenner's pregnancy and experience of parenthood (Wubbena 2016).

Figure 3.2 A Kylie Cosmetics product display in Ulta Beauty. Rick Kern / Getty Images for Ulta Beauty.

The Weather Collection, as the name suggests, is a line of cosmetics with shades and packaging evoking different weather events: lightning bolts, raindrops, and clouds adorn the products, which are also named following the weather theme ("Stratus," "Sunshine," and so on). The collection also uses the pigmentation and consistency of products to evoke different elements, such as water or earth, and includes multiple holographic and shimmer products, evoking rain and lightning. The first promotional video for the collection, which was released on Jenner's accounts as well as that for Kylie Cosmetics, depicts its relationship to weather quite literally: there is rumbling thunder and flashing lightning, along with a moody soundtrack. However, the collection's two eyeshadow palettes are both centered around storms: "The Calm Before the Storm," which features bright, pastel colors, and "The Eye of the Storm," which has darker, edgier shades. The names of some of the eyeshadows, such as "Sweet Storm," "Aquarius," "Destiny," and "True Love," seem to be direct references to Stormi, or perhaps to Jenner's feelings about new motherhood.

Jenner's posts, including content from her Instagram Stories, further establish her personal connection to the products: they show her swatching and modeling different products to "show you guys all the fun detail[s]" (2018). Jenner also confirmed that her daughter inspired the theme: "Right after we chose Stormi's name, her name really inspired me" (Muller 2018). The collection's development and release timeline illustrate that while Jenner was working to maintain the privacy of her pregnancy, she was also working to privatize it: after all, she claimed to have spent "pretty much her entire pregnancy" working on the collection (Muller 2018). Sasso confirms that Jenner used motherhood as an inspiration for the collection, and that it allowed her to "[bridge] her two worlds together" (2018). This coverage frames the reification of motherhood as a touching gesture, animating these commodities with Jenner's maternal affection to literally objectify her motherhood (Gandesha 2016; Bennett 2001). This has become naturalized in brand culture, particularly by (micro)celebrity brands, which emphasize their founders' personalities and lifestyles to encourage perceptions of authenticity and interconnection among consumers (Lehto Brewster and Sklar 2022). The development of the Weather Collection also allowed Jenner to bring her pregnancy narrative further under her private control. By transitioning her maternal experiences from public media property to privatized commodities, Jenner was able to (re)fashion herself from social media socialite to a caring and successful Brand Mom (Lagerwey 2016).

Conclusion

Jenner's Instagram announcement emphasizes that "there was no gotcha moment, *no big paid reveal [I] had planned*" (@kyliejenner 2018a, emphasis mine). Yet, her film, *To Our Daughter* (2018), and timing of the Weather Collection drop suggests that there was in fact a "big reveal" planned, for significant financial gain. The Kardashian-Jenner family was clearly documenting the pregnancy and planning to profit from it, even if it was kept out of the public eye. The narrative structure and abundance of "found" footage in the film, as well as the thoughtfully named products, coalesce to craft a strategically intimate glimpse into Jenner's maternal journey. Jenner's decision to keep her pregnancy private may have been framed as purely personal, but it effectively worked to privatize her pregnancy, reframing it as a private business asset rather than public content (Wubbena 2016).

The coordinated release of her pregnancy documentary, announcement, and the Weather Collection allow Jenner to control her pregnancy narrative, thereby avoiding some of the negative media attention that so many celebrity mothers receive. This is understandable given the punitive coverage of pregnant bodies in postfeminist media culture (Cramer 2015; Petersen 2017); however, the decision to commodify her relationship with her daughter highlights an unsettling trend in contemporary brand culture. The privatization of motherhood has rapidly expanded via the media industries, particularly on social media, which has not only made pregnancy more public but has also increased opportunities for the monetization of pregnancy and parenting content (Banet-Weiser 2021; Hunter 2016). Jenner joins many other "Brand Moms," "momtrepreneurs," and "momfluencers" who use social media to commodify their families through brand endorsements, sponsorships, and self-branded ventures (Lagerwey 2016). This highly gendered and commodified space reflects the pervasive influence of postfeminist media culture, which emphasizes reflexive domesticity, discipline, and entrepreneurial femininity (Gill 2007; Negra 2008). The Kardashian-Jenner family empire, like much of this influencer content, is "structured by the logics of the marketplace," following a teleology of continuous growth that is ominous at best (Jezer-Morton 2021). This growth mentality results in constant expansion into new branded opportunities, further privatizing pregnancy and parenthood.

Jenner's second child, a boy, was born in February 2022 after a more public pregnancy. While Scott and Jenner released another mini-documentary, *To Our Son* (2022), at the time of writing Jenner has not produced a branded venture to celebrate his birth. However, she announced a new line of baby products, Kylie Baby, in fall 2021. Her announcement emphasizes that while bath time is "our special time together," it is "even more special" when using products that "[Stormi] helped me create" ("Coty announces" 2021). This anecdote is ostensibly shared to promote her personal connection to the products and highlight her close relationship with her daughter; however, it also emphasizes how marketplace logics have infiltrated the family to optimize Brand Motherhood (Jezer-Morton 2021; Lagerwey 2016). It is therefore not surprising that Jenner has used fashion and beauty products to (re)create herself as a Brand Mom: that her first postpartum venture was to enshrine her relationship to her daughter in eyeshadow, lip gloss, and highlighter, and that her love for her future son was expressed via sulfate-free bath products. Like Jezer-Morton (2021), I am less concerned about her children's privacy (though such concerns are certainly valid, and worth noting) than I am about the privatization mentality at the heart of her branded efforts. If these marketplace logics continue to shape the representation and experience of motherhood, it will likely produce diminishing returns.

References

Banet-Weiser, S. (2012), *Authentic TM: The Politics of Ambivalence in a Brand Culture*. New York: New York University Press.

Banet-Weiser, S. (2021), "Gender, Social Media, and the Labor of Authenticity," *American Quarterly*, 73 (1): 141–4. Doi: 10.1353/aq.2021.0008.

Barron, L. (2007), "The Habitus of Elizabeth Hurley: Celebrity, Fashion and Identity Branding," *Fashion Theory*, 11 (4): 443–62.

Barron, L. (2015). *Celebrity Cultures*. London: Sage.

Bartky, S. (1990), *Femininity and Domination: Studies in the Phenomenology of Oppression*. New York: Routledge.

Bennett, J. (2001), "Commodity Fetishism and Commodity Enchantment," *Theory & Event*, 5 (1). Available online: https://jscholarship.library.jhu.edu/bitstream/handle/1774.2/32811/5.1bennett.html (accessed March 2, 2022).

Brewster, M. (2014), "Bump Watch: Fashioning Celebrity Pregnancy as Performance and Product," MA thesis, Parsons School of Design, New York.

Butler Breese, E. (2010), "Meaning, Celebrity, and the Underage Pregnancy of Jamie Lynn Spears," *Cultural Sociology*, 4 (3): 337–55. Doi: 10.1177/1749975510380317.

Cherid, M. I. (2021), "'Ain't Got Enough Money to Pay Me Respect': Blackfishing, Cultural Appropriation, and the Commodification of Blackness," *Cultural Studies ↔ Critical Methodologies*, 21 (5): 359–64. Doi: 10.1177/15327086211029357.

Cichowski, H. (2017), "How and When to Announce your Pregnancy on the Internet," *Babylist*, August 2. Available online: https://www.babylist.com/hello-baby/facebook-pregnancy-announcement (accessed June 5, 2021)."

"Coty Announces the Launch of Kylie Baby, the New Brand by Kylie Jenner" (2021), *Coty*, September 28. Available online: https://www.coty.com/in-the-news/press-release/coty-announces-launch-kylie-baby-new-brand-kylie-jenner (accessed April 7, 2022).

Craik, J. (1993), *The Face of Fashion: Cultural Studies in Fashion*. London: Routledge.

Cramer, R. A. (2012), "The Baby Bump is the New Birkin," in S. Tarrant and M. Jolles (eds.), *Fashion Talks: Undressing the Power of Style*, 53–66. New York: State University of New York Press.

Cramer, R. A. (2015), *Pregnant with the Stars: Watching and Wanting the Celebrity Baby Bump*. Palo Alto, CA: Stanford University Press.

Dyer, R. (1998), *Stars*. London: BFI (British Film Institute).

Edwards, L. (2012), "Transmedia Storytelling, Corporate Synergy, and Audience Expression," *Global Media Journal*, 12 (20): 1–12.

Feldman, B. (2016), "Was Taylor Swift Betrayed by her Own Notes App?" *Intelligencer*, July 18. Available online: https://nymag.com/intelligencer/2016/07/was-taylor-swift-betrayed-by-her-own-notes-app.html (accessed December 10, 2021).

Foucault, M. (1997), *Ethics: Subjectivity and Truth*. Edited by P. Rabinow. Translated by R. Hurley and Others. London: Penguin.

Freeman, A. (2018), "Kylie Jenner and the Ultimate Performance of Privacy in a Post-selfie Era," *Dazed & Confused*, February 8. Available online: https://www.dazeddigital.com/life-culture/article/38944/1/kylie-jenner-social-media-pregnancy-privacy (accessed July 9, 2021).

Gandesha, S. (2016), "'Reification' between Autonomy and Authenticity: Adorno on Musical Experience," in S. Gandesha and J. F. Hartle (eds.), *The Spell of Capital: Reification and Spectacle*, 37–54. Amsterdam: Amsterdam University Press.

Gill, R. (2007), "Postfeminist Media Culture: Elements of a Sensibility," *European Journal of Cultural Studies*, 10 (2): 147–66.

Gill, R. and C. Scharff, eds. (2013), *New Femininities: Postfeminism, Neoliberalism and Subjectivity*. London: Palgrave Macmillan.

Goodman, J. B. and G. W. Loveman (1991), "Does Privatization Serve the Public Interest?" *Harvard Business Review*. Available online: https://hbr.org/1991/11/does-privatization-serve-the-public-interest (accessed April 1, 2022).

Granata, F. (2017), *Experimental Fashion: Performance Art, Carnival and the Grotesque Body*. London: Bloomsbury.

Hall, S. ([1973] 1991), "Encoding, Decoding," in S. During (ed.), *The Cultural Studies Reader*, 90–103. London and New York: Routledge.

Harvey, D. (2007), *A Brief History of Neoliberalism*. Oxford: Oxford University Press.

hooks, b. (1992), *Black Looks: Race and Representation*. Boston, MA: South End.

Hunter, A. (2016), "Monetizing the Mommy: Mommy Blogs and the Audience
    Commodity," *Information, Communication & Society*, 19 (9): 1306–20. Doi:
    10.1080/1369118X.2016.1187642.

Ingleton, P. and L. York (2019), "From Clooney to Kardashian: Reluctant Celebrity and
    Social Media," *Celebrity Studies*, 10 (3): 364–79.

Jezer-Morton, K. (2021), "What Worries Me about Making a Family into a Brand,"
    Mothers Under the Influence, Substack, December 10. Available online: https://
    mothersundertheinfluence.substack.com/p/what-worries-me-about-making-a-
    family?s=r (accessed April 2, 2022).

Juneau, J. (2017), "Mom-to-Be Mindy Kaling 'is not telling anyone, not even close
    friends, who the father' of her baby is: Source," *People*, July 18. Available online:
    https://people.com/parents/pregnant-mindy-kaling-not-revealing-father-of-baby/
    (accessed February 20, 2022).

Kirkpatrick, E. (2021), "Jennifer Aniston Says She Used to Take Those 'Nasty,' 'Hurtful'
    Pregnancy Rumors Personally," *Vanity Fair*, December 9. Available online: https://
    www.vanityfair.com/style/2021/12/jennifer-aniston-hurtful-pregnancy-rumors-
    career-over-family-the-hollywood-reporter (accessed August 3, 2021).

Kornhaber, S. (2017), "Pop Culture's Fraught Obsession with Celebrity Baby Bump," *The
    Atlantic*, February 3. Available online: https://www.theatlantic.com/entertainment/
    archive/2017/02/disrupting-the-celebrity-pregnancy-industrial-complex/515589/
    (accessed April 9, 2022).

Kylie Jenner [@kyliejenner] (2018a), "I'm sorry for keeping you in the dark through all
    the assumptions. I understand you're used to me bringing you . . ." Instagram,
    February 4. https://www.instagram.com/p/BeycUmgFTWb/ (accessed April 1,
    2022).

Kylie Jenner [@kyliejenner] (2018b), "[Lightning bolt emoji] The Weather Collection
    [lightning bolt emoji] Launching Feb 28 3pm pst. Check out my stories to see a
    closer look [yellow heart emoji]," Instagram, February 22. Available online: https://
    www.instagram.com/p/BfhH6KblLik/?utm_source=ig_embed (accessed March 10,
    2022).

Kylie Jenner (2018), "To Our Daughter," video, YouTube, February 4. Available online:
    https://www.youtube.com/watch?v=BhIEIO0vaBE&list=LLhFlOQnTt_1TLOs0X
    WNiYjA&index=992 (accessed December 10, 2021).

LaConte, S. (2020), "Mindy Kaling Got Caught by Paparazzi When She was Hiding Her
    Pregnancy, and Her Story about It is Hilarious," *Buzzfeed*, October 10. Available
    online: https://www.buzzfeed.com/stephenlaconte/mindy-kaling-hid-pregnancy-
    caught-by-paparazzi (accessed March 2, 2022).

Lagerwey, J. (2016), *Postfeminist Celebrity and Motherhood: Brand Mom*. New York and
    Abingdon: Routledge.

Lehto Brewster, M. (2020), "Making *Lemonade*? Beyoncé's Pregnancies and the
    Postfeminist Media Gaze," in M. Laing and J. Willson (eds), *Revisiting the Gaze: The
    Fashioned Body and the Politics of Looking*, 147–72. London: Bloomsbury.

Lehto Brewster, M. and M. Sklar (2022), "'Brand, Community, Lifestyle': Fashioning an Authentic, Body Positive Influencer Brand on Instagram," *Journal of Fashion, Style, & Popular Culture*, 9 (4): 501–21.

Marshall, P. D. (2021), "The Commodified Celebrity-Self: Industrialized Agency and the Contemporary Attention Economy," *Popular Communication*, 19 (3): 164–77. Doi: 10.1080/15405702.2021.1923718.

McRobbie, A. (2007), "TOP GIRLS?" *Cultural Studies*, 21 (4–5): 718–37. Doi: 10.1080/09502380701279044.

Monteverde, G. (2016), "Kardashian Komplicity: Performing Post-Feminist Beauty," *Critical Studies in Fashion and Beauty*, 7 (2): 153–72. Doi: 10.1386/csfb.7.2.153_1.

Moulard, J. G., C. P. Garrity, and D. H. Rice (2015), "What Makes a Human Brand Authentic? Identifying the Antecedents of Celebrity Authenticity," *Psychology & Marketing*, 32: 173–86. Doi: 10.1002/mar.20771.

Muller, M. G. (2018), "Kylie Jenner's Daughter Stormi Inspired Her Latest Kylie Cosmetics Collection," *W Magazine*, February 23. Available online: https://www. wmagazine.com/story/kylie-cosmetics-stormi-collection/ (accessed April 1, 2022).

Nash, M. (2012), *Making "Postmodern" Mothers: Pregnant Embodiment, Baby Bumps and Body Image*. London: Palgrave Macmillan.

Nead, L. (1992), *The Female Nude: Art, Obscenity and Sexuality*. London and New York: Routledge.

Negra, D. (2008), *What a Girl Wants? Fantasizing the Reclamation of Self in Postfeminism*. London and New York: Routledge.

Parker, D. and D. Saal, eds. (2003), *International Handbook on Privatization*. Cheltenham and Northampton, MA: Edward Elgar Publishing.

Petersen, A. H. (2017), "How Kim Kardashian Pushed the Boundaries of Celebrity Pregnancy," *Buzzfeed*, June 15. Available online: https://www.buzzfeednews.com/ article/annehelenpetersen/how-kim-kardashian-pushed-the-boundaries-of-celebrity (accessed March 20, 2022).

Peterson-Withorn, C. and M. Berg (2020), "Inside Kylie Jenner's Web of Lies—And Why She's No Longer a Billionaire," *Forbes*, May 29. Available online: https://www.forbes. com/sites/chasewithorn/2020/05/29/inside-kylie-jennerss-web-of-lies-and-why-shes-no-longer-a-billionaire/?sh=1c9616ea25f7 (accessed September 9, 2022).

Radić, M., D. Ravasi, and K. Munir (2021), "Privatization: Implications of a Shift from State to Private Ownership," *Journal of Management*, 47 (6): 1596–1629. Doi: 10.1177/0149206320988356.

Russo, M. (1995), *The Female Grotesque: Risk, Excess and Modernity*. New York and London: Routledge.

Russo, G. (2018), "Keeping Your Pregnancy Off Social Media? You're a Silent Minority," *Romper*, March 9. Available online: https://www.romper.com/p/keeping-your-pregnancy-off-social-media-youre-a-silent-minority-8442640 (accessed March 10, 2022).

Sauter, T. (2014), "'What's on Your Mind?'" Writing on Facebook as a Tool for Self-Formation," *New Media & Society*, 16 (5): 823–39. Doi: 10.1177/1461444813495160.

Savas, E. (2000), *Privatization and Public–Private Partnerships*. London: Chatham House.

Staff Author (2020), "Alexis Bledel is a Mom! Gilmore Girls Star and Husband Vincent Kartheiser Welcomed Son Months Ago," *People*, December 2. Available online: https://people.com/parents/vincent-kartheiser-alexis-bledel-welcome-son/ (accessed April 3, 2022).

Stanley, A. (2013), "Another Cog in the Machinery of Divahood," *New York Times*, February 14. Available online: https://www.nytimes.com/2013/02/15/arts/television/beyonces-documentary-life-is-but-a-dream-on-hbo.html (accessed July 1, 2022).

Tasker, Y. and D. Negra (2007), *Interrogating Postfeminism: Gender and the Politics of Popular Culture*. Raleigh, NC: Duke University Press.

Thompson, W. (2018), "How White Women on Instagram are Profiting Off Black Women," *Paper Magazine*, November 14. Available online: https://www.papermag.com/white-women-blackfishing-instagram-2619714094.html?rebelltitem=9#rebellti tem9 (accessed February 19, 2022).

Tolson, A. (2001), "'Being Yourself': The Pursuit of Authentic Celebrity," *Discourse Studies*, 3 (4): 443–57. Doi: 10.1177/1461445601003004007.

Tulloch, C. (2016), *The Birth of Cool: Style Narratives of the African Diaspora*. London: Bloomsbury.

Turner, G. (2016), *Understanding Celebrity*, 2nd ed. London: Sage.

Tyler, I. (2011), "Pregnant Beauty: Maternal Femininities Under Neoliberalism," in R. Gill and C. Scharff (eds.), *New Femininities: Postfeminism, Neoliberalism, and Subjectivity*, 1st ed., 44–59. Houndmills and New York: Palgrave Macmillan.

Weisgerber, C. and S. H. Butler (2016), "Curating the Soul: Foucault's Concept of Hupomnemata and the Digital Technology of Self-Care," *Information, Communication & Society*, 19 (10): 1340–55. Doi: 10.1080/1369118X.2015.1088882.

Winter, J. (2018), "The Politics of Beyoncé's Pregnancy: Re-articulating Lemonade's Narrative Agency through the Public Construction of Black Motherhood," *MAI: Feminism & Visual Culture*, September 12. Available online: https://maifeminism.com/the-politics-of-beyonces-pregnancy-re-articulating-lemonades-narrative-agency-through-the-public-construction-of-black-motherhood/ (accessed March 2, 2022).

Wissinger, E. (2016), "Glamour Labour in the Age of Kardashian," *Critical Studies in Fashion and Beauty*, 7 (2): 141–52. Doi: 10.1386/csfb.7.2.141_1.

Woodward, E. (2020), "Is this the Decline and Fall of the Kardashian Empire?" *Buzzfeed*, September 12. Available online: https://www.buzzfeednews.com/article/elliewoodward/kardashians-killed-their-own-show (accessed March 3, 2022).

Wubbena, Z. C. (2016), "A Fight for Education and Against Capital: Neoliberalism, News Media and Educational Policy," in Z. C. Wubbena, D. R. Ford, and B. J. Porfilio (eds.), *News Media and the Neoliberal Privatization of Education*, xi–xxxii. Charlotte, NC: Information Age Publishing.

Part 2

Fictional Mothers Onscreen

Unlike the previous part of this section, the chapters here deal with fictional (or fictionalized) filmic representations of mothers—a genre of image in which culturally convenient myths are built by imagined or authored narratives. Via its unique ability to institutionalize meaning through reproduction and distribution, film has been accused of conveying messages of conformity and deference to authority since the earliest writings on mass culture theory; it is therefore a rich site of investigation for how cultural ideals of "good" and "bad" mothers are visualized and disseminated (Hollows, Hutchings, and Jancovich 2000: 2–3).

Costume, of course, plays an essential role in the creation of onscreen images of mothers, layering them with "aesthetic, commercial, patriotic, [and] political [meanings]," all of which contribute to the entrenchment of what it means to look like a "mother," part of what Breward calls the function of fashion onscreen—"shoring up those hierarchies of power associated with class, race, and gender which have ensured the smooth operation of western capitalist economies" (Munich 2011: 2; Breward 2003: 132). This part does not take up the question of how audiences receive these meanings; indeed, the *impact* of the institutionalized image ("motherhood") is the subject of this volume's final part on "Identity." These three authors are concerned instead with the carefully crafted interaction between costume and film narratives that make representations of mothers "seem natural and transparent" when they are in fact anything but (Munich 2011: 2).

Two of these chapters address American films, though one (*The Zookeeper's Wife*) is a major studio production and the other (*Woodshock*) an independent art film. Those differing relationships to the Hollywood system and traditions of narrative offer different possibilities for how maternal characters are portrayed and how their interiority is revealed, but both films still operate within a Western paradigm of onscreen appearances, mores of motherhood, and customs of dress, and speak to Western cultural anxieties (Vidal 2012: 18).

The Zookeeper's Wife is a Second World War period piece and *Woodshock* has strong elements of horror—both genres with established conventions for how mothers are depicted (as saintly and monstrous, respectively), to which these films adhere to varying degrees (Chaudhuri 2006: 93). The essays by Morolake Dairo and Kimberly Lamm reflect upon nostalgia and the sanitization of history (and with it, mothers) as well as how exploring the complex psychology of the mother-child relationship can lead to both terror and liberation.

Importantly, the third essay in this part, by Indira Jalli, considers films from an entirely different studio system—that of the Telugu film industry based in and around Hyderabad, India, often nicknamed Tollywood. In Jalli's telling, fashionability and motherhood have long been presented as incompatible in Tollywood films, with frequently violent consequences for characters who attempt to break that rule. Jalli breaks down a number of sartorial codes used in these films' representations of "good" (demure, traditional, nationalistic) and "bad" (fashionable, Westernized) mothers to help the non-Telugu viewer understand how the visual world of these fictions is organized to reproduce structures of power that exist in the politicized physical world, while the fictional narratives allow for tidy resolutions that reinforce hegemonic expectations without the messes and nuances of reality.

As Rich states, "Patriarchy could not survive without motherhood and heterosexuality in their institutional forms; therefore they have to be treated as axioms, as 'nature' itself" ([1976] 1995: 43). As Jalli demonstrates, in the postcolonial social context, where the legacy of colonial power structures the relations between Indian men and women, with men "previously required to submit to the colonialist male, now assum[ing] the same role, exercising suppressed aggression against females in the home and society," the project of naturalizing gender roles has particularly high stakes (Nasir 2019). And for the fields of fashion and motherhood studies, which both aim to grow more global, this essay aids in broadening the knowledge base to better understand how motherhood is institutionalized through images around the world.

References

Breward, C. (2003), *Fashion*. Oxford: Oxford University Press.

Chaudhuri, S. (2006), *Feminist Film Theorists: Laura Mulvey, Kaja Silverman, Teresa de Lauretis, Barbara Creed*. London: Taylor & Francis. Available online: https://ebookcentral-proquest-com.libproxy.newschool.edu/lib/newschool/reader.action?docID=274415 (accessed September 21, 2022).

Hollows, J., P. Hutchings, and M. Jancovich (2000), *The Film Studies Reader*. London and New York: Arnold.

Munich, A. (2011), *Fashion in Film*. Bloomington, IN: Indiana University Press.

Nasir, Z. (2019), "Feminism and Power in the Postcolonial Societies of the Subcontinent," *The Asia Dialogue*, May 22. Available online: https://theasiadialogue. com/2019/05/22/feminism-and-power-in-the-postcolonial-societies-of-the-subcontinent/ (accessed October 31, 2022).

Rich, A. ([1976] 1995), *Of Woman Born: Motherhood as Experience and Institution*. New York and London: W. W. Norton & Co.

Vidal, B. (2012), "Introduction: Period Film and the Mannerist Moment," in B. Vidal (ed.), *Figuring the Past: Period Film and the Mannerist Aesthetic*, 9–26, Amsterdam: Amsterdam University Press.

4

The Fashionable Mother as Dangerous Contradiction in Telugu Film

Indira Jalli

The present chapter aims to understand how and why the two entities of motherhood and fashion are depicted as incompatible with each other throughout the history of Telugu films and what purpose these depictions serve. Telugu films refer to those produced in the Telugu-speaking Indian states of Andhra Pradesh and Telangana. The Telugu film industry, one of the largest in India but less internationally well known than Bollywood, is also known as Tollywood. For Indian men, women's attire and self-fashioning have been at the core of anxiety since the time of colonization due to the British introduction of numerous social reforms and criminalization of many (local) customs that were anti-women. Both conservative and liberal Indian men have articulated their own views on the subject of Indian women and their dress—indeed, a long ideological and cultural battle has been waged over what an Indian woman should wear, resulting in defining what a middle-class normative Telugu woman wears today (see Bannerji 2001; Hussain 2014). Indian filmmakers have been heavily influenced by all these discourses and generally try to appease the existing patriarchal norms, making films that support and strengthen existing notions of Indian femininity and motherhood.

The "good mother" discourse in India, like in much of the rest of the world, requires the mother to behave in "culturally recognizable and acceptable ways" (Miller 2005: 86). A particular genre of Telugu movies (in fact, the most dominant genre until recently) has revolved around the theme of "good" and "bad" mothers; in such films, a fashionable woman is always depicted as unfit to be a mother. "Good" and "bad" mothers as categories of characterizations will be referred to throughout the rest of this paper without the scare-quotes, but this labeling is meant to refer to the accepted moralizing about their behavior, not the author's judgment. Since a majority of these films are family dramas, it should be understood that the value ascribed to a female character on screen depends on how much importance she gives to her family. Because, as Banerjee and Miller explain, "[Indian] men continue to take women's clothing and self-presentation as the critical signifiers of their inner virtue," the costuming and other modes of presenting women and mothers is key to understanding the films' position on their characters (2003). A woman who spends time in front of a mirror, for instance, is understood to be not spending enough time with her family and, consequently, all her children will be understood to be damaged in one way or another. There are numerous characteristics associated with this stereotype and one of them is that such women are essentially foolish and unfeminine.

A majority of these films revolve around the taming of such bad mothers by aggressive males, usually in the hero role. The hero typically tames her by marrying her daughter/s. The method that these men most frequently use against such women is sexual aggression. In a film like *Alluda Majaka* (It is Not Easy to Deal with Son-in-Law) (Satyanarayana 1995), the hero goes to the extent of raping his mother-in-law because she is arrogant and unfeminine. The reason implied is that a bad woman does not deserve respect and has to be either reformed in order to fit into the sexist family set-up or chased away from all legitimate spheres of society. This chapter tries to explain this complex cultural phenomenon dominant in films from the 1960s to the present. Though the frequency of such films is largely reduced now, it should be noted that the idealized mother figure is still usually portrayed in conservative terms, continually influenced by the history outlined here.

A woman in Telugu films is expected to desexualize herself after she becomes a mother. She has to dress up and behave in a certain way in order to pass for a good mother. Male characters do not have any such obligations. A mother is also expected to defashion herself as she ages. In other words, no older woman is expected to be fashionable on screen except for the sake of comedy. For instance, in certain films like *Nirnayam* (Decision) (Sivan 1995), *Sneham Kosam* (For the Sake of Friendship) (Kuman 1999), *Saukyam* (Comfort) (Kumar Chowdary 2015) and others, grandmother characters behave in a modern way, clad in modern clothes, drinking, or gambling, all played for comedy. This means that very old women are completely desexualized and thus their defeminized activities can provoke laughter rather than anger in the audience. The true bone of contention within the Tollywood filmic universe is those women of acceptably sexually active age, from their mid-teens to late fifties, who, in such films, must not be fashionable if also a mother.

The bad mother character is usually wealthy, greedy, feminist, anti-poor, rejects local culture in favor of Western culture, speaks English, loves to be flattered, is corrupt, criminal, disrespectful to her husband, ultra-modern, and so on. She is seen to stoop to any level in order to reach her goals, which are usually power/wealth-seeking. All these negative characteristics are meant to create antipathy in the audience towards her. These kinds of films end with the arrogant woman realizing her mistake, subjecting herself to the authority of her husband and other males, and behaving in submissive ways.

As stated, the role of fashion in these films is frequently to distinguish between which female characters are good (i.e., normative) and which are bad (i.e., disruptive of the social order). For instance, in the films of the 1960s, small differences in style distinguished arrogant women from the rest of the normative women. These women might keep their hair knot a little higher and more voluminous or be depicted with decorative pins, clips, flowers, etc. in their hair. Her hair may have some curls falling on her face or neck, or the hair would be decorated with plastic, synthetic, or artificial flowers; this feature never appears on normative women. Normative women only wear real flowers, as wearing flowers in the hair is a sign that her husband is alive and she is still auspicious.[1] When it comes to hair pins, normative women tend to wear black hair pins that merge with the color of their hair. They use hair pins only to keep their hair controlled, unlike the fashionable women who use different fancy hair accessories to highlight the beauty of their hair.

Good mothers, as a subset of good, normative women, never wear sunglasses or colorful silk hair scarves, unlike the bad mothers, who always wear them. In fact, a bad mother might wear them quite frequently because she is busy going out for business purposes or for entertainment, both of which are presented as problematic activities. Words like "meetings," "conferences," and "tours" are spoken by bad mothers, while in the family of a good mother, such business-related words would only be spoken by her male family members. Great admiration for the English language is another characteristic of a bad mother. All the bad mothers in these films use English words, even if they are from a remote village and with only a vernacular background. The English spoken by rural bad mothers is played for comedy and to build audience resentment towards the character. English is seen as an ultimate sign of fashion and thus is hated when spoken by a bad mother. Her fascination with English and the Western lifestyle is portrayed as being anti-nation. Conversely, English spoken by men is tolerated, as is their adoption of modern behaviors; no such pressure to embody and protect national identity is applied to male characters.

By the 1970s, bad mother characters began to wear visible make-up, sleeveless blouses, transparent saris, high heels, and loose or bobbed hairstyles. They also began to wear nightdresses in evening scenes. This trend continued in the 1980s. By the 1990s, bad mothers began to wear Western clothes, were shown doing workouts and keeping fit, putting on matching jewelry, wearing thick makeup, lipstick, etc. Throughout these decades, heavy jewelry remained a staple. Another notable feature is that all these women wear their *thali*—the thick gold chain or thick cotton thread smeared with turmeric featuring two pendants, resembling breasts, and black beads, signifying that a woman is married and that her husband is alive—over their saris, whereas normative women usually hide it beneath their *pallu*, the part of the sari that covers a woman's waist, tummy, breast, and left shoulder and then falls down like a mantle (Dube 1988; Banerjee and Miller 2003).

Films have to continually reinvent more and more outrageous entertainment in order to lure audiences to theaters. As a result, a not only unconventional but immoral formula was invented by Telugu filmmakers by the 1980s in which heroes are shown making sexual advances towards the fashionable (bad) mothers of the heroines (good, normative women intended to become good mothers), who indeed were sometimes their mothers-in-law. *Sithadevi* (named for the film's main character) (Sharma 1982) was perhaps one of the first films in which a bad mother, Kanakeswari (played by actor Dubbing Janaki), mother of the young heroine, puts on extra makeup when she learns that her daughter has called her rich boyfriend (the hero) to their house. She sits in front of a huge mirror and applies special makeup. Her daughter asks why she is putting on special makeup that day and she responds, "Your rich boyfriend is coming home today, right? Should we not look special for him?"

Nari Nari Naduma Murari (Lord Krishna between Two Ladies) (Kodandarami Reddy 1990) was perhaps the first movie to initiate the trend of the hero making these kinds of advances in a surprisingly straightforward manner. In this film, the hero sees his fashionable would-be mother-in-law in her bedroom while she is wearing her sari (Figure 4.1).

He keeps praising her beauty, touching her, and even pinching her cheek as the movie goes on, making explicit his sexualization of her. He boasts, "I will enter not just into your bedroom but also into your bathroom." *Alluda Majaka* (Satyanarayana 1995) is perhaps the only film in which the hero marries a bad mother's elder daughter, rapes/sexually harasses[2] his fashionable mother-in-law, and later marries her younger daughter also. By the end of such movies, the bad mother is left lonely, as all the other characters find faults with her, judge her, and

Figure 4.1 The inappropriately fashionable mother in *Nari Nari Naduma Murari* spends much time relishing her own youthful appearance in the mirror, evidence of her vanity and moral weakness. *Nari Nari Naduma Murari* directed by A. Kodandarami Reddy © Yuva Chithra Arts 1990. All rights reserved.

ostracize her. In crisis, all alone, she becomes helpless and timid. The hero then solves her problems by teaching her who is the boss, and the movie ends there. The price this fashionable mother has to pay at the end of the film is to cease her arrogance and become *normal*. She gives up all authority to the males in her family, which is usually her husband, her son-in-law, and/or the hero, and limits herself to cooking, cleaning, and being spiritual. Given that these types of films are essentially comedies, the hero mocking the bad mother and devaluing her as being superficial, stubborn, arrogant, anti-human, unfeminine, etc. is always played for fun. Despite the comedic intentions, the message that women are subordinate to men is taken very seriously.

The most important characteristic of the bad mother, as well as the harshest consequence she is made to face, is that she has failed to bring up her children, especially her daughters, in a feminine way. The first movie that operated as an example of this plot was perhaps *Gundamma Katha* ('The Story of a Woman Named Gundamma) (Rao 1962). *Gundamma Katha* is the first and a beloved humorous film dealing with the themes of fashion and motherhood. In fact, there is no fashionable mother as such in *Gundamma Katha*. The mother of the heroine, Gundabathula Achamma (played by Surakantham), is not fashionable herself but wants her daughter Saroja (played by Jamuna) to have a luxurious, care-free lifestyle. Saroja looks stylish, with a shiny handbag and two plaits (yes, making hair into two plaits for a woman of marriageable age was considered too fashionable for

India in the 1960s), speaks English, gets up late, takes coffee in bed, does not do any domestic chores, is lazy, etc. These features were interpreted as overly fashionable for Telugus of the 1960s. Saroja is also a woman with self-respect, which is portrayed as arrogance in the film. For instance, while her mother dresses—indeed, decorates—her to attend her "marriage looks" (an event where a prospective groom visits his prospective bride's house with his family in order to decide their marriage), she asks, "Am I cattle in the market to show myself like this?" Her question, expressing a reasonable objection to the transactional approach to her body and appearance, is mocked. The film blames Gundamma, the mother, for raising her daughter in such an unfeminine and unconventional way.

This movie features a song called "Lechindi Mahila Lokam" (The World of Women has Arisen), which is a satire on the subject of women's rights. Each stanza ends on a negative note, like how women's rights to education and employment have created unemployment (for men) or how their right to divorce eventually destroys the family structure. *Gumandamma Katha* was a key part of launching the formula that presented fashion and motherhood as antithetical. Later, numerous films were made that directly depict fashion and motherhood as hostile to each other and also how bad mothers eventually destroy the lives of their daughters.

Palleturi Bava (Rural Cousin) (Pratyagatma 1973) is another among the first films to have used the element of fashion to demarcate motherhood into "good" and "bad" types. One can see the deep impact of *Gundamma Katha* on *Palleturi Bava* as both films refer to fashion, motherhood, and women's rights in the same patriarchal tone. The heroine Lalitha (played by Lakshmi) studies in Britain and is totally Westernized. Her father, Bheema Rao (played by Nagabhushanam), is conservative and her mother Deepalakshmi is modern and encourages her daughter to be ultramodern. Lalitha arrives in a shirt and tight pants. Her father comments that she is a boy, not his daughter, because a woman should not wear pants. Rao takes issue with everything that Lalitha wears and does. His first question to her is: "Daughter, why do you keep your hair down like that? Why don't you fold it into a plait?" The hero, Edukondalu (played by Nageswara Rao), is a wealthy rural man and is very conservative. The modern culture that the heroine represents and brings into his rural environment is presented as a disruption and cultural trauma needing to be uprooted at all costs. Lalitha and Edukondalu marry and the cultural tensions between them slowly intensify as the movie goes on. He tries to beat her up on a series of occasions, but she runs away into her room and bolts it from inside. Deepalakshmi wants her daughter to divorce the hero; he visits their house to tell them to drop the case, as for him divorce is a challenge to his masculinity. Deepalakshmi and Lalitha are shown reading a magazine and laughing loudly. Both reading and laughing loudly are considered improper for women, and Lalitha is wearing shorts, exposing her thighs. In this context, the audience understands that Deeplakshmi encourages her daughter to wear fashionable, short clothes. The hero accuses Deepalakshmi of acting "worse than a stepmother" by sending a divorce notice on behalf of her own daughter.

In the Telugu context, as in the Western fairy-tale tradition and other societies where monogamous marriage is the norm, the stepmother is associated with evil, or wickedness (Williams 2010). The reason may lie in anxieties over property. A new woman entering into a family means a potential new heir and hence the splitting of shares in property. A stepmother character is usually much younger than her husband—in many old films stepmother characters are portrayed as almost the same age as his daughter—so there may be a suspicion around her motives for marrying him (Noy 1991). In the classic film *Sarangadhara* (named for the film's main character) (Raghavan and Rao, 1957), for instance, a young stepmother tries to seduce the son of her older husband. The stepmother is also considered smart and wily, as she comes from a younger generation and gains control of the older man with her charm. Needless to say, the accusation that Deeplakshmi is worse than a stepmother impugns her mothering and her very status as a woman.

Edukondalu lectures Lalitha:

> Wearing half clothes is not called civilization. In this country, for a woman what is more important than food is *manam maryada* (sexual virtue)... [She should be] covering the whole body even at the cost of starvation. A good woman is someone who lives without raising her head. It is not civilization for a woman to send a divorce notice just because her husband beats her up in a fit of anger.

Lalitha's father agrees with her husband's argument and tells Lalitha, "Daughter, you won't get these kinds of excellent lessons on civilization even in London." Such scenes in which males give lectures on how a woman should behave were routinely incorporated in films of the 1960s to 1990s.

When she refuses to go with him, the hero shouts, "If she does not come by Friday, I will slaughter and offer all of you as a sacrifice to our village goddess." One night, Edukondalu intrudes in their house and rapes Lalitha; as a result, she gives birth to a baby boy. Her father Rao is ecstatic and tells his wife, "Now, it is not me or my son-in-law, but my grandson who will control you." This suggests that a male heir is highly prized and a male of any age (even one just born)

Figure 4.2 Lalitha of *Palleturi Bava* is shown at left in her ostentatious fashions before she is reformed by force. At right, she has become a mother and her dress reflects the change in her behavior. *Palleturi Bava* directed by Pratyagatma © Prasad Art Pictures 1973. All rights reserved.

carries the potential to tame a woman of any age. Deepalakshmi gives the child away, as she wants her daughter to remarry. Lalitha is furious with her mother for separating her child from her. She asks "Are you a mother? What kind of a mother you are?" Motherhood is shown as bringing drastic changes in Lalitha as she begins to act very orthodox (Figure 4.2). She is "redeemed" by the changes in her behavior, attitude, and attire following her son's birth, while her mother, the original Westernizing, modernizing influence, is punished.

In another movie, *English Pellam East Godavari Mogudu* (An English Wife and a Husband from East Godavari) (Varma 1999), the heroine Sailaja (played by Ramya Krishna) is ultramodern and Western-educated (Figure 4.3). She tries to end a pregnancy with an abortion. Already in the eighth month, it is too late, so she plans to throw the child away when it is born. However, giving birth transforms her into a very traditional woman and she cares for the welfare of her baby. Both Lalitha in the 1970s and Sailaja in the late 1990s behave in conventional ways after they give birth; they now wear only saris and do not wear any make-up or jewelry. They fold their hair into a knot on their neck, a style traditionally reserved for women in their fifties and older. The movies seem to suggest that motherhood makes women biologically, psychologically, and emotionally weak, even when they were previously headstrong and independent. Scholars, including Hilary Lips, have detailed how nineteenth-century physicians and psychologists alike (including Freud, perhaps most influentially) thought that women's reproductive systems determined their whole cognitive functions and behaviors (2020). These films, made decades later, appear to agree, as motherhood teaches the women characters that biology is their destiny and the only way to fulfill their prescribed role is to subject themselves to the sexist local culture. While

Lalitha touches the feet of Edukondalu and pleads with him to take her back, Rao beats his wife Deepalakshmi black and blue, as Edukondalu had beaten Lalitha earlier in the story. Deepalakshmi falls on the floor and pleads with her husband that she has learnt her place and will be obedient to him. The movie ends with fashionable Deepalakshmi and her ultra-Western daughter Lalitha endlessly apologizing to the hero and his family (Figure 4.4).

Figure 4.3 Sailaja, heroine of *English Pellam East Godavari Mogudu*, in her fashionable Westernized attire after studying in Britain, is assertive and has no desire to be a mother. *English Pellam East Godavari Mogudu* directed by Rudraraju Suresh Varma © V.M.C. Productions 1999. All rights reserved.

Figure 4.4 *English Pellam East Godavari Mogudu*'s Sailaja, right, after becoming a mother, renouncing her independent ways, and submitting to her husband. Her turn to traditional dress reflects the change. *English Pellam East Godavari Mogudu* directed by Rudraraju Suresh Varma © V.M.C. Productions 1999. All rights reserved.

Buchi Babu (named for the film's hero) (Narayana Rao 1980) is a film explicitly about how a fashionable woman is unfit to be a mother. It depicts Gundabathula Achamma (played by Suryakantham), a fashionable senior woman who has three daughters and one son; the film shows that all her children are spoiled, as she is a bad mother. She wears sleeveless blouses, sunglasses, and has a bob cut. Achamma also wears slippers in the house, which is considered too modern for Telugus because women with families should be barefoot in the house. Her father-in-law says to Achamma, "You have three daughters. You do not allow one daughter to go to her husband. You have made another daughter a widow. And you don't allow a husband to come to your third daughter." The message of the film is that a fashionable woman is a bad mother and her daughters will end up divorced, widowed, or unmarried. The hero (Nageshwarao) tames the arrogant Achamma and marries her daughter, as is common to the plots of such films where heroes marry the daughters of such bad women to teach them a lesson.

The film *Illalu* (Housewife) (Rama Rao 1981) centers on a woman, Kalpana (played by Jayasudha), who is from a rich family and enjoys a rich, indulgent lifestyle and hates the routine, traditional life of family, husband, and children. When her child is a baby, Kalpana spends all her time gambling and partying. She wears two plaits and a gown, which in itself would have been considered inappropriate for a Telugu mother in the 1980s, who should only have been seen wearing a sari. The dress she wears, unlike a sari, doesn't cover her down to her feet, and doesn't have a *pallu*. She arrives late at night and asks her husband, the hero Kiran (played by Shoban Babu), to get ready for a party. She asks, "Why are you carrying the baby like an old grandmother? Come, let us go to the party." She tells him that it is the maid's responsibility to take care of the baby. He slaps her and tells that she should not step out of the house from that day onwards. She responds that she hates the baby and suggests that he jump into a river with the baby. She leaves the baby with him and returns to her father's house.

After several years, Kiran marries another woman, Jyothi (Sridevi), who treats her stepson as her own. Kalpana comes across Kiran and his family. She is now married again to a wealthy old man. Kalpana's motherly instinct begins to surface strongly when she sees her son again and she falls into depression. One scene depicts her having a dream where she falls at the feet of the hero and pleads with him to give the child back to her. In the dream she wears a sari and keeps her hair in a tight knot on her neck, puts on a red *bindi,* and wears small ear studs. In other words, she attires herself as mother material. When she wakes up, she realizes that it was a dream. In the background a song keeps playing: "If the tree thinks bearing a fruit is a burden, will the earth bear the tree?" The last quarter of the movie is about how deeply Kalpana repents her mistakes. Her repentance and change of heart begin to reflect first in her attire and attitude. She stops wearing Western clothes or modern hair styles. Instead, she begins to appear always in a sari and a small amount of traditional jewelry like small ear studs, a single gold chain, a tight hair knot on her neck, bangles, and a red *bindi* on her forehead. Furthermore, she covers her shoulders completely with the *pallu* of her sari.

The movie ends when Kiran leaves with his family and Kalpana is left standing alone in the dusky evening in a remote hill station. The director took extra care with the visualization and symbolism of the characters, especially Kalpana. The characters' names also indicate their natures: Jyothi means "a bright light," Kiran means "a ray of light," and Prakash means "brightness," while Kalpana means "an illusion." So, the names Jyothi and Kiran indicate that these characters value tradition, represent light and brightness, and also suggest fruitfulness, hope, and the future. Since Kalpana means a mere illusion, she symbolizes fickleness and falsity, and is presented as having no future. In this character, both fashion and the idea of a fashionable mother are false, fake, and fickle, just like Kalpana, the illusion.

Indian religious scriptures are filled with how a woman should behave and how she should be controlled. During colonial times, Indian women became the subject/object of social reform as well as indigenous anxieties and apprehensions about changing socio-cultural fabric (Sarkar 2001). Many writers during these times shared ideas about the subjects of women and culture; indeed, any Telugu magazine produced during colonial times is likely to contain at least one article exhibiting apprehensions as to women's changing status and their freedoms. Telugu filmmakers over the decades of this industry's existence have combined both their own cultural prejudices and these stereotypes; consequently, the portrayal of mothers has remained essentially the same from the 1930s to the present.

The common feature of all the films referenced in this chapter is that the stylish women characters are feminists, entrepreneurs, frequently claim their rights, and more importantly, want their daughters to marry liberal men so that they will have better lives. Their claims and desires are mocked as they are portrayed as arrogant, greedy, tricky, seductive, etc. Meanwhile, those in anti-feminist roles, especially the film's heroes, act good, generous, and honest, so that the dismissal of the fashionable women and curbing of their claims for rights are justified. Women's rights are portrayed as a trivial matter and a source of humor.

For instance, in *Palleturi Bava,* the heroine Lalitha's lawyer tells her to get her front teeth pulled so that it will appear as a sign of domestic violence and thus make it easier to obtain a divorce from the hero. For Telugu filmmakers (who are mostly men), the legal claims of women are the stuff of comedy. Films are made with plots centering around the cultural prejudices against fashionable women so that patriarchy is stabilized and women who seek an evolved lifestyle are criminalized.

Conclusion

Unfortunately, this genre has not disappeared. In some more recent films such as *Allari Ramudu* (Mischievous Ramudu) (G. Gopal 2002), *Naa Alludu* (My Son-in-Law) (Mullapudi 2005), *A Aa* (title representing Telugu alphabets) (Thrivikram Srinivas 2016), and others, the mothers of the heroines are ultra-modern, assertive entrepreneurs who refuse to be cowed by any patriarchal norms. More importantly, they want their daughters to marry evolved men so that they will be treated well by their partners. However, the heroes in each of these films tame these bad mothers and marry their daughters, just as in the earlier examples of films outlined in this chapter. Interestingly, the daughters of these bad women reject their mothers and submit themselves to the heroes.

The Indian nation is perceived as a motherland and women are thus considered an embodiment of the nation. Since the nation is also perceived as an extension of family, it is the responsibility of the woman to limit herself to the role she is traditionally assigned. Since fashion is viewed as an alien, Western element, women who engage in fashionability are projected as not only anti-family but as being anti-national. Thus, being fashionable essentially means being a non-mother, an outsider, and hence always suspect and excluded from the legitimate sphere of the interior, whether of the family or the nation.

Notes

1 Auspiciousness occupies a central place in Hindu ideology as a divine blessing that makes life, fertility, prosperity, and happiness possible.

2 There is a scene in this film suggesting that he has raped one of the three women which include his mother-in-law and her two daughters, but the film does not clarify which woman he violated.

References

A Aa (title representing Telugu letters) (2016), Dir. Thrivikram Srinivas, film. India: Haarika and Hassine Creations.

Allari Ramudu (Mischievous Ramudu) (2002), Dir. G. Gopal, film. India: Friendly Movies.

Alluda Majaka (It is Not Easy to Deal with Son-in-Law) (1995), Dir. E. V. V. Satyanarayana, film. India: Devi Films.

Banerjee, M. and D. Miller (2003), *The Sari*. London: Berg.

Bannerji, H. (2001), *Inventing Subjects: Studies in Hegemony, Patriarchy and Colonialism*. India: Tulika.

Buchi Babu (named for the film's hero) (1980) Dir. Dasari Narayana Rao, film. India: A.A. Combines.

Dube, L. (1988), "On the Construction of Gender: Hindu Girls in Patrilineal India," *Economic and Political Weekly*, 23 (18): WS11–19.

English Pellam East Godavari Mogudu (An English Wife and a Husband from East Godavari) (1999), Dir. Rudraraju Suresh Varma, film. India: V.M.C. Productions.

Gundamma Katha (The Story of a Woman Named Gundamma) (1962), Dir. Kamalakara Kameshwararao Rao, film. India: Vijaya Vahini Studios.

Hussain, P. (2014), "Evolving Semiotics of Adornment in Urban Indian Women," in N. J. Rajaram, G. H. S. Prasad, S. Kumar, and M. Belli (eds.), *Contemporary Issues and Trends in Fashion, Retail and Management*. Hyderabad: National Institute of Fashion Technology. Available online: https://www.researchgate.net/profile/Prabhdip-Brar/publication/331298845_NIFT_CONFERENCE1/links/5c70fe23299bf1268d1e32c1/NIFT-CONFERENCE1.pdf#page=636 (accessed March 20, 2020).

Illalu (Housewife) (1981) Dir. T. Rama Rao, film. India: Babu Arts.

Lips, H. (2020), *Sex and Gender: An introduction*, 7th ed. Long Grove, IL: Waveland.

Miller, T. (2005), *Making Sense of Motherhood: A Normative Approach*. Cambridge: Cambridge University Press.

Naa Alludu (My Son-in-Law) (2005) Dir. Vara Mullapudi, film. India: Sri Bharathi Enterprises.

Nari Nari Naduma Murari (Lord Krishna between Two Ladies) (1990), Dir. A. Kodandarami Reddy, film. India: Yuva Chithra Arts.

Nirnayam (Decision) (1995), Dir. Sangeeth Sivan, film. India: Jayabheri Art Productions.

Noy, D. (1991), "Wicked Stepmothers in Roman Society and Imagination," *Journal of Family History*, 16 (4): 345–61.

Palleturi Bava (Rural Cousin) (1973), Dir. Pratyagatma, film. India: Prasad Art Pictures.

Sarangadhara (named for the film's main character) (1957), Dir. V. S. Raghavan and K. S. Ramachandra Rao, film. India: Minerva Pictures.

Sarkar, T. (2001), *Hindu Wife, Hindu Nation: Community, Religion and Cultural Nationalism*. London: Hurst and Company.

Saukyam (Comfort) (2015), Dir. A.S.Ravi Kumar Chowdary, film. India: Bhavya Creations.

Sithadevi (named for the film's main character) (1982), Dir. Eranki Sharma, film. India: Bhumi Chithra Films.

Sneham Kosam (For the Sake of Friendship) (1999), Dir. K.S.Ravi Kumar, film. India: Sri Surya Movies.

Williams, C. (2010), "'Who's Wicked Now?' The Stepmother as Fairy-Tale Heroine," *Marvels & Tales*, 24 (2): 255–71.

5

Fashion and Motherhood at War

A Costume Analysis of *The Zookeeper's Wife*

Morolake Dairo

The American film industry is a global force in molding and disseminating archetypes—the smoldering temptress, the rebellious teenager, the struggling working-class male, the noble freedom fighter, and various versions of "mother" among them. The lives and values of these characters are visually narrated through their costumes. The character of "mother" has been portrayed again and again in varying ways: expectant mothers, evil stepmothers, grieving mothers, teenage mothers, saintly mothers, murderous mothers, aged mothers, angry "mama bears"—the list is endless. This chapter questions Hollywood's vision of the mother at war, adopting a hybrid case study-content analysis method to investigate the character of Antonina Zabinski, played by Jessica Chastain in the 2017 movie *The Zookeeper's Wife* (dir. Niki Caro). The movie is based on the true story of a Polish couple (Antonina and Jan Zabinski) who operated the Warsaw Zoo and later used its underground chambers to aid the escape of over 300 Jews in Poland during the Second World War (Hoffman 2017; Soll 2017). Antonina is the key character in the film, playing wife, mother, zoo assistant, and accomplice in the hiding of Jews during the Nazi invasion. This study limits its investigation of the character of Antonina to her role as a mother, focusing on various phases of motherhood including pre-pregnancy, pregnancy, and child-rearing to ask how costume design is used to convey ideas about motherhood in a time of war and how the costuming of period film sanitizes both history itself and the role of this historical real-life mother.

Film costumes operate on the level of symbolic representation, at once functional and metaphorical. As imagery, costumes can signify independently of character, body, or narrative, but are still deeply situated in the contexts (both onscreen and off) in which they appear (Bruzzi, quoted in Annila 2014). Clothing is a visual language onscreen that communicates alongside plotting and dialogue and can add to, or detract from, the believability of a character according to its audience. In film, objects, including archetypes (essentially, objectified characters) come to represent the whole of the category to which they belong—their referents. Film scholars, including Aumont et al. (1997), call this the iconic system of representation, or schematic representation. The archetype of "mother" thus functions in this way, similar to other filmic types such as geek, bad boy, or hero; a singular onscreen mother can, through the amplification of certain traits and removal or simplification of others, become a stand-in for the audience's accepted definition of "mother" in general. This discussion is also present in the neighboring chapter on "good" and "bad" mothers in Telugu films, which provides an interesting contrast to the Hollywood model.

Furthermore, historical costume objectifies the past through a similar process of amplification/simplification. According to Hall, representation is "an essential part of the process by which meaning is produced and exchanged between members of a culture" (paraphrased in Annila 2014). Representation of the past through costume therefore not only acts as a visual window into an imagined past, but in fact helps to produce that past in the contemporary understanding. Costumes may contribute to the glorification of past icons or rewrite an accepted story of a historical figure (Dyer 2021). Therefore, the representation of Antonina, a real historical figure, via the costumes designed for her by Bina Daigeler in 2017 and worn on the body of Chastain within the narrative of director Niki Caro's film can be understood as a distillation of the most potent contemporary ideas about not only (white, Western) womanhood during the Second World War but also about motherhood under the pressures of war. We must ask, however, whether this distillation is completely reflective of the realities of war, or indeed of motherhood, as Antonina is portrayed as unfailingly selfless, giving, and self-sacrificial.

Methodology

A content analysis methodology was adopted for this study, with the film's costumes as the primary content. The movie *The Zookeeper's Wife* was viewed from start to finish on three occasions. The first viewing of the film noted the character and plot development, while the second viewing was to observe the costumes of the key character Antonina more closely. All of the costumes worn by Antonina were recorded and organized by scene with a focus on her clothing in relation to style, texture, colors, silhouette, and accessories. Other elements of costuming such as makeup, hair styling, and footwear were also included in this study but were given less attention in the analysis. The third viewing of the movie was used to confirm and review all the notes captured in the previous viewings.

In film costuming, the color of clothing is used to communicate both a character's emotional state and the wider context (in this case, of wartime). Much research exists on the symbolism of colors in relation to emotional states and positive / negative associations with given traits. Kim, Jun, and Kim (2014), for instance, aggregate a number of categorizations determined by other scholars including the Color Science Research Institute of Japan to explain how costume colors can influence the mood and emotions in a movie and also symbolize the mental states of characters. These colors, depending on the character and context, can be interpreted as positive or negative. For example, red can be used to signify passion, love, happiness, and courage but can also be used to signify fear, cruelty, violence, and greed (Jung and Kim 2015; Kim, Jun, and Kim 2014). In the opening scene of *The Zookeeper's Wife*, for example, the costume worn by Antonina—a floral-patterned silk dressing gown worn as she nurtures her young son amidst lion cubs in her bedroom—seems to capture the peace and stability experienced before the Nazi invasion of Poland (Figure 5.1). As the war advances, Antonina's clothing reflects the mood with more subdued colors, such as brown and black. From a positive perspective, according to the research gathered by Kim, Jun, and Kim, brown and black can signify elegance, vigor, truth, stability, and composure,

Figure 5.1 Jessica Chastain as Antonina Zabinski in *The Zookeeper's Wife*. The floral robe provides support for the characterization of Antonina as a caregiver of children and animals. *The Zookeeper's Wife* directed by Niki Caro © Focus Features 2017. All rights reserved.

but within the context of this movie, these colors reflect the conflict and gloom in Warsaw as well as Antonina's frustrations and fears (2014). Color analysis based on these theories is used throughout the study.

This is also a case study of the portrayal of mothers in Hollywood films in general, and mothers in wartime in particular. The choice of *The Zookeeper's Wife* was driven mainly by four factors—relevance to the theme of fashion and motherhood, the era and the setting of the movie in a historical war period, the focus on a female protagonist, and the character of the female protagonist as a wife and mother. The theme of traditional motherhood is further entrenched in this movie, as the movie shows key moments of the protagonist coping with pregnancy and post-pregnancy in a volatile setting.

The Zookeeper's Wife

The Zookeeper's Wife is set in the late 1930s and early 1940s, spanning the period just before the outbreak of war, to the invasion of Warsaw, to the postwar period. It is an adaptation of a non-fiction book by the same title authored by Diane Ackerman in 2007. The book narrates the pre-war activities of the zoo, destruction of the zoo during the Nazi invasion, and transformation of the zoo into a pig farm for the feeding of German forces. It focuses on the participation of the owners in underground resistance efforts, especially Antonina, including secretly housing Jews whom Jan (her husband) rescues from the Warsaw ghetto, in the underground chambers of the Zoo (Max 2007; Seaman 2007). The author acquired most of her historical data from Antonina Zabinski's diaries and used the content to reconstruct her life (Foran 2007).

In explaining the choice of costumes for Antonina, the film's costume designer Daigeler notes that the real Antonina never wore trousers (Focus Features 2017). This was replicated in the movie via a staple wardrobe consisting of only skirts, blouses, dresses, coats, and dressing gowns. The movie hews closely to the fashion of the era in terms of hair, make-up, and clothing (ibid.). Even to tend to the zoo animals, Antonina's character wears feminine blouses, skirts, and day dresses that allow fluid movement.

Second World War Fashion: The Era of Rationing

Famously, clothing was among the goods placed under forced rationing for citizens on the home front during the Second World War. Prices for textiles and garments increased and sales taxes were introduced to curb consumption. Rather than discouraging fashion, the circumstances led to growth and innovation in functional fashion (Clouting and Mason 2018). In Britain, for instance, some handbags were fitted with gas mask compartments in case of a sudden gas spray from enemy planes. In response to blackout periods—imposed darkness to prevent easy targeting by German bombers—luminous buttons, brooches, and handbags were developed to help wearers stay safe and prevent being struck by vehicles on the ground. There were also austerity regulations minimizing the yardage used to produce clothes, including restriction of the number of pockets, lapel sizing, length/style of cuffs, colors, buttons, embroidery, and other embellishment (ibid.; Turner 2019). Styles also had to be versatile, meaning that looks could be changed by adding or removing pieces. Womenswear silhouettes and hat design showed military influence. British and American movies such as *Millions Like Us* and *Gilda* were used to spread the austerity measures for women. Movie characters, reflecting these realities, embraced creativity and ingenuity in those times by borrowing clothing for weddings, knitting, and making do with coupons (Turner 2019). Much of the responsibility for adhering to austerity measures, from making and mending their families' clothing to maintaining the household spirit of sacrifice and patriotism, fell to mothers as keepers of the home. This chapter's bibliography contains additional references on the origin of rationing and its use in Europe during the World Wars.

In Poland, war rationing continued until 1947, as the country recovered slowly from the devastations of the War (Dudek-Woyke 2015; Sulej 2016). As Katarina Sulej writes of the immediate post-war period, "When the women citizens of Warsaw began returning to the capital in 1945, they did so in simple, patched suits and thick woolen stockings marked with traces of home darning" (2016). The realities of clothing rations are visible in some scenes in *The Zookeeper's Wife*, with most of the characters repeating their outfits, including Antonina, over a six-year period—a relative rarity for Hollywood costuming.

Motherhood, Pregnancy, and the Second World War

Motherhood, while perhaps seemingly straightforwardly biological, is in fact a social construction dependent on the values of a particular time and place. In highly volatile periods such as wartime, the category of "mother" takes on meanings unique to those circumstances. Along with the elderly, the sick, and children, mothers and expectant mothers are seen as being at high risk and therefore in need of special protection. At the same time, a mother may find herself running or fighting for her life or that of her children, placing her also in a protective, possibly even heroic, position. Access to basic health care and food may also be scarce, increasing the unique risks of war (Barnes 2018).

During the Second World War, in some countries like Japan, mothers and their babies were used for experiments (Brody et al. 2014). In Germany, wives of soldiers loyal to the Nazi regime were treated as breeders of the "pureblood" Aryan race (Barnes 2018). In other parts of the world including England, pregnant women were among the people classified as vulnerable during the early years of the war and were transferred alongside others, such as people with disabilities, to places deemed safe from enemy bombs. Some Polish women captured by Nazis during the war were raped and those who became pregnant either had to abort or were sent to gas chambers if the pregnancy was beyond the stage of abortion (ibid.). In *The Zookeeper's Wife*, Antonina must birth her baby at home because the hospitals are full of wounded combatants and casualties or shut down or destroyed by explosions and air raids (Bayer 2020).

In times of war, clothing becomes a luxury as food and safety are of more vital importance. Krause (2019) notes that between the 1920s and 1940s, maternity wear was designed and produced to conceal protruding bumps, with expectant mothers embracing smaller prints to hide growing bellies. More commonly, and in line with the "make do and mend" attitude of the rationing economy, pregnant women repurposed other functional clothing for their maternity wardrobe, hand-altering garments to accommodate their transforming bodies and to be worn both during and after pregnancy.

Antonina as Mother

Antonina as portrayed in the film exudes nurturing and self-sacrifice associated with the motherly. She not only caters to her children and husband, but she also cares for the animals in the zoo and, eventually, for Jewish refugees at the expense of her own safety. In the opening scenes, Antonina is the mother of a young boy, Ryszard. As the movie progresses, she becomes pregnant and gives birth to a daughter, Theresa, but the evidence of her supposed motherly nature is extended to the animals in the zoo as well. In a dinner scene, Antonina rushes to the rescue of an unresponsive newborn elephant and resuscitates it as its aggravated mother watches. Antonina also seems to exhibit motherly bearing to the Jewish captives, especially Ursula, a young girl raped by German soldiers in the Warsaw Ghetto and later rescued by Jan. To analyze how Antonina's motherliness is produced and communicated through costume, we recognize that the context of the film's construction of her includes these moments in which her mothering and motherliness extend beyond the relationship to her own biological children.

Femininity Maintained

In the previously mentioned opening scene, Antonina watches over her young son and two lion cubs lying with him on a bed in a floral dressing gown worn over a silky nightdress. The silky nightdress has thin straps and is revealing around the bust section, suggesting that there is still ongoing romance between her and her husband. With the flowing floral silks conveying a time of peace, love, and calm before the war, the implication is also that she is succeeding in both her motherly domesticity (gently caring for human *and* animal babies) and in maintaining suitable femininity and desirability within her marriage. Subsequently, she is dressed in a flared-silhouette floral gown with pumps and red lipstick as she rides her bicycle around the zoo to perform her rounds feeding and checking on the animals—both traditionally attired woman and caretaker. When she encounters her husband shoveling hay, she kicks off her high heels to help him; in just this opening sequence, we witness the film's definition of an ideal mother (feminine, pulled-together, but natural and earthy enough to commune with animals and not too vain to get into the muck with her family).

In the next scene featuring a dinner hosted by Jan and Antonina at their villa located within the zoo premises, Antonina is dressed in a short-sleeved, cowl neck, polka-dot silk blouse tucked into a slim-fit belted black pencil skirt and nude stockings. She also has a white ribbon tied as a headband with no jewelry except her wedding band. In comparison to the other women in the room dressed in highly adorned 1930s finery (coiffed curls, fur capes, tight-fitting sleeveless dresses, ornate jewels), she is conspicuously modest, a reinforcement of her lack of vanity and her virtue. At the party, Antonina answers the cries of her young son and zoo assistant to save a newborn elephant who is unresponsive until she intervenes. The way her caretaking responsibilities (in the form of her son's cries and the newborn elephant's crisis) interrupts her refined hostessing justifies the choice of the more modest dinner outfit—she is a mother, a gracious hostess, but also an assistant zookeeper around the clock. The role of a mother, whether working outside the home or domestically, is multivariate. Culture, including media, reinforces the traditional expectations that a mother will care for children, a home, and a marriage, even (or perhaps especially) in difficult times (Barnett 2004; Fullerton and Patterson 2010). The character of Antonina embodies this procrustean motherly role and is even given a "super-mother" status as she saves the lives of animals and later takes on the care of the hidden Jewish refugees.

Antonina's Costumes in the Film's Context

Beginning with the bombing of the Warsaw Zoo by German forces, we see Antonina's peaceful life destroyed and the chaos of war set in. Her costumes reflect this, with a turn first to somber yet intense colors (burnt orange, burgundy, navy) and scaled-back adornment. This sharp turn indicates a response to trauma that leaves no time for the flirtatious intimacy she had enjoyed with her husband and a prioritizing of protecting her son over her own presentation. Her subsequent abandonment of colorful clothing symbolizes the end of normalcy. In the last floral silk dressing gown we see her in, Antonina comforts her son over the killing of their animals; she masks her own emotions to comfort him, this feminine garment contributing to an image of motherly strength and compassionate stoicism.

As the Zabinskis enact a plan to turn their zoo into a pig farm to feed the German forces, concealing an operation to smuggle Jews to safety, Antonina's grief over the lost animals is paired with a resolution to help as many people as she can. Her desire to care for Ursula is materialized when she removes her own shawl and offers it to this surrogate daughter. We later see Ursula wearing Antonina's burnt-orange sweater—a token of the older woman's sacrifice.

Antonina's sexuality takes on a complicated dimension when she finds herself needing to use it as currency to protect her family and their hidden guests. Lutz Heck, a Nazi zoologist tasked with patrolling the zoo, displays evident attraction to Antonina. Knowing this, Antonina pulls him into an embrace in order to shield his ears from the sounds of the hidden Jewish children in the basement. In extreme circumstances such as war, a woman's beauty is potentially dangerous to her as well as a possible shield for harm. Misunderstanding the relationship with Heck, Jan becomes jealous, and he and Antonina make compensatory love. Antonina becomes pregnant.

Antonina's first scene as a pregnant mother shows her dressed to cover up her growing bulge in a brown jacket and a black gown gathered at the waist, giving some definition. For the first time, Antonina's bobbed blonde hair is pulled back, symbolic of a different phase in her life. In this period, appearance becomes increasingly secondary to Antonina; her pregnancy and the war continue to advance, and her focus is on the survival of her loved ones. A 1945 issue of the Polish magazine *Przekrój*, commenting on the wartime need to de-prioritize appearances, scolded women, "For heaven's sake, ladies, see to something else! No one, after all, looks nice. But really, you can't waste too much time on it, when there are so many important things to do" (translated in Sulej 2016). Where motherhood is often conceived of as a state in which one sacrifices perceived frivolities like fashion, motherhood in wartime enforces this to an extreme degree.

Still, when called upon to perform a duty for her family, Antonina takes labored preparations to dress up. When Jan is captured by Nazi forces due to his participation in the Warsaw uprising, Antonina goes, in a desperate move, to Lutz Heck with the intention of seducing him for information as to her husband's whereabouts. Her bobbed hair is packed loosely but adorned with a white ribbon—the same ribbon she wore in the dinner scene when Heck first took notice of her. She is seen tying it around her head with knowing intention, wishing to recapture a desirability she can again weaponize. A floral dressing gown from one of the pre-war scenes is seen hanging beside her mirror, a reminder of happier times. The juxtaposition of the somber seductress costume against the carefree floral robe shows the ravages of war on this woman and her family, while reminding the audience that the intended seduction of Heck is only another sacrifice by this mother for her husband, children, and others dependent upon her.

It is 1945 and the war is over in Warsaw. Antonina returns to the zoo with her children. She wears the brown coat in which she fled after Heck discovered they had been hiding the Jews. Her hair is longer (as, presumably, haircuts were an impossible luxury). Her clothes are looser than shown in the previous scenes pre-war and during the war, as if to show the access to fewer meals in those times. The final scene shows Antonina painting with Jan (who returns home after capture) dressed in a cream shirt with floral embroidered details on its sleeves; this is the first time since the commencement of the war that her clothing shows some sign of warmth through its floral details.

Conclusion

As the costume designer on this film, Bina Daigeler utilized various elements to communicate the character of Antonina, including color, texture, and repetition.

The repetition of outfits emphasizes the rationing system in the war era and how the purchase of new clothes would have been a luxury even in times of a growing pregnancy.

The choice of apparel also served to signify Antonina's modesty and need to mix femininity with comfort in a role (zookeeper) that would typically require masculine-coded clothing such as trousers, jumpsuits, or overalls. Her maintenance of her wardrobe of blouses, skirts, and pumps through the phases of her motherhood and the war serve to further position the fictionalized Antonina as a saintly, archetypal mother.

Antonina's superhuman strength, compassion, and nurturing ability is also accompanied by other identities in this film; in addition to being a mother, Antonina is also a wife (the primacy of which is evidenced by the film's title), zoo assistant, cook, veterinarian, cunning seductress, rebel. She plays all of these roles in a time of war and extreme uncertainty. As the actress who portrayed Antonina, Jessica Chastain, herself stated, "[i]n this world of macho, violent aggression, Antonina was trying to bring softness and femininity and love to everything she did" (Focus Features 2017). The costume design, incorporating potent symbolism inherent in color, pattern, and adornment, aids in reinforcing the idea that the character's motherly qualities were an integral aspect of her ability to act heroically and righteously.

References

Annila, P. (2014), "Film Costumes as Icons: Three Representations of a Hero's Iconic Film Costume," MA diss., University of Lapland, Rovaniemi.

Aumont, J., A. Bergala, M. Marie, and M. Vernet, eds. (1997), *Aesthetics of Film*. Austin, TX: University of Texas Press.

Barnes, P. (2018), "The Struggles Of Pregnant Women During World War II: 15 Pics," *Babygaga*, May 10. Available online: https://www.babygaga.com/the-struggles-of-pregnant-women-during-world-war-ii-15-pics/ (accessed April 20, 2020).

Barnett, R. C. (2004), "Women and Multiple Roles: Myths and Reality," *Harvard Review of Psychiatry*, 12 (3): 158–64.

Bayer, S. (2020), "Episodes from the Story of the Hospitals of the Warsaw Uprising," *Medical Review—Auschwitz*. Available online: https://www.mp.pl/auschwitz/journal/english/238174,hospitals-of-the-warsaw-uprising (accessed September 28, 2021).

Brody, H., S. E. Leonard, J. B. Nie, and P. Weindling (2014), "U.S. Responses to Japanese Wartime Inhuman Experimentation After World War II," *Cambridge Quarterly of Healthcare Ethics: The International Journal of Healthcare Ethics Committees*, 23 (2): 220–30. Doi: 10.1017/S0963180113000753.

Clouting, L. (2018), "10 Top Tips for Winning at 'Make Do and Mend,'" *Imperial War Museum*, January 11. Available online: https://www.iwm.org.uk/history/10-top-tips-for-winning-at-make-do-and-mend (accessed April 10, 2020).

Clouting, L. and A. Mason (2018), "How Clothes Rationing Affected Fashion in the Second World War," *Imperial War Museum*, January 5. Available online: https://www.iwm.org.uk/history/how-clothes-rationing-affected-fashion-in-the-second-world-war (accessed April 2020).

Dudek-Woyke, A. (2015), "What Poles Ate When There was Nothing to Eat," *Culture.Pl*. Available online: https://culture.pl/en/article/what-poles-ate-when-there-was-nothing-to-eat (accessed April 11, 2020).

Dyer, S. (2021), "How Costumes in Period Dramas Shape our Perception of Royalty," *The Conversation*, May 12. Available online: https://theconversation.com/how-costumes-in-period-dramas-shape-our-perception-of-royalty-157715 (accessed September 9, Dyer).

Focus Features (2017), "Behind the Scenes: The making of Jessica Chastain's costumes in *The Zookeeper's Wife*," *Focus Features*, April 4. Available online: https://www.focusfeatures.com/article/craft_the-zookeepers-wife_bina-daigeler (March 31, 2020).

Foran, C. (2007), "Antonina's Ark," *The Globe and Mail*, December 15. Available online: https://www.theglobeandmail.com/arts/books-and-media/antoninas-ark/article1201597/ (accessed April 12, 2020).

Fullerton, R. S. and M. J. Patterson (2010), "Procrustean Motherhood: The Good Mother during Depression (1930s), War (1940s), and Prosperity (1950s)," *Information & Media Studies (FIMS) Faculty*, 1–31. Available online: https://ir.lib.uwo.ca/cgi/viewcontent.cgi?article=1116&context=fimspub (April 15, 2020).

Hoffman, J. (2017), "*The Zookeeper's Wife* Review—Jessica Chastain Drama is Wildly Inconsistent," *The Guardian*, March 20. Available online: https://www.theguardian.com/film/2017/mar/20/the-zookeepers-wife-review-jessica-chastain (accessed April 10, 2022).

Jung, J., and E. Kim (2015), "A Study of the Costumes and Make-up in the Movie *Anna Karenina*," *Journal of Fashion Business*, 19 (3): 14–30.

Kim, J.-H., Y.-S. Jun, and Y.-S. Kim (2014), "Costume Color Design as a Symbolic Expression in the Independent Film (Bittersweet Life)—Images in Situations of Movie Location," *Research Journal of the Costume Culture*, 22 (1): 167–82.

Kot Ofek, T. (2021), "Appearance, Citizenship and Clothing Controls in Britain, 1939–1951," PhD diss., University of York. Available online: https://etheses.whiterose.ac.uk/29889/ (accessed September 15, 2021).

Krause, A. (2019), "20 Photos that Show How Maternity Fashion has Changed over the Years," *Insider*, November 8. Available online: https://www.insider.com/how-maternity-fashion-has-changed-2019-3 (accessed April 12, 2020).

Max, D. T. (2007), "Antonina's List," *New York Times*, September 9. Available online: https://www.nytimes.com/2007/09/09/books/review/Max-t.html?auth=login-email&login=email (accessed April 4, 2020).

Mower, J. M. and E. L. Pedersen (2012), "United States World War II Clothing Restrictions," in P. G. Tortora (ed.), *Berg Encyclopedia of World Dress and Fashion: The United States and Canada*. London: Berg Fashion Library. Doi: 10.2752/BEWDF/EDch3811.

Roodhouse, M. (2011), "Rationing," in Dale Southerton (ed.), *Sage Reference Encyclopedia of Consumer Culture*. Thousand Oaks, CA: Sage. Doi: 10.4135/9781412994248.

Seaman, D. (2007), "Strange Sanctuary," *Los Angeles Times*, September 2. Available online: https://www.latimes.com/archives/la-xpm-2007-sep-02-bk-seaman2-story.html (accessed April 12, 2020).

Social Issues Research Centre (SIRC) (2011), *The Changing Face of Motherhood*. Oxford: Social Issues Research Centre. Available online: http://www.sirc.org/publik/CFOM.pdf (March 31, 2020).

Sulej, K. (2016), "Fashion in Poland after World War II," *Culture Poland*, August 4. Available online: https://culture.pl/en/article/fashion-in-poland-after-world-war-ii (accessed April 12, 2020).

Soll, J. (2017), "The Revelatory Horror of *The Zookeeper's Wife*," *New Republic*, April 3. Available online: https://newrepublic.com/article/141806/revelatory-horror-zookeepers-wife (accessed April 4, 2020).

Summers, J. (2015), *Fashion on the Ration: Style in the Second World War*. London: Profile Books.

The Zookeeper's Wife (2017), Dir. Niki Caro, film. USA: Focus Features.

Turner, N. (2019), "Costumes Go to War: British Propaganda Films Influence Women to Do Their Part," *Dress: The Journal of the Costume Society of America*, 45 (2): 153–71.

Turner, N. (2022), *Clothing Goes to War: Creativity Inspired by Scarcity in World War II*. Bristol: Intellect.

6

The Fascinance of the Maternal Gaze:

Kate and Laura Mulleavy's *Woodshock*

Kimberly Lamm

Finding Rodarte

In 2005, Kate and Laura Mulleavy, sisters and self-taught designers from California, started Rodarte, a fashion line that revitalizes fashion's imaginative connection to femininity. In a video interview for *Vogue*, the Mulleavy sisters explain how they chose the name Rodarte. The way they tell this story—lyrically following their memories and associations, letting their sentences flow seamlessly into each other—reveals the intimacy of their collaboration and the familial context out of which it emerges. As Kate recalls, they were wondering what to call their company, and their father found an old Pasadena phone directory that included their maternal grandfather's name, Rodarte. When the family became citizens and started using the anglicized name "Rodarts," Rodarte faded away, but it did not disappear. It was there in the phone book, among the rows of names and numbers. This was the first time their mother saw her real name in print, and they took this revelation as a sign. "Obviously," Laura explains, "we need to use our mom's maiden name in its original form" (Mulleavy and Mulleavy 2013). Symbolizing a young woman's life before marriage, and the systems of patriarchal exchange marriage has historically symbolized, the "maiden" name evokes youthful femininity. For the Mulleavys, the maiden name also represents their mother's Latina heritage before assimilating into the erasure white American culture demands. The designers' choice to give their fashion line their mother's maiden name suggests what is at stake in the unabashed love for the sartorial signs of femininity that their work expresses.

Twisted layers of weathered lace; tulle, silk, and satin; outlandishly large taffeta bows and ruffles; polka dots, pastels, and floral patterns; these are just a few of the materials and stylistic signatures the Mulleavy sisters work with to place femininity at the center of their designs. When fashion writers report on their collections, it is clear they strike an emotional chord. Reviewing Rodarte's ready-to-wear line from Spring 2018, *Vogue* writer and editor Sally Singer remarks upon the use of baby's breath in the show and offers an insight that strikes me as crucial for understanding the Rodarte aesthetic and its stakes. Singer writes that the baby's breath was "perhaps the most Rodarte gesture of the day: to remember and elevate the beauty of something so common, so prevalent, and so deeply associated with the romantic imagination of young women" (2017). She goes on to note that this theme—the romantic imagination of young women—also materializes in "laddered tights, inexpensive charm bracelets, and the beaded appliques of accessible formal wear" (ibid.). A description like this, attentive to the details of their designs, makes Rodarte's commitment to femininity even more discernible and suggests how much the fashion world values it. And yet, not everyone shares Singer's enthusiasm. Rodarte's designs have been described by fashion writer Cathy Horyn as "cloyingly naïve" (Horyn 2015). This description of the clothes has, according to Gabrielle Korn, a "distinctly sexist undertone" and illustrates the pervasive dismissal of girls, women, and femininity that Rodarte unabashedly challenges (Korn 2020).

This chapter connects Rodarte's challenge to the pervasive denunciation of femininity to the longing for the maternal animating their work. I pursue this connection by analyzing *Woodshock* (2017), the first feature film they wrote and directed. I turn to this haunted and hallucinatory film not only because so many of Rodarte's designs take their inspiration from the history of cinema—Robert Altman's *3 Women* (1977) was the starting point for the Spring 2018 collection, for example—but because the film is about the loss of a mother and the value of the femininity that can be found in maternal care. In *Woodshock*, the maternal becomes the thread that links femininity, film, and fashion. The film can therefore tell us a lot about the feminist stakes of their vision.

Early in *Woodshock*, Theresa (played by Kirsten Dunst) holds and kisses the body of her terminally ill mother (played by Susan Traylor) and creates a tender passageway for her death by giving her a lethal dose of medical marijuana. Opening the film with a daughter caring for her mother encapsulates the affective dimensions of Rodarte's designs and suggests that a longing for the maternal is part of their work's loving adoration of femininity. Contradicting the pervasive and largely unconscious assumption that women are missing something, Theresa's loss and her memory of her mother's body are full. They animate the film's flow of memories and perceptions and connect the protagonist to a world rich with natural and imaginative resources. At the same time, the film traces Theresa's struggle to find a language to express and inhabit her grief. To explore this struggle and its connections to Rodarte's designs, I draw from the work of artist and psychoanalyst Bracha L. Ettinger. In her essay "*Fascinance* and the Girl-to-m/Other Matrixial Feminine Difference," Ettinger writes of the gaze of "fascination" between the daughter-girl and the woman-mother that allows femininity to thrive beyond its positioning in relationship to men. Ettinger tracks the desires of young women "to be caught in a move of fascination that belongs to femininity," which allows the "woman-mother" and "daughter-girl" to see each other with loving adoration (Ettinger 2006a: 62). It is the gaze of fascinance, which encourages the girl to imagine herself into a "mature elusive femininity" that *Woodshock* realizes and mourns (Ettinger 2006a: 62). The longing for fascinance in *Woodshock* is a point from which to begin understanding the feminist potential of Rodarte's work.

Fashioning a Cinematic World in *Woodshock*

Before *Woodshock*'s first shot, a black screen fills with metallic sounds. They are high-pitched, hollow, and ethereal. The screen then fades into an image that portrays a pattern created by the stately columns of the California redwoods and the cool, dark shadows between them. Glimpses of sunlight and blue sky appear high and far in the background. A small barefoot figure wearing a white slip dress appears from behind one of the trees. Almost indiscernible, her body emphasizes the redwoods' otherworldly heights that extend far beyond the frame. This figure is Theresa, the dreamy and troubled protagonist of *Woodshock*.

"Woodshock" is a colloquial term for the disorientation one can feel in the thick of the forest, and the Mullaveys' choice to use it for their title connects the film's exploration of loss to the California redwoods. In these opening images, Theresa speaks in the voiceover with a gravelly whisper to an unidentified interlocutor and recalls getting lost in the woods one summer: "when I turned around you were gone." She also remembers the desire to stay lost after she was finally found, and with this recollection, the camera circles the base of the redwoods and focuses on Theresa lying face down in a tree's sculptural twists and gnarled, knotty forms. Lying with the tree, letting her body become part of its textured crevices, Theresa draws attention to the gigantic width of the trunk. She wants the wood to hold her. In one close-up, she embeds a hand into a textured crevice and looks up with a tearful and loving admiration.

Like a refrain, images that evoke the color, shape, and texture of wood appear throughout *Woodshock*. Wood is the source of the film's sensory palette. It is often suffused in a warm amber light, and the tactility of wood carries memories and sensations that exceed the capabilities of sight. These portrayals of Theresa engaging with the redwoods reflect how much nature is a source of inspiration for the designers. (Their father is a botanist.) As it frames Theresa's body, wood registers the depth with which she mourns her mother, a mourning the film connects to the destruction of the redwood forest.

These opening scenes in the forest inaugurate a rhythmic leitmotif of Theresa dissolving, disappearing, and becoming increasingly indiscernible, a stranger to herself and alienated from the world she inhabits. *Woodshock* is, above all, a moving portrait of Theresa. She moves among the sublime columns of the redwoods, but also appears within images composed of floral wallpaper, mirrored reflections, lace curtains, and prismatic light. As Theresa wanders through the film to find a language that could express her grief, the cinematographer Peter Flinckenberg layers her portrayal with an array of techniques—soft focus filters, lens flares, and double exposures—all of which create porous cinematic images that evoke the complexity of her psychic life as it comes undone. Many views of Theresa look like stylized pictures from fashion spreads in glossy magazines and show that *Woodshock* draws on a history in which film and fashion emerged in tandem. As fashion scholar Caroline Evans explains, it was a fascination with women moving, appearing, and disappearing that linked film and fashion in the early twentieth century (Evans 2011). The Mulleavys bring this fascination to *Woodshock* and draw on it to plumb the depths of feminine subjectivity.

Film and fashion are inseparable in the Mulleavys' imagination, and both aesthetic practices point to the impact of their mother on their creative lives. They often talk about the fact that their mother nurtured their passion for film. In the pages of *Vanity Fair*, Marnie Hanel reports that their mother "let her daughters play hooky so that she could give them another kind of education" (2011). Movies replaced school. It is in this context that Laura notes that film fostered their interest in clothing. As she explains, "[their] first relationship to clothing didn't come from what our mom was wearing. It came from film" (ibid., 2011). Often a mother's attire gives a daughter her "first relationship" to clothing, but the Mulleavy sisters received this inheritance less directly, through their mother's encouragement to engage with film and receive "another kind of education."

This education was rich and deep enough to inspire a lifetime of creativity. Articles and interviews that accompanied the release of *Woodshock* attest to their love for and thorough knowledge of cinema. Identifying the films they admire, and describing how those films captured their attention, the Mulleavys make it clear they value cinematic images that create and attest to intersubjective encounters. This investment becomes clear when they describe Altman's *3 Women*: "Strange and wondrous ... these characters intermingle almost like a dream ... Millie unpacking her groceries and narrating it to herself ... Pinky dressed in her many nightgowns, longing to be anyone but herself ... and Willy, desolate, standing amid her pastel, surrealistic murals" (Mulleavy and Mulleavy 2017). The ellipses evoke the blurred connections among the female protagonists, and through the description of the costumes—"Pinky dressed in her many nightgowns"—the Mulleavys show that clothing is not only part of the visual landscape Altman creates, but attests to the desires of the characters to fashion worlds in which they can become other to themselves.

In their collections that draw inspiration from cinema, Rodarte can allude to a film's signature costumes, but their engagement does not stop there. Their designs evoke the visual world a film creates. For the Fall 2016 collection, Rodarte created a collection that draws from Francis Ford Coppola's *The Godfather* (1972). This collection alludes to the costume designs of Anna Hill Johnstone, and particularly the lace veils that have a prominent place in the film's wedding scenes. One dress composed of black lace and accented by a veil evokes the imminent death of Michael Corleone's Sicilian bride Apollonia. Another dress is made of sheer burgundy fabric with a warm brown tint that is layered over swaths of burgundy red. Dark flowers with white centers cover the bodice and create a trellis that moves diagonally across the torso. In an interview, Laura explains that they wanted to evoke the feeling of Gordon Willis' cinematography and get that "perfect red wine color" (Bravo 2022). When asked what specifically about Coppola's film they appreciate, Kate replies that she is "mesmeriz[ed]" by its "cohesiveness" (ibid.). In Coppola's "grand vision," she explains, "everything comes into effortless storytelling. He's an incredible world builder" (ibid.). This "world building" is something the Mulleavy sisters strive for in their work. This ambition refutes the assumption that femininity is too superficial, sweet, and passive to tap into the aggressive drive world building requires. They stage this refutation not by denying femininity or reinforcing the connection between masculinity and aggression; instead, the Mulleavy sisters fashion a world in which femininity is recognized for its depth, strength, and value.

Visualizing the Loss of Fascinance

Woodshock begins with Theresa giving a lethal dose of marijuana to her mother, which allows her to slip away from the pain of terminal illness and die peacefully. The film is set in Humboldt County, and marijuana is a significant part of the cultural landscape in which this assisted suicide takes place. The drug and its hallucinatory states create the imaginary spaces and deeply felt sensations in which the daughter's grief, and her connection to her mother, are revealed. After Theresa drops poison from an amber bottle into the joint she will help her mother smoke from, there is a perfectly symmetrical shot of two interconnected spaces that formally attests to their connection. On the right is Theresa's mother lying in bed, propped up by two pillows against a wood headboard. The sheets are off-white and sunlight filters through the white curtains. On the left is Theresa walking through a dark corridor. As she moves toward the room where her mother sleeps, Theresa creates a vertical line and light illuminates her body in rhythmic intervals. This spatial contrast sets up the significance of the next scene in which their bodies are entwined together in a soft, sleepy, and intimate embrace.

This portrayal of intimacy continues with an image of Theresa's hands gently tying and arranging the tan-colored ribbons placed at the laced edges of her mother's nightgown. This delicate gesture represents the gendered labor mothers are generally expected to perform, but it also evokes the reciprocity of maternal care. Once dressed by the mother, the daughter now carefully arranges her bed clothes. This act also suggests the designer's attention to the detail of a dress, and the mother's imminent death gives this attention significance. Touching her mother's face, Theresa asks her if she's "sure she wants to do this" (take the drugs that will allow her to die). She takes her daughter's hand, which reveals her IV, and kisses it. The mother turns to her daughter, looks at her with loving admiration, and tells her, slowly, she couldn't do this without her. Both Theresa and the care she gives are valued. The mother's look suggests what the daughter is about to lose—what Bracha Ettinger calls "the gaze of fascinance"—and what the directors have found and realized on the terrain of the cinematic image.

I am drawn to the work of Ettinger to read *Woodshock* because it tracks the intricate psychic processes through which young women inherit the feeling of femininity's value from the adoring eyes of maternal figures. The gaze of fascinance, a central concept of Ettinger's oeuvre, is the visual, affective space that holds the feeling of being valued. Ettinger's project might seem like a simple matter of feminist assertion, but it is more radical than that, as the historical dismissal of femininity, a premise of masculine dominance, is difficult to excavate and dismantle. Psychoanalytic thought, the primary field in which Ettinger works, has certainly contributed to this dismissal. As Ettinger explains, psychoanalysis has a "long tradition of ignorance concerning the woman-to-woman, non-Oedipal relations" (Ettinger 2006a: 61). And yet, she developed the gaze of fascinance by working within and against this "long tradition of ignorance," as it leads her to what psychoanalysis simultaneously represses and reveals: psychic relations among women. The attention psychoanalysis pays to the psychic impact of maternal care on early infant life offers resources for thinking about the place of femininity in the patriarchal unconscious and how it might transform.

The gaze of fascinance creates virtual spaces in which acts of women seeing women and girls as "fascinating" can be discerned and understood. With etymological connections to witchcraft, sorcery, and spells, to be fascinated is to be deeply interested. An act of "transgressive hospitality," the gaze of fascinance welcomes femininity's differences and finds them captivating (Ettinger 2006a: 66). Ettinger argues that this loving gaze precedes and exists to the side of patriarchal systems of value in which femininity is recognized for mirroring back the centrality of masculine subjectivity. In the field of desire created by fascinance, the girl is valued in and of herself. She is seen within a loving vision that will "envelop and subjectivize her as a potentially ravishing being" (Ettinger 2006a: 67). What better way to describe the Rodarte aesthetic?

The gaze of fascinance is a development of Ettinger's concept of the matrixial, which comes out of her attention to the "feminine/prenatal encounter" as a liminal space in which multiple subjectivities emerge together as both linked and separate (Ettinger 2006b: 48). The matrixial is, as Ettinger explains, the "archaic m/Other with whom the girl once dwelled in an ancient *time-space of encounter*" (Ettinger 2006b: 64). She also describes it as the "unconscious border space of the several" (Ettinger 2006b: 68). While this encounter with multiplicity emerges from the intrauterine, the concept of the matrixial doesn't valorize the womb or essentialize it as the core of femininity. The matrixial does, however, address what Griselda Pollock names the "sexual specificity of the feminine in every subject," which opens on to "acoustic, sonorous, and tactile potentialities" that "move beyond the limits of bodies and the boundaries between inside and outside" (2006: 3, 20). Revealing how this rich border-defying aesthetic emerges from maternal care, Ettinger writes that "the mother's gaze, like her voice, enveloped us, touched us, but also eluded us" (Ettinger 2006a: 42). The matrixial is distinct from the strict binaries of phallic logic that "positions the feminine negatively, below the threshold of any kind of symbolization" (Pollock 2006: 2). That is, the matrixial is a "differential potentiality before and beyond" recognizable gender identifies and particularly, the "strict separation of masculine and feminine" (Ettinger 2006a: 68). With its connection to the envelope of maternal care, it makes sense that Pollock would draw upon figures of fabric and weaving to explain the matrixial. Weaving is, according to Pollock, "a potent and necessary metaphor, an image of a decentered field, a textuality, a texture, vibrating threads" (2006: 6).

Woodshock takes up the threads of fascinance, but the film is also pushing against the fact that for the most part, this adoring maternal gaze is buried under the presumed value of masculinity and its capacity to position femininity negatively. This burial prevents it from becoming a readily available mode of seeing girls, women, and the aesthetic practices—like fashion—with which they are associated. Negative reviews of *Woodshock* illustrate how easy it is to draw from the pervasive dismissal of femininity. A reviewer in *Vanity Fair* begins by exploring the alignment of fashion and cinema but ends up using fashion to trivialize *Woodshock* and highlight its flaws. He writes that the film could "desperately use some extra detailing at the level of character and psychology," and then goes on to describe its conclusion as "misery chic" (Lodge 2017). Such formulations tell us what we already know: feminism, never mind a feminism inflected by fascinance, is not readily available when people respond to a film that tries to fashion a world in which femininity is valued. Fascinance is an exception to the general rule of masculinity as the most valued point from which to see and encounter the world.

Woodshock grapples with masculinity's stubborn psychic hold. After the death of Theresa's mother, this aspect of the narrative comes into the foreground, and Theresa becomes pulled between two men: Keith (played by Pilou Asbaek), her boss at a dispensary for medical marijuana, and Kirk (played by Joe Cole), her boyfriend. Keith gave Theresa the marijuana that allowed her mother to die. Intrusive and strange, he exudes the distortions of aggressive impulses barely kept under wraps. Kirk is quiet, subdued, and caring, but also frustrated by Theresa's grief. He works in a lumber yard for a living and wants to provide for Theresa. Keith competes with Kirk, and for both men, Theresa is a way to prove their masculine worth by showing that they can provide for women and master exchange relations. Their attachment to this iteration of masculinity contributes to making a daughter's grief strange. And yet, Keith and Kirk are not sinister; they awkwardly struggle with the power they try to embody. The Mulleavys' nuanced portrayal of these characters connects to Ettinger's argument that the matrixial gaze of fascinance is not a substitute for phallic value and it does not flip the terms of its hierarchy. As Pollock explains, the matrixial "surfs beneath/ beside the phallic. It emerges beside the process of a deconstruction of the latter's blind domination of the subjective field, while itself never emerging as another, hence phallic, contender" (2006: 6). In other words, the matrixial gaze of fascinance does not compete with the splits and oppositions of Oedipal subjectivity, but instead "open[s] spaces for what co-exists" with it (Pollock 2006: 6).

In a world premised on the value of masculinity, the gaze of fascinance is hard to find, and the death of a mother, which can represent the symbolic death of maternal femininity, can compound the difficulties a girl is likely to encounter on the path to womanhood. Ettinger describes these difficulties by posing the following question: "Can a girl become a woman if she cannot receive admiring recognition of her femininity from another woman-Mother?" (2006a: 67). *Woodshock* makes the loss of this "admiring recognition" visible, but also creates cinematic images that reveal how art can be a place for rediscovering its loving reciprocity. Early in the film, Keith offers an observation that opens a way for Theresa to begin composing an image of herself accessing the gaze of fascinance. When she returns to her job at the marijuana dispensary, she despondently puts labels on glass jars and bristles at Keith's obtrusive bodily presence as he moves through this space with its cool colors and metallic sounds. And yet, Keith reveals that a part of him is soft, attentive, and tuned into her loss. When Theresa is sitting in a silver chair before a room of marijuana plants illuminated with fluorescent lights of deep fuchsia, he looks at her from across the room and then says, somberly, "I know it's kinda weird, but sometimes you look like your mom."

Following Keith's insight about maternal resemblance, there is an abrupt cut to a mirrored image of Theresa rummaging through cardboard boxes in her mother's home. She finds a cream-colored slip with a deep neckline trimmed in lace. Holding it with loving adoration, she slowly pulls it close to her chest. In the next shot, Theresa stands in front of a mirror looking at herself wearing the article of clothing she just found. Mirrors on the other side of the room also create reflections of her body so there are three linked portrayals of Theresa wearing the slip that belonged to her mother, each one perceived and visualized from a different angle (Figure 6.1). The slip is Theresa's inheritance of fascinance. It materializes her loving connection to her mother, the touch of her skin, the feel of her body from the inside out, and the sensuous care with which she is associated. The mirrored reflections suggest that the slip allows Theresa to see and hold the traces of her mother's gaze as she perceives herself. The Mulleavys

Figure 6.1 Kirsten Dunst as Theresa in Kate and Laura Mulleavy's film *Woodshock*. Printed with permission of the photographer.

have composed a cinematic sculpture of Theresa inhabiting the material traces of her mother's body to access and enter what Ettinger identifies as "mature elusive femininity" (2006a: 62).

The silk slip with lace trim becomes a manifestation of Theresa's psychic state as it continues to unravel. An explicit illustration of that unraveling takes place when Theresa builds a structure on the outer periphery of her mother's home with narrow pieces of wood. She undertakes this messy and labor-intensive project while wearing the slip. At odds with the idea that femininity is not aggressive, there is an extended scene that portrays Theresa pounding the stakes into the ground with a rock. The night fog illuminates the silk garment and provides an ethereal contrast to the obsessive force she brings to this work. Hitting the wood, she creates a rhythmic sequence of loud cracks and thuds. It is unclear what this project symbolizes, but it feels akin to world building. Perhaps it maps a space for her mother's home that both contains Theresa's grief and extends it further outward. What is clear is that Theresa pursues it aggressively and her mother's slip highlights the fact that femininity can be part of that pursuit, not outside of it.

Theresa undertakes this world-building project in an altered, sleepwalking state. She wakes up and notices her slip and the sheets are soiled with dirt. From inside the house, the camera pans across the front yard to represent Theresa's line of sight as she witnesses the sticks of wood scattered in a haphazard row. Kirk stands behind her as she looks out the window in disbelief. She asks him, "You think I did this?" With simmering anger and disgust, he takes note of the dirty and torn garment she wears and says with punitive force, "look at you. Look at what you did out there. I'm not cleaning up for you." After this exchange, she starts to take the slats of wood down and throw them into a pile, but then she decides to build the structure again. There are great images of Theresa crossing the yard with an angry determination. The slip and its link to femininity isn't an impediment; almost at one with her skin, it follows the force of bodily movement. But something spooks her, and she runs into the house in fear. Petrified, she sits on the floor and up against a wall hugging her knees to her chest. Embodying this iconic pose from horror films, Theresa watches herself continue to ram stakes into the ground. In the middle of this self-reflexive hallucination and out-of-body experience, she receives a call from Keith requesting her company and *Woodshock* starts to tip into horror.

Dark Undertones and Aggressive Depths

The Mulleavy sisters are fans of horror films. Their knowledge and love of the genre made its way into their Fall 2008 collection, which features "slasher" dresses that elegantly move between what Caroline Evans calls the "borders of beauty and horror" (2003: 5). Dyed black, white, and bright blood red, the diaphanous fabric of these dresses is swirled, torn, gathered, and ripped. It is almost as though each dress has emerged from a slice of a film still in which the messy aftermath of a murder, clothes and skin torn asunder, becomes an abstract design. In one gown, the red spills into the nets of bright angelic white, dissipating like blood in water. There is also a short cocktail dress from this collection composed of swaths of netted fabric gently linked together with raw twine. The front of the dress has a long streak of blood-red sequins and an array of spontaneous drips and splatters. Reporting on this collection for *Vogue*, Laird Borrelli-Person taps into the aggression these "slasher" dresses express and writes that they "prove [Kate and Laura Mulleavy] have plenty of teeth. And sharp ones" (2008). These designs aggressively destabilize the borders between bodies and show that horror expresses a desire to materialize intersubjective relations. Horror is about intense interdependency.

For their Fall 2020 collection, which was staged in the nave of St. Bartholomew's church in Manhattan, Rodarte cited Coppola's *Dracula* (1992) and displayed clothing that attested to gothic and sinister strains of femininity. "Dramatic" doesn't quite capture the rich colors and textures of the dresses in this collection: bright red silk, black leather fringe, indigo velvet with metallic tints. Many of the dresses are composed of sheer nets of silvery layers that look like, according to

Gabrielle Korn, "bejewelled spiderwebs" (2020). Rodarte brings the idea of a seductively woven trap to the love the collection expresses for, in Korn's words, "fantastical, powerful, dark female tropes" (ibid.). Rodarte's celebration of femininity does not repress or shy away from the aggressive depths condensed within these tropes.

Slightly opaque and difficult to follow, the narrative of *Woodshock* reveals how Theresa's psychic unhinging leads to murderous violence, and it is this dimension of the film that reveals her connection to femininity's aggressive depths and dark undertones. Driving Theresa home from a party, Keith tells her that an older customer, Ed (played by Steph Duvall) is terminally ill. Keith says to her, "He needs us ... but I didn't think you could go through with it again." With despairing longing, Theresa is pulled by the idea of Ed's suffering. She drives to his house and watches him sink into a chair on the porch. Set against the dusky blue night sky illuminated by the moon, it is clear he is hovering at death's painful edge. Theresa brings the poisoned weed to the shop for Ed to buy, but accidentally sells it to Johnny, a young man who is reluctant to participate in the destructive iterations of masculinity that pulsates through this world. After Keith tells Theresa that Johnny is dead, she is consumed with guilt and starts to psychically shatter. She begins to smoke the poisoned weed she gave to her mother; the narrative slips further away from linearity; the boundaries between fantasy and reality blur; and Theresa becomes increasingly destructive. When she stabs her finger with a knife and drags the blood across the lace tablecloth, Theresa creates an ominous sign.

Cuts, blood, and violence seem to give Theresa psychic relief. It also allows her to make visible her mother's death and the absence it leaves in her life. After Keith invites her over, because he "could use some company," she dresses up in a black sequin dress, a sharp contrast to the pale creams of the slip she wears through much of the film's second half. She puts on jewelry and paints her lips with the juice of blackberries. The images of her crushing a berry, using it like lipstick, eating it, and then licking the red stains from her fingertips encapsulate *Woodshock*'s sensuous relationship to violence.

First, Theresa goes to Ed and tells him about her mistake. After hearing her confession, he dies. Horrified, in a frantic and deranged state, she rushes to Keith's house. He is in the midst of ironing—an act that connects intimately to the work of dressing, of designing, and of traditional mothering—and rows of colored glass beads hang from his ceiling. Keith tries to comfort Theresa, wraps her in a blanket, and wonders what has happened to her. After pleading with him to explain "why can't he say it," she screams, "we helped kill her. We killed her."

Unable to calm her, Keith goes to the phone to call Nick. They struggle, and Theresa ends up burning his face with the hot iron and then bashing his face in with it. The rhythmic thuds of the iron hitting Keith's face echoes Theresa pounding the wood stakes into the mud with rocks. Trying to watch this shockingly brutal scene, but impulsively turning away, I was reminded of Robin Wood's observation that the "fascination with horror films is their fulfillment of our nightmare wish to smash the norms that oppress us and which our moral conditioning teaches us to revere" (Wood 1978: 27–8). Keith isn't a villain, but he does represent an effort to contain Theresa in normalcy. He sees her as a way to assert his masculinity, and traditionally this assertion has relied upon the decidedly normal devaluation of femininity. This dismissal of femininity, and the accompanying idealization that it is always moral, giving, and good, and therefore without aggressive depths and dark undertones, is repressive, and as *Woodshock* shows, consequential.

After this gruesome scene, Theresa is once again in the woods. Her face and body are covered with bloody slashes and she is only wearing the silk slip, soiled with dirt and ragged with rips. She places her body against the trunk of a tree and she becomes a blurry trace of light. Like an ecstatic wood nymph, she begins levitating along the enormous heights of the gigantic redwoods and in the dark spaces between them. This movement culminates the otherworldly dimensions of the film, Theresa's psychic unraveling, and the imaginative distortions of her grief. At the same time, by defying gravity, Theresa's radical movement aligns with the magical heights and deep history embedded in the trees. Her flight seems to unleash the energy and aggression that is stifled by the pervasive denunciation of femininity and its compensatory idealization. While Theresa's crimes are linked to the crime of destroying the forest, her ascension along the steep vertical lines of the redwoods expresses a wish for another world.

Conclusion

A daughter's story of losing her mother, *Woodshock* reveals what fascinance is and what the loss of it means. Fascinance connects to the desire to cherish rather than exploit the earth and its inhabitants that are, like the redwoods, vulnerable and rich with resources. This hallucinatory film, with a violent undercurrent that manifests through Theresa's loss, shows that dismissing or underestimating femininity, seeing it as devoid of dark undertones and aggressive depths, makes it ricochet into danger. But even if fascinance, maternal care, and femininity are easy to lose in a world that continues to be written by the stubborn legacies of patriarchal masculinity, the Mulleavy sisters reveal that it can be found in aesthetic practices such as theirs that fashion a world for femininity.

References

Borrelli-Persson, L. (2008), "Rodarte Fall 2008 Ready-to-Wear," *Vogue*. Available online: https://www.vogue.com/fashion-shows/fall-2008-ready-to-wear/rodarte (accessed May 2022).

Bravo, T. (2022), "Rodarte Designers Kate and Laura Mulleavy on their 'Godfather'-Inspired Fashion Collection," *San Francisco Chronicle*. Available online: https://datebook.sfchronicle.com/movies-tv/rodarte-designers-kate-and-laura-mulleavy-on-their-godfather-inspired-fashion-collection (accessed May 2022).

Ettinger, B. L. (2006a), "*Fascinance* and the Girl-to-m/Other Matrixial Feminine Difference," in G. Pollock (ed.), *Psychoanalysis and the Image: Transdisciplinary Perspectives,* 60–93. Malden, MA: Blackwell.

Ettinger, B. L. (2006b), "The Matrixial Gaze," in B. Massumi (ed.), *The Matrixial Borderspace*, 41–92. Minneapolis, MN: University of Minnesota Press.

Evans, C. (2003), *Fashion at the Edge: Spectacle, Modernity, and Deathliness.* New Haven, CT: Yale University Press.

Evans, C. (2011), "The Walkies: Early French Fashion Shows as a Cinema of Attractions," in A. Munich (ed.), *Fashion in Film*, 110–34. Bloomington, IN: Indiana University Press.

Hanel, M. (2011), "From Sketch to Still, the Visual History of Rodarte in *Black Swan*," *Vanity Fair*, January 7. Available online: https://www.vanityfair.com/hollywood/2011/01/from-sketch-to-still-the-visual-history-of-rodarte-in-black-swan (accessed May 2022).

Horyn, C. (2015), "Finding Magic in the Trash at Rodarte," *The Cut*. Available online: https://www.thecut.com/2015/02/cathy-horyn-rodarte-oscar-de-la-renta.html (accessed May 2022).

Korn, G. (2020), "Rodarte's Fall 2020 Show Was So Pretty, It Hurt," *Refinery 29*. Available online: https://www.refinery29.com/en-us/2020/02/9402649/rodarte-nyfw-fashion-show-fall-2020-vampire-goth (accessed May 2022).

Lodge, G. (2017), "Film Review: Kirsten Dunst in 'Woodshock.'" *Vanity Fair*. Available online: https://variety.com/2017/film/reviews/woodshock-kirsten-dunst-1202546279/ (accessed May 2022).

Mulleavy, K. and L. Mulleavy (2013), "Vogue Voices." Available online: https://www.vogue.com/video/watch/vogue-voices-rodarte (accessed May 2022).

Mulleavy, K. and L. Mulleavy (2017), "Rodarte's Top 10." Available online: https://www.criterion.com/current/top-10-lists/313-rodarte-s-top-10 (accessed May 2022).

Pollock, G. (2006), "Femininity: Aporia or Sexual Difference," in B. Massumi (ed.), *The Matrixial Borderspace*, 3–40. Minneapolis, MN: University of Minnesota Press.

Singer, S. (2017), "Rodarte: Spring 2018 Ready to Wear," *Vogue*, July 2. Availale online: https://www.vogue.com/fashion-shows/spring-2018-ready-to-wear/rodarte (accessed May 2021).

Wood, R. (1978), "Return of the Repressed," *Film Comment*, 14 (4): 25–32.

Section 2

Material: Experience

If, as Rich explains, the institution of motherhood is essentially an extension of patriarchy, then, "The woman's body is the terrain on which patriarchy is erected" ([1976] 1995: 55). Indeed, this is where motherhood and fashion perhaps most obviously overlap: both have been imposed on the bodies of women and feminized people in ways that have kept them from experiencing the full freedoms available to men.

Rich's "mothering" is taken here to be not just an experience, but an *embodied* experience, whether that includes birthing children or being consumed by their care—and any experience that takes place in and on the body is one necessarily tangled up with fashion. In all human cultures, the human body is a *fashioned* body, meaning one whose look and feel are partly determined by culture, whether they are technically dressed or not. As Entwistle explains, dress operates as "the interface between the individual and the social world, the meeting place of the private and the public" (2000: 7). The mothering body, therefore, experiences both the private and public spheres (its relationship to which has been variously determined throughout history and across territories) at least partially depending on how it is dressed.

The chapters in "Material" depart very consciously from the idea, established in the sub-sections on "Image," that "[the institution of] motherhood has alienated women from our bodies by incarcerating us in them" (Rich [1976] 1995: 13). This notion of bodily incarceration is somewhat literalized in a single garment that reappears throughout this section, and to which fashion and fashion studies bear a complex ongoing relationship: the corset.

While it remains impossible to pin a single meaning onto the centuries-old foundation garment with infinite iterations, uses, and appearances, I see the constraint and restriction of the corset as an apt metaphor for how mothers are meant to conform to traditional expectations. The chapters in this section that use the maternal corset as a site of analysis are also concerned with the discourse surrounding it, demonstrating how cultural negotiations of the meaning of dress also place boundaries around how people experience mothering at the most elemental, physical level. With a diverse mix of sources (including surviving garments, advertisements, design patents, and advice literature), the first three chapters here aim to untangle the narrative of the period in which the corset for pregnancy came under intense scrutiny.

Though corsets of various kinds are still very much worn today—including during pregnancy, though they may be masquerading as "shapewear" or "belly bands"—the maternity and breastfeeding corsets in this section are historical, primarily deriving from the nineteenth and early twentieth centuries. While this might point to a bias toward that period in fashion studies scholarship in general (and therefore the richest vein of secondary sources upon which to draw), it also interrogates the last time a major shift occurred in the Western ideology of mothering (towards a model that is labor-intensive, emotionally expansive, noble, fulfilling, and somehow utterly "natural") emerged, the ramifications of which we continue to live with today.

Motherhood scholar Sharon Hays calls this prevailing ideology "intensive mothering" and traces its origins to the late Victorian era, when the protection of children's innocence was newly believed to require the exclusive care of a protective, virtuous mother (1996: 29). Previously, children's fragility and high childhood mortality rates necessitated less emotional investment in them, but in the new Western industrial environment, where home and work were for the first time separated into distinct spheres, a new image of mothering as "pervasive sentimentality mixed with purity, piety, and patriotism" arose (ibid.). It was these new social conditions for the rising middle-class mother that led to her cultural equation with and essential confinement to hearth and home. Even knowing that this picture of motherhood is less than two centuries old, and aware that it only ever applied to relatively affluent, mainly white people, we find it a remarkably difficult ideology to shake off even now.

Despite sharing a time period, each of the three chapters takes a distinct approach to interrogating how dress was used to police the motherly body. Karen Case's chapter dives deeply into the highly polarized medical conversation around mothers' responsibility to their fetuses as well as to the comfort of those around them. Lauren Downing Peters uses archival design patents to show how the pregnant body was perceived as a problem that could be solved by design, and Claire Salmon addresses breastfeeding and the postpartum period—a phase as rife with cultural contradictions and anxieties as pregnancy—as the corset gave way to the bra, for nursing and otherwise.

The last chapter of the section, on Comme des Garçons' famous "Lumps and Bumps" collection, bursts forward in time just as Rei Kawakubo's padded designs allowed the feminized body to burst beyond the constraints of "natural" shape. Katrina Orsini suggests a connection between the advances in obstetric medicine allowing visual access inside the womb to Kawakubo's playful abstraction of the physical protrusions of pregnancy that freed them to roam around the body. The desire to see inside the maternal body is consistent with the discourses of discipline that continue to be enacted upon it—what Steele refers to as the "internalized corset" of diet and exercise regimes, or what Liu and Wang refer to as the "third shift of bodywork" mothers are expected to perform (Steele 2003: 143; Liu and Wang 2021). As we so often see by bringing fashion history into conversation with the present, change is not always as rapid or complete as the fashion system might like us to believe.

This jump in time, from the onset of the intensive mothering paradigm to the era of postmodern abstraction, leaves a swath of the twentieth century unexamined. That period, the first in which commercial maternity wear was widely available and the bodies of pregnant people were fashioned by it, deserves rich, material-focused research as well. The brilliant book *Designing Motherhood: Things that Make and Break Our Births* includes discussion of the tie-waist skirt, that pre-Lycra "midcentury maternity game changer," and the big-business industry that's developed since its debut (Millar Fisher and Winick 2021: 104). If such garments continue to be recognized for their significance to fashion history and ability to tell the story of how the ideology of intensive mothering shifted and morphed through the twentieth century, they will hopefully appear in greater numbers in museum collections, garment-based studies, and material culture histories.

Designing Motherhood contributor Malika Verma also highlights the role played by the sari in the pregnancies of millions of people in South Asia and the diaspora, suggesting another avenue for globally minded research into garments whose uses transform through the lives of pregnant people and mothers. There remain so many garment-based stories of motherhood to tell. The forthcoming chapters intend to get the ball rolling.

References

Entwistle, J. (2000), *The Fashioned Body: Fashion, Dress and Modern Social Theory*. London: Polity.
Hays, S. (1996), *The Cultural Contradictions of Motherhood*. New Haven, CT: Yale.

Liu, Y. and W. Wang (2021), "Discipline and Resistance in the Representation of Motherhood: Postpartum Recovery Discussion on *Xiaohongshu*," *Feminist Media Studies*, March 11.

Millar Fisher, M. and A. Winick (2021), *Designing Motherhood: Things that Make or Break Our Birth*. Cambridge, MA: MIT Press.

Miller, D. (1998), *A Theory of Shopping*. Ithaca, NY: Cornell University Press.

Rich, A. ([1976] 1995), *Of Woman Born: Motherhood as Experience and Institution*. New York and London: W. W. Norton & Co.

Steele, V. (2003), *The Corset: A Cultural History*. New Haven, CT: Yale University Press.

7

The Corset Crusade

Dress Reformers and the Maternity Corset

Karen Case

In the 1833 text *Tokology*, Alice Bunker Stockham, physician, "19th-century sex radical," and the first to make public that maternity corsets led to birthing complications, recalled a conversation at a medical conference with a prospective mother (Silberman 2009: 324; Block 2007: 168). A "bright, intelligent young married" attendee quietly and confidentially had queried Stockham regarding at what point in a pregnancy a woman should stop wearing a corset. Stockham writes that, tired after a day of lectures, she answered loud enough to be overheard by attendees: "The corset should not be worn for two hundred years before pregnancy takes place" (1883: 107). As a no-nonsense physician vested in women's health care, Stockham's response wasn't entirely sensitive to the woman, but she highlighted the confusing controversy regarding maternity corsets for prospective mothers and took a firm stance against corseting or tight lacing during pregnancy.

From 1820, and well into the 1900s, male and female physicians and writers for popular and professional periodicals and books addressed the maternity corset. There were those who saw corsets or tightlacing as a fashionable societal obligation, while others felt that female muscles before and after birth were too weak to support a pregnancy. Many, like Stockham, admonished the women who wore them. Pregnant women's confusion was evident in an advice letter written by the anonymous Mrs. G. S. P. to Dr. William Augustus Evans. Evans included it in his text, *How to Keep Well: A Health Book for Home*, published by Sears and Roebuck and Co.:

> I should like your opinion regarding a point on which I find that women and
> physicians with whom I talk and books that I read differ greatly. The point is
> this—should a pregnant woman wear corsets? By some I am told that to support

the abdomen is to weaken the muscles which normally should support the uterus and its contents, while others say that to go without corsets when one is used to them is apt to cause backache and will certainly make the abdomen sag permanently. Now, if a woman is anxious to do the best thing for both her child and herself, would you advise her to wear or not to wear a maternity corset throughout her pregnancy?

1917: 1284

His reply was simple. "A woman who has been accustomed to corsets should wear a maternity corset during pregnancy" (ibid.). This stance was directly opposed to physicians like Stockham, as well as the male and female dress reformers who rebelled against tight lacing as an overall unhealthy practice, branding the maternity corset as heinous to the unborn child and detrimental to the overall advancement of the human race. The movement to abolish tight lacing, dubbed the "corset crusade" by an anonymous author in the 1887 journal *Annals of Hygiene*, faced an uphill battle given the corset's symbolic meaning as a "badge and mark of aristocratic pride" (Edwards 1887: 117). Dr. J. C. Culbertson, editor of the weekly medical journal, *Cincinnati Lancet-Clinic*, described it as "a hen fight between the stayers and the belly fats" (T. C. M. 1899: 515).

Each side argued "science." Industry advertisers maintained that corset making was "calculated to remedy all defects in form and enable women to attain the symmetrical shape so essential to a stylish figure" (Borosdi 1909: 281). The Simpson Crawford Company in New York remarked that they employed "experts who have made intelligent corset fitting a study for years" by advancing "the new standard of dress reform corsets" (ibid.). Those opposed to maternity corsets ranged from sexologists, physicians, popular women's advice authors, editors, and dress reformers, all of whom enjoyed considerable and deliberate influence on the consumption habits of women and mothers. This chapter examines their arguments, published in American medical and popular journals, as well as advertisers' claims directed at expectant mothers.

The urgency of reformers' outcries against the maternity corset as a health risk was due partly to women's societally agreed-upon destiny, namely "that supreme effort of nature necessary to the creation of a human being" (Edwards 1887: 117). A mother wearing a corset was considered to be doing so at "frightful cost" to herself and the "innocent creature introduced into the world" (ibid.). According to Dr. Caroline Eliza Hastings, dress reformer, physician, as well as founder and president of Boston's first women's medical society, corsets were "instruments of torture" (ibid.). Dr. Mary J. Stafford Blake, like Alice Stockham, was one of the first female gynecologists in the United States. She argued that for women wearing a corset was like being "cruelly pressed" (1874: 23). Although less painful than "the thumb-screws of the inquisition," it was just as harmful to the body, due to the "unyielding steels" and "firm plates of metal attached as clasps to her belt" (ibid.).

As female doctor dress reformers, women like Blake and Hastings were operating under the societal assumption that every woman would become a mother. Susan Cruea asserts that intellectual women of the time "were condemned as 'unfeminine,' since a woman's 'heart' was valued over her 'mind,' the mind being associated with the masculine" (2005: 189). True women became mothers with heart, rearing the next generation of sons and daughters as a fulfillment of a national and biological imperative and destiny. Thus, the strident voices of dress reformers within the medical establishment that called for abolition of maternity corsets were doing so for the sake of healthy, comfortable pregnancies and safe births more than for the comfort and freedom from constraint for women as individuals. Despite their intellectual and reformist stance, these women negated their own and other women's selfhood and, while holding a public leadership role, they fostered all women's deference to a maternalist destiny.

In contrast to the normalized ideal of a corset-dependent, trim silhouette, dress reformer, magazine editor, and savvy domestic pundit Sarah Josepha Hale cautiously promoted a political as well as fashion agenda in the popular periodical *Godey's Lady Book*. A widow and poet, Hale is best known for her poem, "Mary Had a Little Lamb" and for initiating Thanksgiving as a national holiday in the United States; however, her covert leadership can be gleaned from her adroit influencing of her readership regarding more progressive societal views and ideas regarding fashion. Hired by Louis Antoine Godey in 1837, Hale held the editorship of *Godey's Lady Book* for forty years. Under her editorship, it became the highest circulated periodical in the United States. Hale not only used her columns, but also carefully selected prose that could subtly sway readers to her opinions. For example, Mrs. L. H. Sigourney, poet, and her co-editor at times, despite mythological imprecision, wrote a poem as a one-sided dialogue with the flower Narcissus as a child. It queried, "Narcissus pale, Had you a mother, child, who kept you close over your needle, or your music books? . . . I'm afraid she shut you from the air and tanning sun, to keep you delicate,—or let you draw your corset lace too tight" (Sigourney 1842: 72). The poem critiques the mother for her aversion to the natural world and speaks to the domestic realm as harmful to the child's health. The voice calls for the natural world and the absent mother is viewed as jointly responsible for not only the health and mortality of the child, but also for perpetuating harmful beauty standards that result in literal and figurative entrapment.

Women's submission to their mothers' fashionable norms drew a catty misogyny from male doctors. The periodical *Scientific American* reported that "A learned doctor, referring to tight lacing, avers that it is a public benefit, inasmuch as it kills all the foolish girls, and leaves the wise ones to grow to be women" ("Tight Lacing" 1847: 307). Health reformer, eugenicist, and brother to the cornflake entrepreneur, Dr. John Harvey Kellogg maintained that though the "baneful effects of corset-wearing" women "shield themselves, declaring that their corset does them no harm" (1893: 243). He maintained that "ladies do not really know when their clothing is tight about the waist and when it is loose" (ibid.). As evidence of this, he provided an illustration from an unidentified newspaper that reported on "a young lady who accidentally broke a rib in the attempt to gain another half-inch on her corset string" (ibid.). Kellogg concluded, "She well deserved the accident, no doubt" (ibid.). There may have been some envy on Kellogg's part. He noted, in his seminal work, *Plain Facts for Old and Young*, that the female constitution was stronger than a man's, clarifying that women held to "a superior degree the quality known as endurance. She will endure for months what would kill a robust man in as many weeks" (Kellogg 1882: 43). Not only did Kellogg praise women's "elimination of the wastes of the body" as more efficient than a male's, he also stated that females were stronger given that they had been "ground down under the heel of fashion for ages, 'stayed,' 'corseted,' 'laced,' and thereby distorted and deformed in a manner that would be fatal to almost any member of the masculine sex" (ibid.).

Others saw corseting as a natural manifestation of women's development. In perhaps what could be a metaphor for a woman's acquiescence, Dr. Howard Atwood Kelly suggested that, as early as preadolescence, a young girl experiences corset "rebellion at first," gradually giving in until she "adapts her feelings to it and finally defends it" (1912: 70). Doctors commented on women's limited sentience and heightened endurance while simultaneously admonishing and praising them for adhering to the necessity of corsets for beautification. An excerpt from the *St. Louis Medical Review* was reported in the *Journal of the American Medical Association*, describing a corset advocate: "The charges against the corset and tight lacing are, in a measure, opposed by Ewing, who reports the case of a young lady who had worn corsets since the age of 8, and had a typical fashion-plate figure, a magnificently developed bust and middle chest" (1903: 470). Dr. Ewing viewed the making of a "bust" and "fashion-plate" figure as more essential than the comfort and health of girls and women.

Fat was a significant concern of the Victorians and was believed to be tied to corporeal and sexual indulgences. Cesare Lombroso, an "influential figure of late Victorian criminology," linked fat to "prostitutes," in his coauthored text written with Guglielmo Ferrero (Bonzom 2018). They quote Dr. Alexandre Jean Baptiste Parent-Duchatelet, an "eminent" French hygienist of the nineteenth century who compared female sex workers to the irrational, disordered Parisian sewers (Harsin 1993: 863). The authors maintained that "obesity marks women at about age 25 to 30"; but that fat "is rarely noticeable in young girls or beginners" (Lombroso and Ferrero 2004). Colleen Gau, independent scholar of clothing, suggests that the term "loose woman" was related to corset use, implying that women "wore their undergarments loose or open to accommodate their customers' time constraints" (1998: 14). The expediency of the sex act was believed to be the reason to keep the ties untied, as opposed to these women's general discomfort caused by a corset.

The corset served not only to control unwanted fat, but a maternity corset could mask a pregnancy, thus covering up a legitimate marital sexual encounter and allowing a wife additional time for social access or to hide an unmarried transgression. To the Victorians, even marital sexual encounters were suspect. Although sex was considered essential to married life, it was so only if it was "moderate" and "did not incite sensual desires" (Seidman 1990). Victorians felt "compelled to detail its proper use . . . Their strategy involved compartmentalizing sex or cordoning it off from other spheres of life" (ibid.). Corseting was one way of keeping private matters between couples under wraps. For the unmarried "transgression," the corset during pregnancy might well have seemed an essential garment for the expectant mother. It deflected from the obvious sexual act and acted as a temporary cover for mother and baby.

For pregnant women, shame and fear existed simultaneously in the wearing and not wearing of a corset. Shame was attached to publicly revealing the visible result of intercourse; as aptly stated by Sarah Blewitt, the maternity corset allowed women to feel they could "make closed—and impregnable—what has clearly been opened and impregnated" (2015: 117). Thus, not only did a corset keep the abdomen in check, it provided a dubious "cover," allowing women to socialize within the public realm in a state generally considered private. According to Lilian Craton, fat "deflects questions of pregnancy," serving as "a metaphor for pregnancy" by "mimicking a pregnancy" or providing "a practical tool for the pregnant woman" (2009: 113). This provided the pregnant women with a choice to keep the narrative solely about her as opposed to the dual story of "mother with child." Jennifer Scuro suggests that once a pregnancy is revealed, the dominant social narrative concerns mother and child, with a woman's agency occurring only within the context of her pregnancy and her action's impact on the child (2017). Thus, basic activities and objects previously within her purview, such as food, exercise, dress, and undergarments, could be used to shame.

The acceptance of the maternity corset and unchallenged fat shaming may lend credibility to Jane M. Ussher's theory of the societal fear of the "fecund female body" (2006: xi). As anthropologist Rebecca Gibson maintains, a woman without a corset was viewed as nature uncontrolled (2020). For the expectant mother, not wearing a corset might be likened to nature unleashed, giving way to the pregnant woman as "threatening Other" (Santos 2016). This "other," according to Cristina Santos, works to combine "male fears and anxieties surrounding the female transformation from innocent virgin to sexually initiated (and empowered) women to the pregnant body" (ibid., 60). Citing philosopher Rosi Braidotti, she argues that the pregnant person becomes "morphologically dubious," linking her to heightened suspicion given her ability to contain life (Braidotti 1997, quoted in Santos 2016: 64). Corsets may well have been a form of societal containment of such power.

Mel Davies reinforces the idea of societal constraints, suggesting that, "In a period when maintenance of status was so emphasized, very few would have been prepared to risk excommunication from the ranks of the respectable by ignoring the dictates of fashion," and in this case the dictates were "to maintain a controlled, restricted silhouette even when carrying a child" (1982). As late as 1920, professor and doctor B. J. Jeffries and J. L. Nichols, opposing the maternity corset—albeit for the dubious reason of protecting only white mothers and children given fears of a declining birth rate—chided in *Search Light on Health: The Science of Eugenics*, "Many women lace themselves in the period of their gestation in order to meet their society engagements" (1921: 305). Their text sold over a million copies and, interestingly, heavily cites Alice B. Stockham (Leonard 2005; Jefferis 1921: 305).

These social obligations played out on the body left upper- and middle-class mothers with the task of not only maintaining respectability for themselves but also for their daughters before, during, and after their childbearing age. Controlling a daughter's size was the prerogative of mothers, who viewed their daughters' waist as something tied to not only physical beauty but also respectability in the marriage marketplace. Olivia P. Flynt of Boston was a progressive manufacturer of corsets. She explained that tight lacing or corset use was tied to mothers' sentiments towards their daughters: "We express regret that they have placed corsets upon their daughters and they reply: Dear me, the child is larger than I was when I was married and really larger than I am now; I cannot have her grow so large and thought you would give me something to shape her up" (1882: 4). Providing an illustration of the critical damage done to young women, Flynt recalled that "a fond mother brought her only daughter to have a beautiful dress made for her coming-out party." Describing the stance of the young woman, Flynt states that she "stood with a hand above each hip, crowding down and squeezing herself into the smallest space … and again her mother pulled away at the lacings" (ibid., 4–5).

Her story concludes with the dress being made, "and many more. […] The beautiful Miss G was engaged before the end of her first season, and one year from the night she entered society was married and went abroad; in less than another year her corpse was returned to her mother. She could not survive motherhood" (ibid., 5). Flynt's telling reinforces the narrative of the monstrous mother acting as an enforcer of social norms at the expense of her daughter's health. While certainly more morbid, this echoes the absent mother of Narcissus. Voices such as Flynt's, in conjunction with the pro-and-con waffling of medical authority, contributed to the confusing discourse regarding the relationship between corsets and the health of young women and the infants to whom they were expected to give birth.

Others who spoke out against the maternity corset, such as Stockham and Fowler, were progressive on the dissemination of information on sexuality. This left them in financial ruin at the end of their lives due to public and civil moral sentiment. Such retribution took the form of not only having their reputations destroyed, but also their livelihoods through publishing and writing. Their life histories evidence how threatening it was to provide information to women regarding prioritizing their health and the wellbeing of their babies over adhering to advertised beauty norms.

As a publisher of not only her own books, but also of others' works, Alice Bunker Stockham wrote in the areas of marriage, women's health, and childrearing. An advertisement for Stockham's publishing company appeared in the *Columbus Medical Journal* of 1909, with a picture of the then 76-year-old. It was accompanied by an author description, most likely written by Stockham, stating that she "has been writing and teaching along lines devoted to a better understanding of the laws of health as applying to Motherhood, Parenthood and the care and rearing of children-especially the baby" (1909: 373). Her work, according to Lydia McDermott, was intended to not only provide women with information, but also "to convince women to own themselves" (McDermott 2016: 140). Stockham's publishing company was halted by Anthony Comstock,

US Postal Inspector and anti-vice activist who charged her with sending through the mail indecent and obscene content.

More subtle pressures and implicit coercion via advertisers were used against Orson Squire Fowler, who was attacked for his views on sexuality, most notably his work entitled *Creative and Sexual Science*. A writer in the Chicago *Tribune* condemned Fowler as writing "Under the cloak of science" to spread "the seeds of vice" (Young 1990: 127). Fowler was an outspoken opponent of maternity corsets. Architect, phrenologist, and sexologist, he called tight lacing a "suicidal and infanticidal practice," expressing mock surprise that it was supported and "perpetrated even by Christians" (Fowler 1870: 770). Fowler asked whether Christ loved the corseted "the more they are laced," questioning, "how can infanticides and suicides enter the kingdom of heaven?" He provided marital advice to the male reader regarding how to "choose" a wife and mother to his children, warning: "Let those who had rather bury than raise their children, marry tight-lacers." As if writing about a commodity, Fowler suggested that men should select women who are "naturally full-chested" and who "will be likely to live long and bear vigorous children." He forewarned prospective husbands that those "who would not have their souls rent asunder by the premature death of wife and children, are solemnly warned not to marry small waists; for in the very nature of things, such must die young, and bear few and feeble offspring" (ibid., 769). He also linked the detriment of the middle and upper classes to women's use of the corset, maintaining that "If this murderous practice continues another generation, it will bury all the middle and upper classes of women and children, and leave propagation to the coarse-grained but healthy lower classes." In perhaps one of the most blaming statements to mothers, he writes, "Reader, how many of YOUR weaknesses, pains, headaches, nervous afflictions, internal difficulties, and wretched feelings were caused by your own or mother's corset-strings. Such mothers deserve execration" (ibid.). Fowler died in 1887, remaining a relatively obscure figure except for his having been a proponent of the discredited phrenology, and with a tarnished reputation due to his publications on sexuality.

Like that of Stockham and Fowler, advice of all kinds was available for a price in different forms of Victorian self-help books regarding caring for the pregnant body and the infant that would follow. Female authors popularized the subject area of mothering and childrearing, and advertisers peppered medical journals offering pregnant mothers guidance that was often contradictory. "A maternity corset should be set down as an absolute necessity," writes Helen Berkelley-Lord in the American women's fashion magazine *The Delineator* (1911: 423). "A great many women leave their corsets off entirely at this time, but they run a great risk in doing so. It is not apt to ruin their figure irretrievably, but it is quite likely to do them serious internal injury by discarding the support of a corset just when they need it most" (ibid.). Thus, maternal fears resulted from the threat to their "figure" as well as the need for the corset due to what one advertiser suggests as a "dragging or prolapse" of the muscles. The Goodwin Corset advertised in the *American Journal of Obstetrics and Diseases of Women and Children* was heralded as "solving the problem for the painstaking physician," stating that obstetricians find it "the corset that is anatomically and hygienically correct" (1912: 12). The *Journal of the American Medical Association* had an advertisement concerning the La Grecque Maternity Corset which meets with "the physician's approval and gives great comfort and security" (1910: 20).

Perhaps due to the need to sell books, popular women writers were pragmatic regarding tight lacing during pregnancy. Some spoke to the "charm" of appearing pregnant. Annie Jeness Miller writes in *Mother and Babe*, "It has often seemed to me that motherhood is robbed of much of its charm by the unsightly way in which women endeavor to disguise their condition" (Miller 1892: 18). Still, as though to appease their conscience, these writers included statements that offered warnings regarding the consequences of tight lacing. For example, Hester Pendleton, author of *The Parents' Guide to the Transmission of Desired Qualities to Offspring, and Childbirth Made Easy* (1876), admits to the difficulty of throwing fashion dictates aside, but advises loose laces, while stressing severe ramifications for mother and infant:

> I by no means recommend that those mothers to whom long custom has rendered corsets necessary, should at once lay them aside. They ought, however, to be very careful to wear them sufficiently loose to admit the free enlargement of the womb in an upward direction, and to substitute thin whalebone blades for the stiff steel in common use. If this precaution be neglected, both mother and infant may be seriously injured and ruptures or other local ailments induced.
>
> Ibid., 173

In this same text, Pendleton refers to the "almost unlimited control of a mother over the physical organization of her child" via the wearing or not wearing of a maternity corset. She cites the example of Mrs. B., "a lady moving in a fashionable circle," and a woman Pendleton describes as having "a fine natural constitution and good mental organization" and a desire to remain in "society as long as possible." Mrs. B. "laced herself so tight as to conceal her situation for six or seven months" with the result being that "her first three children were sickly and weak, weighing not more than three or four pounds at birth." Following an accident during her fifth pregnancy, Mrs. B. was forced to forgo the corset "and as she was cut off from the brilliant festivities of winter, she resorted to reading," eventually giving birth to a healthy nine-pound baby boy (ibid., 183). Similar to Sarah Josepha Hale and her artful editorship used to convince mothers of the harm involved in using a corset, Pendleton uses this moral tale, providing the pregnant woman with a story stressing her moral obligation to her baby's health by forgoing the corset.

Fully recognizing the power of social norms of dress, female medical professionals also acknowledged that women would be reluctant to leave corset use behind during pregnancy. Elizabeth Scovil, a Canadian nurse, author, and friend to Florence Nightingale, suggested that physical harm could befall women as the result of corset use, but acknowledged that, "It is difficult to overcome bad habits," maintaining that "the laying aside corsets and doing away with tight bands about the waist will not immediately revolutionize the faulty method of years" (1896: 112). Scovil makes the mother and child indistinguishable by blurring their identities and placing all responsibility on the mother for a healthy infant: "The expectant mother does not breathe for herself alone. She has to inhale a sufficient amount of oxygen to purify the blood as well as her own and she needs every inch of lung surface at her command to make adequate provision for both" (ibid., 113).

Doctors, with the aid of medical texts, asserted their authority by pathologizing birth (O'Brien Hallstein, O'Reilly, and Giles 2019: 228). Medical textbooks such as *An American Textbook of Applied Therapeutics: For the Use Practitioners and Students*, edited by James Cornelius Wilson, assisted by Augustus Adolph Eshner, contained a chapter on "Pregnancy and Other Disorders." The authors were resigned, stating, "few women will probably dispense with corsets while pregnant" (Wilson and Eshner 1897: 1272). Dr. Mary Ries Melendy pathologized the infant at the hands of the mother by offering an early form of mother blaming (Reimer and Sahagian 2015: 1). Describing herself as "an eminent physician of Chicago ... having the unparalleled record of twenty-five years of general practice without the loss of a single case originally placed in her hand," she admonished those who "aspire to the reputation styled 'a fashionable woman'" and who have their "Tight corsets grudgingly loosened a quarter of an inch at a time" and "still retained as the months pass" (Melendy 1914: 16, 185). According to Melendy, these women will bear the consequences; their infant may come "into the world dead or deformed ... Perhaps her baby deprived of certain of its faculties; or it may be that it possesses life and all of its special senses and organs in such a diminished degree that the whole of its future becomes a pain rather than a joy, while its miserable puny structures remains a lasting reproach" (ibid., 185). An example of "mother blame," Vanessa Reimer and Sarah Sahagian write in "Contextualizing the Mother-Blame Game" that "mother-blame is omnipresent" and "perpetuated in daily attitudes and interactions" (2015: 1). Despite her invisibility as a physician within the male-dominated specialty of gynecology, Mary Ries Melendy provides historical evidence of this mother-blame starting in utero because of the maternity corset.

Matthew Derbyshire Mann, delivering the President's Address in 1895 to the American Gynecological Society, discounted the female physicians who had warned against maternity corsets and discussed the limited response to eliminating the maternity corset by stating:

> It does not seem to me that the profession has taken sufficiently strong grounds on this very important matter. Beyond an occasional explosion against corsets and tight-lacing, comparatively little has been done. A few men have been working at the problems involved, but they seem to have made little impression upon either the profession or the public.
>
> Ibid., 605

Mann quotes Dr. John Harvey Kellogg, maintaining that it was not just tight lacing "which does the great majority of civilized women injury, but a dress which fits the form so snugly ... Not only may snug-fitting dresses do harm, but loose-fitting waists if confined by a snug belt are just as bad" (ibid.).

It is impossible to know who was loudest and most listened-to regarding the maternity corset. What is evident is that manufacturers responded to physicians' calls to create looser-fitting corsets. For example, Lucien C. and I. Dever Warner produced and patented the Dr. Warners' Health Corset designed according to "strictly physiological principles, [preserving] the beauty and grace of the form better than most other corsets, [and] with the least injury to health and comfort" (Smith 1991: 98). By the 1880s, the brothers were calling themselves "'practical' dress reformers" unlike the more "utopian" dress reformers, who called for the complete elimination of the corset (ibid.). Hygienic corsetry was "intended for bodily support" and thus was serving the health care needs of women as opposed to the fashion industry" (ibid., 104).

Although the wearing of a maternity corset was contested territory with contradictory assertions drawn by writers and medical professionals in popular as well as medical journals, the common assertion was that women who were pregnant needed protection. Opinions fluctuated as to what kind of protection and the expectant mother was cautioned on multiple points, ranging from her own and her infant's health, as well as the need to keep her figure and her muscles contained. Advertisers who worked within the corset field were pleased to offer advice as well as deliver multiple models designed according to physician's specifications.

"Within a stone's throw" of New York City's Fifth Avenue and Broadway, the New York offices of the International Corset Co. opened with a new year's announcement proclaiming that it was bringing out for the season "a splendid maternity corset which possesses many features of superiority not found in other lines" (New York Offices 1913: 64). Described as being "in a class by itself, both with respect to appearance and durability" it was constructed so that,

> At each side of the corset there is a series of tucks under which is found a lacking that allows for the required expansion. As it is found necessary to let out the corset the tucks may be ripped and later gathered in again, making the corset perfectly satisfactory for regular wear. An elastic gusset over the abdomen also provides for expansion.
>
> Ibid.

Although the apparent need for expansion was never directly tied to the pregnancy which would require it, the author concluded that "It is a most scientifically constructed corset and should meet with an unqualified success" (ibid.).

In the *Dry Goods Economist*, the Ferris "Good Sense" Corsets and Waists advertisement leads with the headline, "Make a Reputation on Maternity Corsets," asserting that their product would become "The Vital spot in your corset section" (1915: 2). Ferris promised that "Once you get the name of selling maternity corsets that are safe, sane, comfortable-and still help in keeping the appearance attractive-you have a trade against which competition is powerless. You have a specialty" (ibid.). The Ferris company also highlighted the need for a "successful saleswoman," who "knows that giving a woman physical aid at a trying time" was much the same experience as that of a nurse. Such offerings of support both physical and affiliative provided for "personal interest on both sides and—in common parlance-is mighty good business policy" (ibid.). In the 1915 *Corset and Underwear Review*, which was a Haire publication, directed at those in corset sales, a maternity corset advertisement declared, "The mother to be is a tremendous purchasing power, and deserving of the best" (New York Offices 1915: 14).

Chicago-based company H. W. Gossard, when describing their maternity corset, acknowledged "the tediousness of the months before the birth of a child," promising that this time "may be greatly alleviated" by wearing "a Gossard Maternity Corset" (H. W. Gossard advertisement 1914: 65). It assured the woman who was pregnant that such a corset could so "greatly improve the appearance that there need be no hesitation about appearing in public" and that it would make "possible both the usual social life and the exercise necessary to the health of the mother and child" (ibid.). Keeping household duties in mind, the company maintained that for a woman who was pregnant, "The fear of a false step is banished by perfect support, healthful walking is not a task, while the usual household duties may be continued" (ibid.). Relating their maternity corset to the health of a mother's infant, they remarked that "The baby endowed with a perfect body and robust physique receives a priceless birthright" and their maternity corset was key to "guarding the mother's health" and improving the health "of the baby" (ibid.).

Conclusion

Advertisers' claims may have reinforced a sense of security for women soon to be mothers. However, with promises of an attractive appearance and physical mobility outside the home, the expectant mother may have also entered the twentieth century as confused about the healthfulness, morality, and respectability of wearing or not wearing a corset during pregnancy as was Stockham's 1830's young conference attendee eighty years prior. Advertisers responded to their confusion by attempting to safeguard expectant mothers from their fears of "a false step" and kept them assuaged by assurances of scientific and physician-led design, nurse-like saleswomen, and babies robust with perfect bodies. For the woman who believed such promises, the point in her pregnancy by which she should stop wearing a corset seemed to be never.

References

Berkelley-Lord, H. (1911), "Should Women Wear Corsets?" *The Delineator*, 423.

Blake, M. J. S. (1874), "Lecture I," in Abba Goold Woolson (ed.), *Dress-Reform: A Series of Lectures Delivered in Boston, on Dress as it affects the Health of Women*, 23. Cambridge, MA: Roberts Brothers.

Blewitt, S. E. (2015), "Hidden Mothers and Poetic Pregnancy in Women's Writing (1818–present day)," PhD diss., Cardiff University.

Block, J. (2007), *Pushed: The Painful Truth about Childbirth and Modern Maternity Care*. Cambridge, MA: Da Capo Lifelong.

Bonzom, A. (2018), "Female Offenders at the Confluence of Medical and Penal Discourses: Towards a Gender-Specific Criminology (1860s–1920s)." *Cahiers victoriens et édouardiens*, 87 (Spring). Available online: https://journals.openedition.org/cve/3624 (accessed October 1, 2021).

Borsodi, W., ed. (1909), *Advertisers Cyclopedia of Selling Phrases; A Collection of Advertising Short Talks as Used by the Most Successful Merchants and Advertisement Writers; Classified and Arranged so as to Facilitate the Expression of Ideas and Assist Merchants in General Lines of Business and Specialists in Special Lines in the Preparation and Compilation of Advertising Copy*. New York: Advertisers Cyclopedia Co.

Braidotti, R. (1997), "Mothers Monsters and Machines," in K. Conboy, N. Medina, S. Stanbury (eds.), *Writing on the Body: Female Embodiment and Feminst Theory*, 59–79. New York: Columbia University Press.

Craton, L. (2009), *The Victorian Freak Show: The Significance of Disability and Physical Differences in 19th-Century Fiction*. Amherst, NY: Cambria Press.

Cruea, S. M. (2005), "Changing Ideals of Womanhood during the Nineteenth-Century Woman Movement," *General Studies Writing Faculty Publications*, 1. Available online: https://scholarworks.bgsu.edu/gsw_pub/1 (accessed October 1, 2021).

Davies, M. (1982), "Corsets and Conception: Fashion and Demographic Trends in the Nineteenth Century," *Comparative Studies in Society and History*, 24 (4): 611–41.

Edwards, J. F., ed. (1887), "The Corset Crusade," *Annals of Hygiene*, 2 (3): 117. Available online: https://www.google.com/books/edition/The_Annals_of_Hygiene/fdYrAAAAYAAJ?hl=en&gbpv=1&bsq=coset%20crusade (accessed November 17, 2022).

Evans, W. A. (1917), *How to Keep Well: A Health Book for the Home*. New York: Sears, Roebuck and Co by Appleton and Company.

"Excerpt from the St Louis Medical Review" (1903), *Journal of the American Medical Association*, 40 (1): 470. Available online: https://www.google.com/books/edition/Journal_of_the_American_Medical_Associat/mLJJAAAAYAAJ?hl=en&gbpv=1&bsq=St.%20Louis%20Medical%20Review%20Corset (accessed 17 November 2022).

Ferris Corsets and Waists advertisement (1915), *Dry Goods Economist* 6 (2), February 27.

Flynt, O. P. (1882), *Manual of Hygienic Modes of Under-Dressing for Women and Children*. Boston, MA: Kirby.

Fowler, O. S. (1870), *Sexual Science: Including Manhood, Womanhood, and Their Mutual Interrelationships; Love Its Laws, Power Etc*. Philadelphia, PA: National Publishing Company.

Gau, C. R. (1998), "Historic Medical Perspectives of Corseting and Two Studies with Reenactors," PhD diss., Iowa State University.

Gibson, R. (2020), *The Corseted Skeleton: A Bioarchaeology of Binding*. New York: Palgrave MacMillan.

Goodwin Corset advertisement (1912), *The American Journal of Obstetrics and Diseases of Women and Children: A Monthly Journal* June 1912, 12.

H. W. Gossard advertisement (1914), *Good Housekeeping Magazine*, 58 (6): 74.

Harsin, J. (1993), "Paris Sewers and Sewermen: Realities and Representations by Donald Reid," *Journal of Modern History*, 65 (4): 863.

Hastings, C. E. (1874), "Lecture II," in A. G. Woolson (ed.), *Dress-Reform: A Series of Lectures Delivered in Boston, on Dress as It affects the Health of Women*, 54. Cambridge: Roberts Brothers.

Jefferis, B. G. and J. L. Nichols (1921), *Search Light on Health: The Science of Eugenics*. Naperville, IL: J.L. Nichols & Co.

Jeness Miller, A. (1892), *Mother and Babe*. New York: Jeness Miller Co.

Kellogg, J. H. (1882), *Plain Facts for Old and Young*. Burlington, IA: I.F. Segner.

Kellogg, J. H. (1893), *Ladies' Guide in Health and Disease: Girlhood, Maidenhood, Wifehood, Motherhood*. Battle Creek, MI: Modern Medicine Publishing Co.

Kelly, H. A. (1912), *Medical Gynecology*. New York: D. Appleton and Company.

La Grecque Maternity Corset advertisement (1910), *Journal of the American Medical Association*, 55 (2): 20.

Lane Bryant advertisement (1915), "The Corset and Underwear Review," October. New York: Haire Publishing Company. Available online: https://www.google.com/books/edition/The_Corset_and_Underwear_Review/NYE1AQAAMAAJ?hl=en&gbpv=0 (accessed November 17, 2022).

Leonard, T. C. (2005), "Retrospectives: Eugenics and Economics in the Progressive Era," *Journal of Economic Perspectives*, 19 (4): 207–24.

Lombroso, C. and G. Ferrero (2004), *Criminal Woman, the Prostitute, and the Normal Woman*, trans. N. Hahn Rafter and M. Gibson. Durham, NC, and London: Duke University Press.

Mann, M. D. (1895), "The President's Address: The Relations of Lithaemia to Disease of the Pelvic Organs in Women," *Annals of Gynaecology and Pediatry*, 8 (9), 599–608. Available online: https://www.google.com/books/edition/Annals_of_Gynaecology_and_Pediatry/8L5YAAAAYAAJ?hl=en&gbpv=0 (accessed November 17, 2022).

McDermott, L. (2016), *Liminal Bodies, Reproductive Health and Feminist Rhetoric: Searching the Negative Spaces in Histories of Rhetoric*. New York: Lexington Books.

Melendy, M. R. (1914), *The Laws of Nature Revealed the Science of Eugenics and Sex Life*. Philadelphia, PA: W.R. Vansant.

New York Offices of the International Corset Co. advertisement (1913), *The Corset and Underwear Review*, January, 64. New York: Haire Publishing Company.

O'Brien Hallstein, L., A. O'Reilly, and M. Giles, eds. (2019), *The Routledge Companion to Motherhood*. London: Taylor & Francis.

Pendleton, H. (1876), *The Parents' Guide for the Transmission of Desired Qualities to Offspring, and Childbirth Made Easy*. New York: S.R. Wells & Co., Publishers.

Reimer, V. and S. Sahagian (2015), "Contextualizing the Mother-Blame Game," in V. Reimer and S. Sahagian (eds.), *The Mother Blame Game*, 1–18. Bradford, ON: Demeter Press.

Santos, C. (2016), *Unbecoming Female Monsters: Witches, Vampires and Virgins*. Lanham, MD: Lexington Books.

"Tight Lacing" (June 1847), *Scientific American*, 2 (39). New York: Munn & Co.

Scovil, E. R. (1896), *Preparation for Motherhood*. Philadelphia, PA: Henry Altemus.

Scuro, J. (2017), *The Pregnancy Does Not Equal Childbearing Project: A Phenomenology of Miscarriage*. Lanham, MD: Rowman & Littlefield.

Seidman, S. (1990), "The Power of Desire and the Danger of Pleasure: Victorian Sexuality Reconsidered," *Journal of Social History*, 24 (1): 47–67.

Sigourney, L. H. (1842), "Gossip with a Bouquet of Spring Flowers," *Godey's Lady's Book and Ladies' Magazine*, 25 (July–December).

Silberman, M. (2009), "The Perfect Storm: Late Nineteenth-Century Chicago Sex Radicals: Moses Harman, Ida Craddock, Alice Stockham and the Comstock Obscenity Laws," *Journal of the Illinois State Historical Society (1998–)*, 102 (3/4): 32–67.

Smith, B. (1991), "Market Development, Industrial Development: The Case of the American Corset Trade 1860–1920," *Business History Review*, 65 (1): 104.

Stockham, A. (1883), *Tokology*. Chicago, IL: Sanitary Publishing Co.

Stockham, A. B. (1909), "The Stockham Books," *Columbus Medical Journal*, 33 (1): 373.

T. C. M. (1899), "The Stayers and the Belly-Fats," *Cincinnati Lancet and Clinic (1878–1904)*, 42 (21) (May 27): 513.

Ussher, J. M. (2006), *Managing the Monstrous Feminine: Regulating the Reproductive Body*. New York: Routledge Press.

Wilson, J. C. and A. A. Eshner (1897), *An American Text-book of Applied Therapeutics: For the Use Practitioners and Students, Pregnancy and Other Disorders*. Philadelphia, PA: W.B. Saunders.

Young, D. L. (1990), "Orson Squire Fowler: To Form a More Perfect Human," *Wilson Quarterly*, 14 (3): 120–7.

8

Design for Borderline Bodies

Lauren Downing Peters

While pregnant people have always needed to get dressed, "maternity wear," a category of clothing designed specifically for expecting mothers, is a relative latecomer in the history of fashion. Until the late nineteenth century, the usual life cycle of clothing and the cost of fabric necessitated alterations through which a woman's everyday garments were incrementally modified to accommodate her expanding form (O'Brien 2010: 501). It wouldn't be until the advent of mass garment manufacturing that specially designed maternity garments would become widely available to American consumers (Tarrant 1980: 117). In addition to being affordable, a defining feature of these maternity garments was the way in which they utilized new manufacturing and design technologies to optimize both the experience and aesthetics of pregnancy.

Among the first purveyors of commercially produced maternity wear was Lane Bryant, a woman who is better known for her pioneering contributions to the history of plus-size fashion than for making clothes for pregnant women. Long before she began selling "stoutwear" (the forerunner to today's "plus-size" fashions), however, Bryant gained notoriety with her "No. 5" maternity dress. The one-piece dress, which Bryant first created for a customer in 1904 and later patented in 1911 (Mahoney 1950: 8), featured an innovative waistband that could be adjusted to accommodate the wearer's changing shape during her pregnancy and through to the postpartum period. In addition to eliminating the need for the wearer to purchase or make new dresses at each stage of pregnancy—a practice that was as wasteful as it was impractical—it was said that Lane Bryant maternity dresses did not bear any of the "stereotypical hallmarks of the maternity look" and helped the wearer to completely conceal her "condition" (Lane Bryant advertisement 1924: 16). This dress, and the design philosophies that underpinned it, would lay the groundwork for the company's foray into stoutwear several years later.

While the leap from maternity wear to stoutwear may at first blush seem surprising, for Bryant and her partner, Albert Malsin, the leap, at least from a design perspective, was a natural one. Indeed, in period advertisements, the company boasted about its ability to accommodate those who were "hard-to-fit," including tall, petite, pregnant and, perhaps most famously, "stout" women. With their distended waists, the pregnant body and fat body were far more alike than they were different, at least compared to the early twentieth century's elongated hourglass ideal. Garments designed to accommodate the pregnant form were therefore easily adapted to those inclined to stoutness, while also serving a similar purpose: to bring the body more in line with prevailing beauty ideals. The design discourses around both the pregnant and fat body therefore also shed light on how they exist in the cultural imaginary as "liminal" or "temporary"—or merely states that a woman passes through in *pursuit of* or on her *return to* so-called bodily perfection.

As I have argued elsewhere (Peters 2021: 101–2), there is a lot that can be learned through the study of dress about the complex and often contradictory expectations brought to bear on feminized bodies. Design patents, which are often overlooked in fashion and dress history, can lend even more insight into how dress has been used to try to solve social and sartorial problems as they provide a technical lens onto the design process. Through an investigation of early-twentieth-century maternity wear and stoutwear design patents and advertisements (especially those published by Lane Bryant and Albert Malsin), this chapter addresses the ways that design was utilized to address the "conditions" of pregnancy and overweight and their remedies—including "balancing," "concealing," and "confining" the body with dress. By further drawing upon Longhurst's, Douglas', and Kristeva's writings on "borderline" and "unruly" bodies, this chapter considers the ideologies, beliefs, and value systems that render both pregnant and fat bodies incomplete absent various design interventions.

*   *   *

On May 2, 1911, Albert Malsin filed a patent for a women's maternity garment with the United States Patent Office. Bearing a striking resemblance to the tailor-made "No. 5" maternity dress Lane Bryant originally created in 1904, it was designed with a discreet elasticized waistband that could easily be adjusted "without the necessity of altering its length or shape" (Figure 8.1). While an ostensibly straightforward solution to a somewhat complicated problem, Malsin's key design innovation—and thus the rationale for seeking patent protection—was the clever way in which he integrated the adjustable waist without visibly interfering with the clean lines of the dress. As described in the patent, the effect

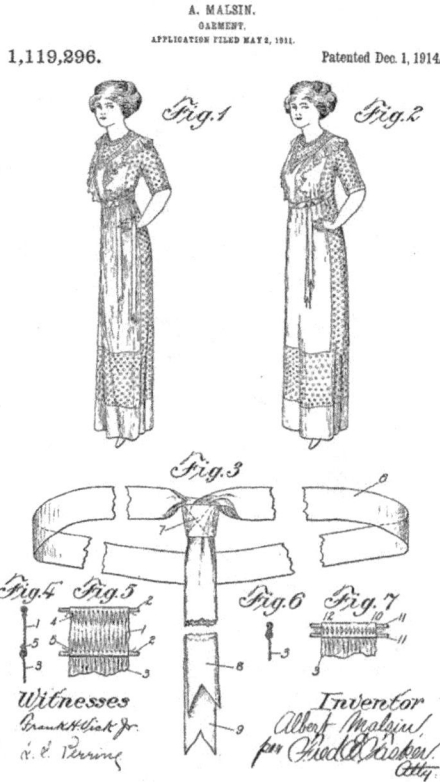

Figure 8.1 Design patent filed by Albert Malsin for a maternity garment with a discreet elasticized waistband that could easily be adjusted "without the necessity of altering its length or shape." Albert Malsin, Patent for a Maternity Garment, US1119296A (May 2, 1911).

was achieved by camouflaging the adjustable waistband with either gathered or pleated fabric to avoid "exposing the character of its construction."

Advertisements published in the fashion press in the months after the patent was granted reinforced the notion that these dresses not only accommodated the wearer's changing form "without removing a hook" but were also at the height of fashion. Indeed, by 1911, two-piece dresses comprised of a separate bodice and skirt had fallen out of vogue. Most maternity garments, however, were still constructed in this manner, and thereby had the unwelcome effect of conspicuously drawing attention to the wearer and thus her condition as well.

Throughout much of Western history, the clothing of pregnant women neither flaunted nor hid signs of pregnancy; rather, pregnancy clothing was merely a woman's everyday clothing adapted to accommodate her expanding form. It was only during the later Middle Ages and the Renaissance that the pregnant form approached anything resembling a beauty ideal (Furer 1968: 8). Between the sixteenth and eighteenth centuries, maternity styles—especially those worn outside of the home—would become increasingly constricting as women tried to negotiate fashion with pregnancy. For over 300 years, most women declined to abandon their corsets during pregnancy; rather, they simply incrementally modified them with gussets, laces, and stomachers as they grew larger (Fisk 2019: 427). Although some physicians and moralists questioned the safety of this practice, it would go on to reach its ignoble apex during the Victorian period (Kelly 1998: 1). While, contrary to popular belief, Victorian women did not stay at home throughout the duration of their pregnancies, they were expected to conceal their distended stomachs when in public (O'Brien 2010: 502). During this period of "confinement"—a term that, in practice, referred more to the act of confining the abdomen than to that of remaining confined to the home—it was not uncommon for pregnant women to wear heavily boned, although slightly adapted, corsets that created an hourglass silhouette. As Summers writes, social taboos and general Victorian prudery demanded that a woman go to great and oftentimes uncomfortable lengths to conceal her pregnancy as it was "the most obvious demonstration of a woman's carnal animality, as well as a reminder of the female body's predilection for unseemly, squeamish and occasionally painful bodily functions" (2001: 39). The pregnancy corset therefore functioned to uphold the chaste image (or illusion) of the Victorian mother, while also "working to contain and imprison the unruly, fecund body" (Erkal 2017: 11).

Amid growing medical consensus about the potential dangers (including miscarriage and stillbirth) of binding the abdomen during pregnancy (Kelly 1998: 2), rigid Victorian corsetry gradually gave way to new styles of pregnancy corsets that seemed to prioritize both the mother's and baby's wellbeing over fashion. So-called "health" corsets advertised in the fashion press in the first decades of the twentieth century traded baleen and steel for elastic and promised "perfect abdominal support" for "better babies" (H. W. Gossard Co. advertisement 1913: 27). Lane Bryant was among the manufacturers of these new-and-improved corsets which, as the company claimed in an advertisement, "relieve all strain from vital organs, producing proper poise, correct breathing, [and] eliminating the usual fatigue" (Lane Bryant advertisement 1915: 113). Patents filed for similar designs likewise stressed the need to create styles that more gently supported the abdomen and that relieved lower back pain without "injurious lacing" (Figure 8.2).

These designers' concerns with the painful side effects of pregnancy were well aligned with a growing body of literature that medicalized childbirth and

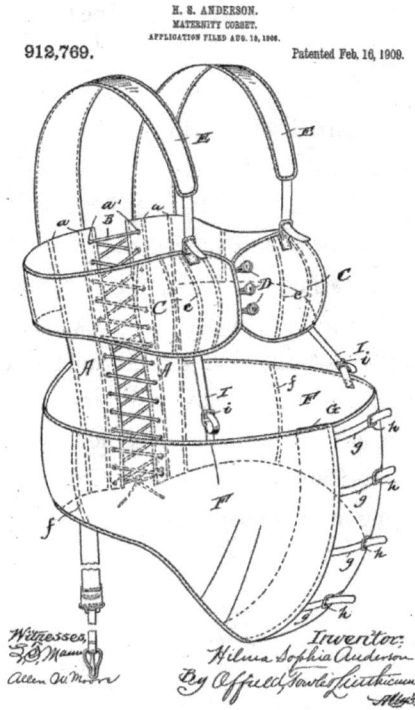

Figure 8.2 Design patent filed by Himla Sophia Anderson, an example of the type of maternity corset designed with the health of both the pregnant wearer and developing fetus in mind. Himla Sophia Anderson, Patent for a Maternity Corset, US912769A (August 18, 1908).

addressed the link between maternal health and that of the developing fetus (Waterhouse 2007: 54)—the neighboring chapter in this volume by Karen Case explores this literature more thoroughly. These garments also, however, reflected the evolution of female beauty and bodily ideals, as well as women's changing roles in society.

By the time "healthier" maternity corsets were being advertised in the pages of the women's and fashion press, women had begun agitating for greater social, economic and political freedoms, and were increasingly spurning the practice of daily corseting, at least in the highly restrictive Victorian style (Fields 1999: 355). As Steele has argued, women's social liberation thus coincided with the liberation of the body as they traded external supports for an "internalized corset" of flesh and muscle (2003: 143). While the extent of this physical liberation is debatable, what isn't is the fact that most women continued to wear corsets and girdles well into the twentieth century in order to gently reshape their bodies in the image of the youthful, slender beauty ideal. Like the sleek, one-piece dresses that emphasized the liberated body, these new corsets were themselves less cumbersome and materialized what Schwartz has referred to as the "new kinaesthetic" of early-twentieth-century physical culture in which the ideal body assumed a machinelike, almost weightless quality (1992: 105). Rather than abandoning the armatures of beauty altogether, however, women came to rely upon an overwhelming array of mass-produced consumer goods—from scientifically designed corsets to gimmicky quick fixes and cure-alls—that (somewhat paradoxically) assisted them in achieving the streamlined ideal.

As is evident in both patents and advertisements, maternity wear was not exempt from this broader impulse to optimize not just the appearance of the body but also the experience of pregnancy. While innovations such as a convertible breastfeeding dress, which featured an easy-to-open front flap that

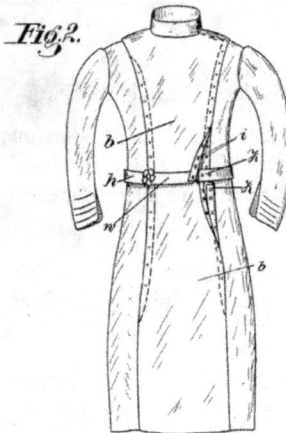

Figure 8.3 Design patent for a convertible breastfeeding dress, featuring an easy-to-open front flap allowing quick and discreet access to either breast. Kathe Hartman, Patent for a Maternity Garment, US1199069A (Filed September 18, 1913).

allowed the mother to quickly and discreetly expose either breast, cleverly addressed universal sartorial pain points that came with birth and motherhood (Figure 8.3), other innovations more explicitly merged function with fashion. In the same Lane Bryant advertisement promising that their maternity corset could relieve pain and fatigue, for instance, the company also argued that it "harmonizes the figure lines throughout the entire period [and] prevents clothes from binding" (Lane Bryant advertisement 1915: 113).

Other maternity design patents filed by Malsin evidence a similar impulse to streamline the silhouette. The aforementioned 1911 patent for the adjustable-waist maternity dress (see Figure 8.3) emphasizes not just the novelty and utility of the innovation but also the way in which it effectively creates a "neat" and "attractive" appearance without compromising the integrity of the design. While the goal of the adjustable-waist maternity dress was not ostensibly to camouflage or conceal the distended, pregnant abdomen, neither of the figures appears visibly pregnant. In this case, "neat" and "attractive" thus seem to imply that the function of innovative, scientifically designed maternity clothing should be to diminish the appearance of pregnancy. It isn't necessary to speculate on Malsin's intentions, however; the aesthetic innovations of Lane Bryant's adjustable maternity dress were explicitly spelled out in advertisements that described the dresses as "especially designed to create proper balance for the figure" and to "conceal all effect of a maternity dress." Even though social taboos around discussing pregnancy were beginning to lift in the early twentieth century, maternity design continued to perpetuate the idea that the pregnant body wasn't something to be flaunted.

Beyond merely solving problems, Swanson argues that early-twentieth-century design innovations, such as maternity corsets and adjustable dresses, were not just "heavily patent-protected technological wonders" on par with other design innovations of the period; they were also "deeply embedded within . . . the social construction of gender and sexuality" (Swanson 2011: 60). In upholding the early-twentieth-century construct of fashionable femininity—namely the archetype of the liberated woman—these patents foreground not just comfort and ease of wear, but also the ways in which these designs help to streamline and slenderize the body by camouflaging any visible signs of pregnancy. In the specific case of Malsin and Bryant's adjustable maternity gown, the waist is not only adjustable; it adjusts in such a manner as to prevent the hemline from unflatteringly rising at the front as the body grows larger. The pleat details at the waist similarly serve the dual purpose of camouflaging the adjustable belt as well as the stomach.

While the impulse to conceal the visible signs of pregnancy can be glimpsed in most maternity garments from approximately the sixteenth century onward, what is decidedly different about early-twentieth-century maternity wear is the way in which it utilizes more modern, "hands off" technological interventions to alter the appearance of the body. Different from Victorian corsetry that physically reshaped the body, early-twentieth-century maternity wear employed technologies and techniques of camouflage to meet the same ends and without any injurious health effects. Such innovations, as Lemus argues, didn't just help the pregnant woman achieve a fashionable outward appearance; they also fashioned the "modern" pregnancy in which various technological interventions ensured both the health of the mother and the fetus, but also the woman's ability to inconspicuously and confidently go about her normal social routines without fear of judgment or reproach (Lemus 2011: 161–5).

*   *   *

As Millar Fisher and Winick observe, the experience of pregnancy in the modern West is one that has been shrouded in shame and embarrassment (2021: 14–15). From at least the sixteenth century, bodily fatness has been rendered similarly marginal in the cultural imaginary (Forth 2019: 8). Both conditions—that of being fat and that of being pregnant—underscore the West's discomfort with what Douglas describes as "matter out of place" within regimes of clearly defined standards of health and beauty (Douglas 1966: 44–50). Those whose bodies place them at the fringes of aesthetic acceptability are therefore subject to censorship, exclusion, and ridicule. Early-twentieth-century consumer culture, however, instilled the idea that with enough physical and monetary investment, individuals could take control of their self-image (Featherstone 1982: 18–33). It is therefore unsurprising that the proliferation of consumer goods created to eradicate fat coincided with an intensification of negative attitudes toward individuals perceived as overweight (Schwartz 1986: 88–9). A widening array of new tools and technologies—from scales to height and weight charts, to standardized sizing—precipitated this shift as they permitted bodily deviance to be seen and measured with greater accuracy. As the threshold between fat and thin grew narrower, Lane Bryant was one among many early-twentieth-century companies to capitalize on consumers' bodily insecurities. While in decades prior, fat women would have employed dressmakers or sewed their own clothing from paper patterns (a process that was as time consuming as it was challenging due to the necessity of grading patterns to be larger), mass-produced stoutwear promised cheap, off-the-rack solutions to complex problems. Indeed, just as their maternity dresses helped to conceal the oftentimes messy and abject realities of human reproduction, so too did their innovations for fat women—from reducing corsets to "scientifically designed' slenderizing dresses—promise to mitigate the stigma of overweight.

While Lane Bryant catered to a number of "hard-to-fit" types in the first decade of the twentieth century, it wouldn't be until 1913 that Malsin would take out a patent for a specially designed stoutwear garment. Similar in style to the adjustable waistband maternity dress for which he filed a patent in 1911, the one-piece dress featured a convertible component that allowed the waist to be made smaller or larger. Different from the maternity dress, however, the skirt was designed to be only partially attached to the bodice and featured surplus, overlapping fabric that could be arranged to "fit the wearer whether in normal or abnormal condition, and have a neat appearance" (Malsin 1913). Malsin's adjustable skirt was but one among many stoutwear patents filed in the first decades of the twentieth century that attempted through various means to mitigate the appearance of overweight. As Keist and Marcketti found, the majority of these patents were for support garments, such as corsets and brassieres, that smoothed and compressed excess flesh to reshape the fat body in the image of the slender ideal (2019: 203). While this, essentially, was the way that conventional corsets functioned, patent authors observed that the stout woman's excess flesh could displace or spill over a normal corset. These new designs thus added features that variously held the corset in place, redistributed the flesh or, in some sensational cases, even promised permanent weight loss (ibid., 204–5). Longline corsets that straightened abdominal curves were particularly challenging to fit to the fat body as they didn't provide anywhere for the displaced flesh to go (ibid.). While Malsin didn't create any corset patents explicitly designated as stoutwear, he did file one for a longline corset in 1916 that through a complex lacing system self-adjusted to fluctuations in the wearer's size and to redistributions of their flesh caused by her natural movements (Figure 8.4).

Malsin, however, would prove to be less interested in physically reshaping the body than in utilizing scientific design principles, borrowed from fields as disparate as Gestalt Psychology and architecture, to merely effect the *appearance* of bodily slenderness. In a series of long treatises that were published in major American newspapers and fashion trade publications in 1916, he would further expound on his design philosophy. In one such article, Malsin espoused a theory of "scientific stoutwear design" that rejected the commonly held notion that fat women should wear rigidly tailored garments rendered in drab and monochromatic color palettes. To the extent that such styles had grown outmoded, Malsin argued that they only served to make the fat woman's body even more conspicuous. Instead, he believed that stoutwear should generally follow the fashionable line (i.e., streamlined, one-piece dresses) and employ

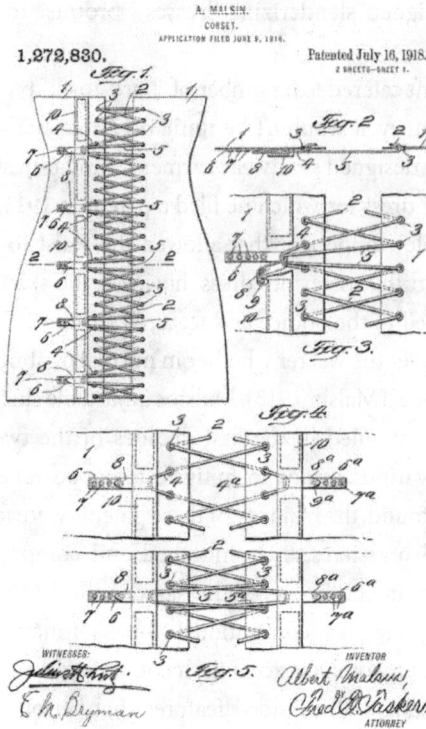

Figure 8.4 Patent filed by Malsin for a long-line corset with a complex lacing system self-adjusted to fluctuations in the wearer's size and to redistributions of their flesh. Albert Malsin, Patent for a Corset, US1272830A (Filed June 9, 1916).

sophisticated optical theories in the design and construction process to create the mere illusion of slenderness. "Like the architects of the Great Gothic Cathedrals," he argued, "stout people should strive to produce in their clothes [the effects] of height, slenderness and airy grace" (Malsin 1916a: 76). By helping women to camouflage their excess weight in this manner, he explained how designers could make "a notable contribution not only to the good looks of a large percentage of American women but also their good health." He concluded the article with the following insight:

It is worry about the appearance they make rather than concern about their health which leads women to undertake reducing treatments that are often exceedingly harmful. Now that it is possible for a woman to create an illusion of…slenderness by simply choosing proper clothes she no longer need to go to war with Nature over the too generous layers of flesh, with which she has been endowed.

Ibid.

In advertisements from the period, the company (smartly) minimized the moral considerations and complex scientific theories that informed their approach to stoutwear design and instead focused on style and slenderness. In an advertisement published in the pages of *Vogue* in 1918, for instance, the company claimed that "no tailor or dressmaker, however exclusive, can compete with the skill and experiences which enable us to simulate slimness and greatly reduce the apparent size." Not unlike those featured in Lane Bryant's maternity advertisements, the accompanying figure bears none of the stereotypical hallmarks (i.e., distended waist, double chin, etc.) of overweight; rather, her body assumes the easy, liberated comportment of the modern woman—her body thoroughly transformed by the "graceful, length-giving lines" of her "charming" broadcloth suit.

*   *   *

In the early twentieth century, a new bodily ideal was in ascendance. Youthful, streamlined and, perhaps most importantly, *free* from both Victorian notions of appropriate femininity and the era's correspondingly rigid dress styles, the body of this "new woman" couldn't have been more different than the encumbered bodies of both the fat woman and the pregnant woman. Not only were their bodies physically heavy, but they also did not easily conform to the era's simpler styles which, with their straight seams, tubular construction and dropped waists, only served to accentuate distended abdomens and wide hips. Moreover, standardized sizes, which established the threshold between "standard" and "non-standard" bodies, were largely unaccommodating of those who were larger or differently shaped. Put simply, theirs were bodies that were out of sync with the architectures, rhythms, and aesthetics of modern life.

Both the pregnant body and the fat body occupy what Langhurst describes as a "borderline state" to the extent that they "disturb identity, system and order by not respecting borders, positions and rules" (Longhurst 2000: 33). In addition to occupying a "borderline" state, it could be argued that these bodies (as well as the conditions of pregnancy and overweight more generally) also exist in a state of perpetual liminality. Oliver, drawing upon Kristeva, argues that the pregnant body presents a model of a "subject-in-process" to the extent that it stands in opposition to the Cartesian model of the sealed and complete subject (Kelly 1993: 11). Not only does the pregnant body exist in a state of becoming; it also exists in a state of return—a return to an "ideal" female form that is tight and contained. A similar argument could be made about the fat body, which, beginning in the early twentieth century, became a principal target of consumer culture. Now that it was possible to quickly and efficiently eradicate (i.e., with diet foods or pills) or camouflage (i.e., with dress) fat, it was no longer permissible for a woman to be contentedly (or even mildly) overweight. Indeed, just as the pregnant body was to "snap back" to its prior form shortly after giving birth, so too had fat come to be regarded as a transitory state in a woman's eternal pursuit of bodily perfection. Not all methods to attain the ideal were created equal, however.

Mass-manufactured maternity wear and stoutwear promised expedient and modern ways for their wearers to attain, or at least inch closer to, the slender ideal. Different from more old-fashioned and, as some believed, dangerous methods of altering the shape of the body—from corsetry to reducing diets—these were purportedly safer and healthier alternatives that, as Malsin argued, did not "compete with Nature" (1916b: 46). As Millar Fisher and Winick argue, however, "The design for the arc of human reproduction is full of incidents in which designers imposed their ... convictions onto their ... consumers in the name of solutions or solving problems 'for them,' many times without informed—or any—consent" (2021: 22). A similar argument could be made about designs for fat people.

What then are we to make of the scientifically designed, *technological marvels* discussed here? Did they provide solutions for their wearers, or did they merely function to make abject, unruly bodies more knowable to a public that was uncomfortable with ambiguity? The unsatisfying answer to both questions is, in all likelihood, *yes*. Indeed, as can be established from both the patents and advertisements discussed here, these designs adopted new, less harmful and obtrusive approaches to solving very real social problems—from pregnancy-related back pain to the sting of weight discrimination—at the same time they reinforced the perception of bodies as borderline, abject, and incomplete absent the intervention of design.

References

Douglas, M. (1966), *Purity and Danger: An Analysis of the Concepts of Pollution and Taboo*. New York: Routledge.

Erkal, M. M. (2017), "The Cultural History of the Corset and Gendered Body in Social and Literary Landscapes," *European Journal of Language and Literature Studies*, 3 (3): 109–18.

Featherstone, M. (1982), "The Body in Consumer Culture," *Theory, Culture & Society*, 1 (1): 18–33.

Fields, J. (1999), "'Fighting the Corsetless Evil': Shaping Corsets and Culture, 1900–1930," *Journal of Social History*, 33 (2): 355–84.

Fisk, C. (2019), "Looking for Maternity: Dress Collections and Embodied Knowledge," *Fashion Theory*, 23 (3): 401–39.

Forth, C. E. (2019), *Fat: A Cultural History of the Stuff of Life*. London: Reaktion.

Furer, B. S. (1968), "Maternity Dress Designs," MS thesis, Oregon State University, Corvallis.

H. W. Gossard Co. advertisement (1913), *Vogue*, October 15: 127.

Keist, C. and S. B. Marcketti (2019), "Supporting Acts: Patents for Undergarments for Stout Women, 1891–1956," *Clothing and Textiles Research Journal*, 37 (3): 200–14.

Kelly, L. D. (1998), "Crossing the 'Bearing' Straits: Women's Maternity Dress in the 19th Century," *Studies in Popular Culture*, 21 (1): 1–12.

Kelly, O. (1993), *Reading Kristeva: Unraveling the Double-bind*. Bloomington, IN: Indiana University Press.

Lane Bryant advertisement (1915), *Vogue*, April 15: 113.

Lane Bryant Maternity Wear advertisement (1924), *Chicago Tribune*, November: 16.

Lemus, C. K. (2011), "'The Maternity Racket': Medicine, Consumerism, and the Modern American Pregnancy, 1876–1960," PhD diss., Northern Illinois University, DeKalb.

Longhurst, R. (2000), *Bodies: Exploring Fluid Boundaries*. London: Routledge.

Mahoney, T. (1950), *50 Years of Lane Bryant*. New York: Lane Bryant.

Malsin A. (1911), Patent for a Maternity Garment, US1119296A.

Malsin, A. (1913), Patent for a Stoutwear Garment, US1119297A.

Malsin, A. (1916a), "How Science is Helping 'Stout' People to Look Less 'Stout,'" *San Francisco Examiner*, April 16: 76.

Malsin, A. (1916b), "What Science is Doing for 'Stout' People," *Richmond Times-Dispatch*, April 23: 46.

Millar Fisher, M. and A. Winick (2021), "Introduction," in M. Millar Fisher and A. Winick (eds.), *Designing Motherhood: Things that Make and Break Our Births*, 14–22. Cambridge, MA: MIT Press.

O'Brien, A. (2010), "Maternity Dress," in V. Steele (ed.), *The Berg Companion to Fashion*, 501–3. London: Berg.

Peters, L. D. (2021), "Pregnancy Corset," in M. Millar Fisher and A. Winick (eds.), *Designing Motherhood: Things that Make and Break Our Births*, 101–2. Cambridge, MA: MIT Press.

Schwartz, H. (1986), *Never Satisfied: A Cultural History of Diets, Fantasies and Fat*. New York: The Free Press.

Schwartz, H. (1992), "Torque: The New Kinaesthetic of the Twentieth Century," in J. Crary and S. Kwinter (eds.), *Incorporations*, 70–126. New York: Zone Books.

Steele, V. (2003), *The Corset: A Cultural History*. New Haven, CT: Yale University Press.

Summers, L. (2001), *Bound to Please: A History of the Victorian Corset*. London: Berg.

Swanson, K. W. (2011), "Getting a Grip on the Corset: Gender, Sexuality, and Patent Law," *Yale Journal of Law and Feminism*, 23 (57): 57–116.

Tarrant, N. E. (1980), "A Maternity Dress of about 1845–1850," *Costume*, 14 (1): 117–20.

Waterhouse, H. (2007), "A Fashionable Confinement: Whaleboned Stays and the Pregnant Woman," *Costume*, 41 (1): 53–65.

9

Mother's Milk is Best of All

Breastfeeding Garments from 1880 to 1930

Claire Salmon

The end of the nineteenth century was marked by a number of social and political changes that would go on to permanently affect the social fabric of Western populations throughout the twentieth century. In this chapter, different disciplinary perspectives will be utilized to explore the change that occurred to women's breastfeeding garments from 1880 to 1930. By comparing and contrasting the approaches taken by medical historians, gender historians, and fashion historians, the evolution of women's breastfeeding garments (from the corset to the bra) can be tracked through the social and medical implications that facilitated their invention. During this time period, there was a significant change in the cultural significance of motherhood within Western culture that is still informing the expectations of motherhood today. Different interpretations of this change are introduced by various historical disciplines, but through the lens of fashion history, it is possible to understand exactly where all these discourses overlap: the persistent policing of the maternal body.

In order to understand the change that occurred in the cultural significance of motherhood through the evolution of women's maternity garments, it is essential to take a multi-pronged analytical approach. This chapter will reference art historians, gender historians, and medical historians to attempt a holistic understanding of the forces that shaped the design of maternity clothing at the turn of the twentieth century. During the Victorian era, pregnancy was considered very taboo and best kept from the public eye. This taboo around pregnant women was largely accepted because it upheld the image of women as virginal and innocent beings even after marriage, and pregnancy was widely understood to be the result of the loss of a woman's virginity (Summers 2021: 39). These ideas are vastly different from the cultural understanding of pregnancy in the twenty-first century that positions pregnancy as women's ultimate biological and emotional fulfillment. This change in ideology that began with the mother who delegated the care of her infant and ended with the dedicated, dutiful motherly ideal that survived throughout the twentieth century can be tracked through the changes that took place in her undergarments.

Corset and Pregnancy

As the previous chapters in this section detail, at the end of the nineteenth century, it was still customary for women to wear a corset as part of their daily foundation garments. While there was an increased awareness around their negative effects on women's health, corsets had been a staple of women's foundation garments since the late Renaissance (Steele 2001). Women living in the early twentieth century had seen their mothers wear corsets, as had their grandmothers before them, and so forth. Corsets were such an established part of women's wardrobes that they continued to wear them during pregnancy and breastfeeding.

Although corsets created especially for pregnant and nursing bodies did come to exist (and will be further explored in this paper), most middle- and lower-class women could not afford to buy new clothing simply because they were pregnant (Ventura 2015a: 213). Consequently, they would wear their corsets as normal, tight lacing as the pregnancy progressed in order to continue to fit into their clothing, before finally retreating into the home when they could no longer be appropriately dressed in public.

The effects of tight lacing a corset on a pregnant body were heavily discussed by doctors, critics, and dress reformers, a discourse that Karen Case's chapter in this volume explores. In the parallel conversation about corsets' effect on breastfeeding, doctors argued that tight lacing over a number of years could cause women to develop inverted nipples, making breastfeeding considerably more difficult if not impossible (Matthews Grieco 1991: 23). Writers scolded pregnant and nursing women for wearing corsets, "accusing them of putting vanity above the health of their unborn child" (Steele 2010: 502). Leigh Summers explores the problematic language used by critics of maternal corsetry and suggests that (contemporary and Victorian) texts on the topic focus on the effects of the corset on the fetus, never on the mother, reducing her to a uterus.

The refusal to acknowledge the pain endured by the corseted pregnant or nursing woman was cultivated by the failure of doctors and dress reformers to talk about maternal corsetry with any empathy toward the mother. "This kind of denunciation made moral criminals of individual women who persevered with corsetry during pregnancy, and made pregnant women, as a 'class', responsible for birth defects and 'race degeneration'" (Summers 2021: 45). This situation, which forced women to choose between their reputation, their babies, and their social lives, actually facilitated the invention of a new undergarment: the maternity corset.

Maternity Wear

In addition to being created especially for pregnancy, with laces that could be loosened at the sides to allow room for the expanding belly, maternity corsets were also created especially for breastfeeding. The corset in Figure 9.1 is an excellent example of this design.

Dated to 1900, it sits perfectly between the non-maternity corset of the nineteenth century and the nursing bra of the twentieth. In addition to all the usual features of a corset like boning and lacing at the back, it features additional lacing at the sides that allow the wearer to loosen and adjust the tightness around their abdomen as their bodies change throughout pregnancy. It also features a

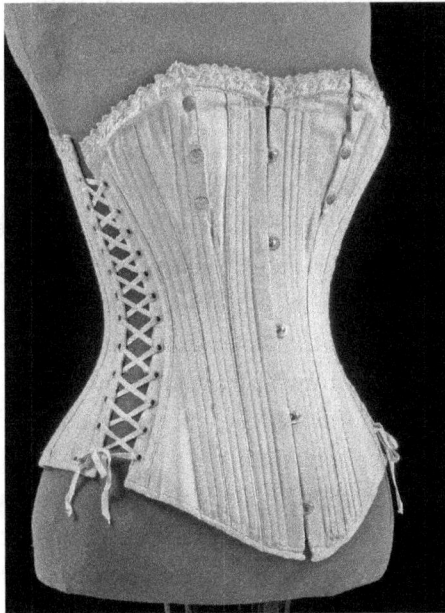

Figure 9.1 Maternity corset *c.* 1900. Victoria and Albert Museum, London.

series of buttons along each breast that would allow the wearer to breastfeed postpartum, without having to get fully undressed. A garment like this was thoughtfully designed to be suitable, comfortable, and durable for women throughout all the stages of maternity. It perfectly encapsulated the changes in ideology around maternity during this time as the focus started shifting to women's experience of maternity and design changes occurred to meet their needs.

During the second half of the nineteenth century, doctors struggled to understand why women were not breastfeeding. Some women could afford to hire a wet nurse to breastfeed their baby while others raised their children "by hand." This meant feeding them artificially, whether with animal milk, infant formula, or pap (a mix of bread and unpasteurized milk). During this time, infant mortality rates were high and, despite the invention of infant formula in the 1860s, doctors still urged all women to breastfeed. At the outset of this medical campaign for breastfeeding, what doctors failed to understand was the difficulties that women faced in doing it. Doctors suggested that women should breastfeed every hour and a half. For upper-class women, who could only breastfeed in the privacy of their homes, this meant they were unable to leave the house at all. For working-class women, on the other hand, taking time off work to care for a baby meant a significant loss of income, as the factory or farm was no place for a child. As such, despite well-documented consequences, wet-nursing and hand feeding remained popular choices for women.

Wet-nursing, despite its popularity, was a problematic and oftentimes dangerous practice. In order to be a wet nurse, a woman had to have recently given birth to a baby of her own. However, by primarily caring for and feeding the baby of her employer, it was not uncommon for the wet nurse to lose her own. In addition to this immeasurable personal sacrifice, wet nurses were also socially alienated and had their moral value judged and measured in order to determine the quality of their milk. Wolf explains that this negative effect on their reputation was due to the belief that, "the act of breastfeeding [was] associated with poverty, vulgarity, ignorance and sin" (2001: 157). Nonetheless, it remained a viable option for upper-class mothers who could not or would not breastfeed, for any number of reasons.

Doctors and critics were quick to mock the young Victorian mother who was portrayed as vain, superficial, and in some cases, dangerously careless. The people who were responsible for creating that stereotype were unable to comprehend why women were refusing to breastfeed. In most cases, they believed it was because women were more preoccupied with their social and sartorial

Figure 9.2 "The Fashionable Mamma," James Gillray, 1796. James Gillray, 1796, The Fashionable Mamma, Wellcome Institute Library.

engagements than they were with motherhood. Cartoons such as the one in Figure 9.2 featured a very popular character: the uninterested mother.

She was caricatured and mocked by doctors, artists, and journalists alike, all growing more frustrated with their lack of success at persuading women to breastfeed. Leslie Williams explains this cultural phenomenon as, "three kinds of male discourse—(artistic, poetic and medical)—all dealing with the vexing question of how best to persuade fashionable, literate, presumably upper-class women to breast-feed" (1992: 99). Wolf argues that "upper and middle class women who decided not to nurse their own babies did not choose their own comfort and convenience over their baby's health. Rather, they chose between an activity that was appropriate for their class and an activity that was increasingly inappropriate" (2001: 157). Unlike women from lower classes, cultural modesty codes did not allow upper-class women to expose their breasts in public. That was not their only deterrent from breastfeeding, however, as social gatherings in the evening (and in the case of working-class women, hazardous workplaces) did not allow for children and therefore prevented mothers from nursing on demand. Lastly, before the availability of the nursing corset, the construction of women's garments made breastfeeding impossible because they compressed the breasts and made the nipples inaccessible to a baby.

At the turn of the twentieth century, doctors continuously encouraged women to give their babies breastmilk in preference over artificial food. However, the belief that variables in a woman's life could affect the quality of her milk persisted. These variables could range from race to climate to marriage status, but the correlation between inadequate milk and infant mortality was understood. In American cities, posters and advertisements were distributed and published by health organizations urging women to breastfeed with slogans like, "Don't Kill Your Baby! Mother's Milk is Best of All" (Wolf 2001: 1). Posters like the one in Figure 9.3 exemplify how governments and health organizations put the blame for infant mortality solely on women.

A physician in 1911 wrote that a woman who chooses not to breastfeed is, "guilty of a neglect that is little short of criminal" (Wolf 2001: 16). Wolf explains that information about germs and disease causation began to spread in Chicago

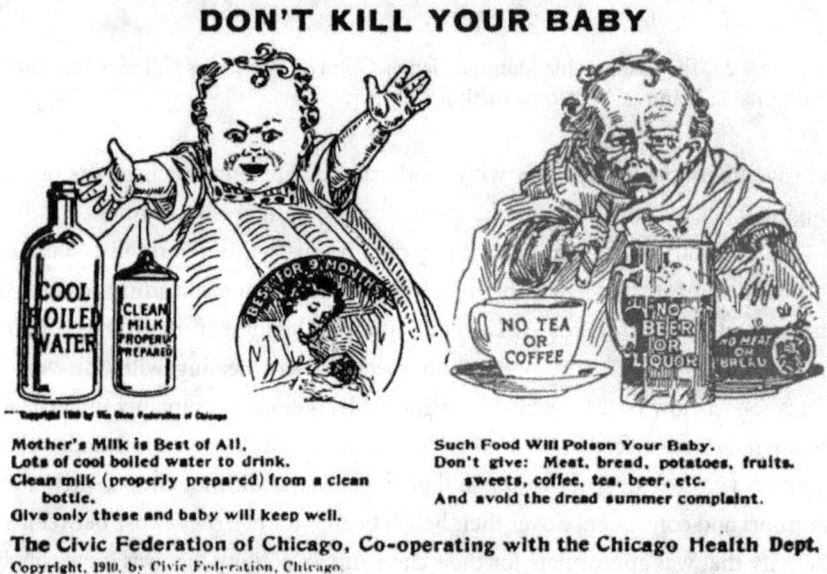

DON'T KILL YOUR BABY

Mother's Milk is Best of All.
Lots of cool boiled water to drink.
Clean milk (properly prepared) from a clean bottle.
Give only these and baby will keep well.

Such Food Will Poison Your Baby.
Don't give: Meat, bread, potatoes, fruits, sweets, coffee, tea, beer, etc.
And avoid the dread summer complaint.

The Civic Federation of Chicago, Co-operating with the Chicago Health Dept.
Copyright, 1910, by Civic Federation, Chicago.

Figure 9.3 Posters like this one exemplify how governments and health organizations put the blame for infant mortality solely on mothers. Bulletin Chicago School of Sanitary Instruction, 1910.

in the 1910s by way of government-sanctioned education campaigns. Women, being the sole preparers of food, were the target audience and consequently directly addressed by these initiatives. Wolf argues that this spurred the belief that only meticulous, well-informed mothers could keep their babies alive, and it sparked a distrust of breastmilk due to lingering beliefs that variables in a woman's life could affect the quality of her milk and that inadequate milk was a direct cause of infant mortality (ibid., 40). By pinning the effects of circumstance onto mothers themselves and making them solely responsible for their baby's life, these campaigns weaponized shame and guilt as a tool to foster the ideal that being a good mother (a well-informed, present, and meticulous one) is inherently attached to the idea of being a good person and a moral citizen. This was a major shift in the cultural perception of motherhood that still informs how motherhood is perceived today.

In Europe, doctors and activists used a different tactic to persuade women to breastfeed. Art historian Gal Ventura credits the emerging interest in breastfeeding and decline in infant mortality rates in France to the push made by artists to depict upper-class women breastfeeding (2015). In addition to portrayals in art, feminist societies formed at the end of the century that promoted maternal breastfeeding did so as an "essential feminine civic duty promoting the state's development" (Ventura 2015b: 21). This artistic glorification of the breastfeeding woman, along with all the accompanying discourse from doctors, governments, and activist groups, cultivated the ideal of the doting mother that we know today.

The discourse that took place among doctors, critics, women, journalists, and artists has proven to be an incredibly useful resource for historians to examine the role that maternity played during the turn of the century. Victorian women were expected to give birth to the next great generation of British imperialists and this responsibility was taken very seriously. As women's rights movements took wing, opposers to it took issue with women's departure from the home and its duties. Because motherhood was to be their only source of fulfillment, mothers having interests, obligations, or social desires outside the home was generally discouraged. The idea that through motherhood women were responsible for the future of their country was internationally widespread.

During the nineteenth century, women often placed out their infants, either with a wet nurse or with a community member, so that they could continue to participate in their work or social duties. The shift that occurred at the turn of the century created a new motherly ideal, one who was entirely fulfilled by an adoring and sacrificial motherhood. The dangerously careless mother who left her child in the care of a wet nurse was replaced by the doting mother who cared for her baby so attentively that she could breastfeed them anytime, anywhere. This ability, to breastfeed anytime, anywhere, was afforded to them by the adoption of specially created garments like the nursing corset. And although this new maternal ideal was objectively a male construct, the invention of these maternity accessories actually demonstrated women's agency in design. The ideal of the selfless, nurturing mother has become so fixed in Western consciousness that the refusal to breastfeed is considered to be extremely selfish or a result of coercion from an external source. But women's refusal to breastfeed until the end of the nineteenth century did not stem from selfishness or coercion from their partners; instead, it stemmed from a discord between inadequate medical recommendations that did not consider their lived experiences and their own volition (Ventura 2015b: 19). The invention of the nursing corset and other maternity accessories allowed women to step into this new role of motherhood with an independent sense of agency.

The invention and popularity of the nursing corset was short-lived and coincided with the final years of corsetry as a whole. But despite its short lifespan, the nursing corset represents an important shift in garment design that focused primarily on functionality based on women's lived experiences. According to Ventura, through their refusal to submit to medical recommendations and retire to the home, women had agency in the invention of this garment and were thus able to shape these commodities rather than be shaped by them: "The jarring synthesis of the stylish mothers' requirements and of the doctors' demands influenced the industry at the end of the century, engendering a new accessory bridging the two worlds: the nurse's corset" (2015b: 15). She goes on to explain how this garment allowed women to breastfeed at will, unaided and without undressing, thus performing their social and maternal duties. In conjunction with the idea that corsets allowed women to participate in the public sphere, and that corsets were an impediment to breastfeeding, the invention of the nursing corset allowed women to participate in both.

One iteration of the nursing corset is previously explored and shown in Figure 9.1. This is the type of nursing corset that would have been available to an upper-class mother. This type of corset, paired with an evening gown, would have allowed an upper-class woman to simply pull down her neckline, unbutton the corset's metal closures and immediately begin breastfeeding. This design allowed her to complete all these steps unaided, and without the risk of dirtying her clothing, in addition to allowing women to continue dressing in the same clothing they would have worn before pregnancy. Along with the cultural change in perception of motherhood as no longer being a private matter and instead an intrinsic quality of womanhood came the sexualization of the motherly figure. Ventura explores this feature by explaining how, "the uncovering of the torso by means of a low neckline dress allowed upper class women to uphold the link between motherhood and sexuality" (2015b: 17). This design allowed women to re-enter the public sphere without having to choose between proper motherhood and social duties.

For women of different social classes, different iterations of the nursing corset came to be. Ventura details the uniforms wet nurses were required to wear by their employers in nineteenth-century France, including loose dresses with buttons on the front to expose the breast with ease (2015a: 216). This type of breastfeeding garment, where only a couple of buttons are undone in order to expose the nipple, is referred to by Ventura as "peep and hide." She theorizes that this type of garment, created to be as modest as possible to allow for public nursing, abstracted, dehumanized, and desexualized the breast, unlike for the upper-class woman who uncovered her entire breast and indulged in the sexual and moral validation of being a good mother. In the United States, as part of the medical initiatives towards breastfeeding, Dr. J. H. Hess designed a special uniform for the wet nurses employed by his hospital. This uniform included a garment called a corset-waist that featured a movable flap over each breast. Each nurse would receive six of these garments and was encouraged to wash them frequently (Fildes 1988: 257). The flap could be unfastened and thrown back to expose the breast. The corset-waist was made of muslin and made to be worn low on the torso so as to avoid adding pressure to the breasts. While women who were employed as wet nurses experienced the brief existence of the nursing corset, most working-class women did not. They were expensive, and the majority of the working class could not afford to buy new clothing simply because their circumstances had changed.

Women's desire for respectability was exerted through the construction of their public image and that image encompassed motherhood and their appearance. The image they were aiming to construct might have been dictated by patriarchal ideals of femininity and gender roles but if that image was well constructed, it offered them as much power and agency as was available to women at that time. As perceptions of women's roles changed due to reform, suffrage, and war, there was a brief gap where women were given the space to define themselves. That is the space in which amenities for breastfeeding were demanded. These amenities include the implementation of (safe) mixed feeding, the invention of hygienic and convenient breastfeeding garments, nursing accessories such as pumps and bottles, and more cohesive and accessible medical support. The invention and eventual disappearance of the breastfeeding corset is a useful tool through which it has been possible to review all the aspects that affected the lives of women who engaged with maternity in the nineteenth and twentieth centuries.

The End of Maternal Corsetry

The efforts of Dress Reformers to bring about a new silhouette at the end of the nineteenth century have been extensively documented by medical, social, and fashion historians. Though none of these historians have looked into the design changes that happened specifically in maternity clothing, changes in women's foundation garments are otherwise discussed. After the Exhibition of Public Health and Safety in 1876, corset advertisements began to emphasize their comfort and healthfulness (Fildes 1988: 81). As previously detailed, during the end of the nineteenth century, the idea that corsets were harmful became more widespread. New corset designs appeared, claiming to be more comfortable and healthier. The efforts of Dress Reformers, along with societal changes such as the invention of the bicycle, effected various changes in women's clothing but the reflection of those changes in their undergarments came in the way of lower necklines until eventually, the corset covered the hips and thighs while leaving the breasts uncovered, which in turn prompted women to experiment with bust enhancers. These transformations reflected the changing perception of women's bodies and their bodily autonomy.

This renewed interest in women's breasts could also explain (or be explained by) the general adoption of breastfeeding. Medical historian Jacqueline H. Wolf also attributes the rising interest in breasts to the newfound acceptability of romantic marriages. She poses the argument that women would want to emphasize their physical attributes in order to attract a romantic partner (2001: 24). Though it is impossible to say when or how exactly the brassiere was invented, society's newfound interest in enhancing the breasts certainly played a part. Some historians credit its adoption to the sudden popularity of the tango, a dance that required free movement in the waist that was impossible to achieve with a corset on (Ewing 1989: 120). Other historians credit it to various designers, such as Paul Poiret, who discarded the use of corsets in their shows (Newton 1974: 145). Either way, the brassiere greatly facilitated breastfeeding for nursing mothers without any great design changes. The early designs of the brassiere generally included

Figure 9.4 Nursing brassiere, 1923, Treasure Cot Co. Nursing Brassiere, 1923, Treasure Cot Co. Catalog, National Art Library.

two pieces of fabric and covered and separated the breasts, but their main objective was to provide a more natural feminine shape than the corset.

In addition to their general popularity, it quickly became clear that the brassiere was a better choice for nursing women. It did not aim to compress the breasts like the corset did, which caused major discomfort to lactating women, and it allowed for better hygiene practices. Figure 9.4 shows an illustration of a nursing brassiere advertised in a maternity catalog that emphasizes its ease of use.

Textile historians Jane Farrell-Beck and Colleen Gau explore in their book, "Uplift: The Bra in America," how new mothers in the 1920s were given brassieres by hospitals postpartum because they were easier to clean than other foundation garments. They write: "New mothers were instructed to keep breasts aseptically clean and support them with a brassiere, a convenient substitute for the cumbersome binder that was regularly used in hospitals. Brassieres gave comfort to swollen, tender breasts and aided in cleanliness of body and clothes. Absorbent pads could be held in place by the brassiere" (2002: 30). Nevertheless, despite the fact that Western culture had moved on from the Victorian taboo interpretation of pregnancy, even in the 1920s when maternity clothing was being overtly advertised as such, illustrations continued to model the clothing on non-pregnant bodies.

Women's breasts and babies were also often abstracted from their bodies and agency. The prioritization of the fetus' health over the mother's, as discussed above, illustrates how the womb (and its fruits) were viewed as a separate entity from the woman. Lori Duin Kelly employs a quote from a nineteenth-century doctor to exemplify this terrifying rhetoric: "the very name woman—womb man—man being the generic term for the race, and womb the adjective, [...] refer to this same childbearing apparatus and to NOTHING ELSE" (1998: 53). According to this belief system, a woman's womb did not belong to her, and according to Wolf, neither did her breasts. As women and men increasingly sought romantic marriages, breasts became sexualized and that sexualization diminished their physiological importance. "A woman's breasts now belonged to her husband as much as, if not more than, to her infant," writes Wolf (2001: 24). This renewed focus on the breasts can also be examined through advertisements for creams and pills that claimed to help their development, along with the rising popularity of breast padding. The concern that breastfeeding would negatively impact the appearance of the breasts, expressed in a magazine quoted by Wolf, demonstrates how women believed that the desirability and availability of their breasts was owed to their husbands (ibid., 25).

The rare visual representations of motherhood that were available at the time were the sentimental portrayals of maternal breastfeeding that had helped shift the narrative around motherhood to one of doting adoration. According to Ventura, portrayals in art of maternal breastfeeding "demonstrated the sharp contrast between the 'dignified mother' and the wet nurse who sells her body like a prostitute" (2015a: 220). The glorification of the values of family and motherhood transformed breastfeeding into a new status symbol that could testify to the status of the household. This newfound acceptance of breastfeeding, though it still unfortunately bore the cost of unwanted sexualization, helped women of the period to exit the home and move into public spaces without having to sacrifice their maternal obligations. Ventura argues that this was a step forward for women's liberation that was facilitated by the nursing corset. And while Ventura makes an interesting case, Leigh Summers counteracts her point by stating that maternity corsets, advertised as supporting the pregnant body, actually supported the prevailing ideology that demanded its invisibility (2001: 42). Both points of view are valid and further illustrate how controversial and personal these discussions can be, and how important it is to be sensitive to the lived experiences of women when addressing issues that concern them and when designing products for their bodies.

Conclusion

In spite of the multiple explanations given by historians as to why women were not breastfeeding during the second half of the nineteenth century, they finally began to do so at its end. After all the campaigning done by doctors, feminists, governments, and journalists, breastfeeding slowly became the norm and the wet-nursing profession is mostly extinct today. The invention of various breastfeeding accessories indicates a point in time where women exercised agency over design. Though they might not have necessarily been the designers themselves, their extended refusal to breastfeed and reluctance to stop tight lacing during pregnancy effectively forced designers and doctors to take their needs into consideration in order to create a product that would meet their needs. The changes that occurred in women's undergarments, from the corset to the nursing corset to the brassiere, effectively reflect the changes that occurred in the cultural perception of motherhood: from the distasteful loss of purity, to the careless monster, to the dedicated, dutiful motherly ideal we know today.

Whether it was women who shaped these commodities or the commodities that shaped women, the existence of the nursing corset was brief. Since upper-class women are the ones who had purchasing power, and therefore influence over products, according to Ventura's model for understanding this design change, the nursing corset would have morphed into the nursing brassiere once upper-class women took up breastfeeding. However, this theory would underestimate all the other factors put forth by the medical historians, anthropologists, gender, and fashion historians who have explored the reason women finally took up maternal breastfeeding.

Due to the fact that there is no historical consensus on the change that took place in maternity undergarments at the start of the twentieth century, it is important to consider it from multiple disciplinary perspectives. The intersection of fashion history, medical history, and social history can provide a broad spectrum of components that ultimately came together to examine this change. In her book *Don't Kill Your Baby*, Wolf examines the aspects of medical history that affected the transition from the wet nurse to the bottle, including medical and government initiatives to encourage breastfeeding. Gal Ventura, an art historian, explores the changing perceptions of the bourgeois breastfeeding woman through her appearance in French art including the social customs and trends that allowed her to exist. Fashion historian Lori Duin Kelly describes the sartorial options that existed for the pregnant and nursing woman at the end of the nineteenth century. Leigh Summers, who has a background in gender studies, discusses the shortcomings of doctors and historians in empathizing with the difficult choices that Victorian and Edwardian mothers had to make. It is only through the examination of all the different aspects that could affect something as controversial and personal as breastfeeding that a conclusion can be reached about how this change in social norms was reflected sartorially. The invention and eventual disappearance of the breastfeeding corset is a useful tool for reviewing all the aspects that affected the lives of those who engaged with maternity in the nineteenth and early twentieth centuries.

References

Barnes, R. and J. B. Eicher (1991), *Dress and Gender: Making and Meaning in Cultural Contexts*. Oxford: Berg.

Bruna, D., ed. (2016), *Fashioning the Body: An Intimate History of the Sillhouette*. New Haven, CT: Yale University Press.

Carter, A. (1992), *Underwear: The Fashion History*. New York: Drama.

Cunningham, P. A. (2002), *Reforming Women's Fashion 1850–1920: Politics, Health and Art*. Kent, OH: Kent State University Press.

Esterik, P. V. (2015), "What Flows through Us: Rethinking Breastfeeding as Product and Process," in T. Cassidy and A. El Tom (eds.), *Ethnographies of Breastfeeding*, , xv–xxiv. London: Bloomsbury.

Ewing, E. (1989), *Dress and Undress: A History of Women's Underwear*. London: Batsford.

Farrell-Beck, J. and C. Gau (2002), *Uplift: The Bra in America*. Philadelphia, PA: University of Pennsylvania Press.

Fields, J. (2007), *An Intimate Affair: Women, Lingerie, and Sexuality*. Berkeley, CA: University of California Press.

Fildes, V. A. (1988), *Wet Nursing: A History from Antiquity to the Present*. Hoboken, NJ: Wiley-Blackwell.

Kelly, L. D. (1998), "Crossing the 'Bearing' Straits: Women's Maternity Dress in the Nineteenth Century," *Studies in Popular Culture*, 21 (1): 1–12.

Lepore, J. (2009), "Baby Food," *The New Yorker*, January 11. Available online: https://www.newyorker.com/magazine/2009/01/19/baby-food (accessed March 6, 2019).

Levitt, S. (1986), *Victorians Unbuttoned*. London: Harper Collins.

Matthews Grieco, S. F. (1991), "Breastfeeding, Wet Nursing and Infant Mortality in Europe (1400–1800)," in S. Matthews Grieco and C. A. Corsini, *Historical Perspectives on Breastfeeding: Two Essays*, Historical Perspectives, no. 1, International Child Development Centre, 15–63. Florence: UNICEF.

Newton, S. M. (1974), *Health, Art and Reason: Dress Reformers of the Nineteenth Century*. London: John Murray.

Poli, D. D. (1997), *Maternity Fashion*. New York: Drama.

Sohn, M. and E. Bye (2015), "Pregnancy and Body Image: Analysis of Clothing Functions of Maternity Wear," *Clothing and Textiles Research Journal*, 33 (1): 64–78.

Steele, V. (2001), *The Corset: A Cultural History*. New Haven, CT: Yale University Press.

Steele, V. (2010), *The Berg Companion to Fashion*. Oxford: Berg.

Summers, L. (2001), *Bound to Please: A History of the Victorian Corset*. Oxford: Berg.

Treasure Cot Co. (1928), *Maternity Wear Catalog*. London: Treasure Cot Co.

Ventura, G. (2015a), "Breastfeeding, Ideology and Clothing in Nineteenth-Century France," in Shoshana-Rose Marzel and Guy D. Stiebel (eds.), *Dress and Ideology*, 211–29. London: Bloomsbury Academic.

Ventura, G. (2015b), "Nursing in Style: Fashion versus Socio-medical Ideologies in Late Nineteenth-Century France," *Journal of Social History*, 48 (3): 1–29.

Willet, C. and P. Cunnington (1951), *The History of Underclothes*. Mineola, NY: Dover Publications.

Williams, L. (1992), "The Womanly Art of Breastfeeding: Art and Discourse in Nineteenth Century Britain," in Ronald Dotterer and Susan Bowers (eds.), *Politics, Gender and the Arts*, 96–111. London: Associated University Presses.

Wolf, J. H. (2001), *Don't Kill Your Baby: Public Health and the Decline of Breastfeeding in the 19th and 20th Centuries*. Columbus, OH: Ohio State University Press.

10

Rei Kawakubo and the Bound Pregnant Body

Katrina Orsini

In 1996, designer Rei Kawakubo sent her Comme des Garçons Spring 1997 ready-to-wear collection down the runway. *Body Meets Dress—Dress Meets Body* featured fifty-seven looks sporting sculptural "lumps and bumps"[1] that appeared to be pads or filler sewn into the bodice of the dresses. The atypical shapes that questioned high fashion silhouettes were met with resoundingly negative reviews from critics. Fashion writer Hilton Als published in *Artforum* that, "Yet another girl sports a pod placed directly on her stomach; when she stood in profile, she looked as if she had been defeated by pregnancy or was simply disinterested in the effect her cosmetic pregnancy had on us" (quoted in Granata 2017: 38–9). While Als' maternal reading of the line may be correct, his strongly negative reaction to both the collection and the pregnant body reveals the true brilliance of the collection. Rei Kawakubo's designs, and consequently the reactions to it, work to expose ill-conceived notions regarding the unsealed body in the Bakhtinian sense, particularly our deep-seated discomfort with the pregnant body. The notion of the bodily grotesque as defined in the 1930s by Mikhail M. Bakhtin has often been explored through critical fashion studies and will be expanded upon below. Bakhtin pinpoints the bodily grotesque in direct opposition to the Classical form through the breaking of body borders. Where the Classical body is sealed and contained, the grotesque body is open and unruly. Where the Classical body is individual and complete, the grotesque body is multiple or transforming.

Als' reaction and those of his contemporaries who voiced similar opinions immediately reveal two of the issues highlighted in Kawakubo's collection: first, as Francesa Granata points out in her book *Experimental Fashion*, the gynophobic nature of any public confronted with pregnant bodies, and second, the responsibility given to a pregnant person to ensure that those around them are comfortable. Als not only decides that the model is "defeated" by her pregnancy, but, even more egregiously, he is bothered that she is indifferent to the effect her pregnancy has on the audience. He unwillingly reveals his desire for a time when the maternal body will become unpregnant and return from this temporary deviation to its "normal" state, or the state most comfortable for him as a male viewer representing society at large. Ironically, Als' reading of the model as "disinterested in the effect" her pregnancy has on those around her is correct. The difference is that Als reads this as negative, and in Kawakubo's line this is presented as neither positive nor negative, simply a state of corporeal being, a silhouette worthy of inclusion in the fashion space.

Als' desire to eschew the pregnant body is not unique to fashion critique. Pregnancy has long been a site and source of cultural spectacle, particularly in the medical field. Between live-witnessed births and cadaver dissections, pregnant bodies are a longstanding site for male posturing as doctors and anatomists worked to separate the womb's activities into mother and child, instead of understanding and treating the architecture of one growing body in the way midwives did. This may be because the idea of the unsealed, pregnant body functions as a grotesque under our contemporary patriarchy: it "unsettles the concept of a singular self: neither one nor two, it disturbs the normative unified subject" (Betterton 2014: 123). In her book *The Female Grotesque*, Mary Russo locates the social pregnant body somewhere between public spectacle protruding into space and the horrors of the filth and degradation associated with the "lower bodily stratum" (1994: 8). In contrast to the idealized, Classical body which is "transcendent and monumental, closed, static, self-contained, symmetrical, and sleek ... The grotesque body is open, protruding, irregular, secreting, multiple, and changing" (ibid.). For most of recorded history, the grotesque body has been shaded with curious negativity while the fashion industry has upheld the standards of beauty reflected in the Classical body.

To make sense of the human life cycle, obstetricians, anatomists, designers, and artists alike would draw and distribute their findings, often depicting the fetus outside of the womb as an autonomous subject, either reflecting their predetermined interests or to avoid the need to confront complex feminine interiority. Eventually, the invention of medical sonograms in the mid-twentieth century allowed the public at large to view the fetus alone. Sonograms mark an important turn in obstetric health—one that changes the focus from safely getting the baby out to being able to get *in* to see the baby (Matthew and Wexler 2000: 143). Images such as sonograms have given rise to the "transparent body," a social construct in which the interiority of the womb is made public and gestational biology is rendered visible (Betterton 2014: 87).

The fetus portrayed as a singular and autonomous being reached new heights in 1965. A fetus in a transparent amniotic sac floated on the April 30 cover of *Life* magazine, drifting across what can only be described as the star-speckled void of outer space. Under the color photograph by Lennart Nilsson read the headline, "The Drama of Life Before Birth," and the description captioned the image as a "Living 18-week-old fetus shown inside its amniotic sac—placenta is seen at right." Placenta "seen" at right is a generous description of an eighth of the organ cropped out of frame, attached to no other person. "Living" and "before birth" also turned out to be duplicitous claims. *Life* later admitted that Nilsson's photographs were taken outside the womb, procured after surgical abortions or spontaneous miscarriages (Cosgrove 2013). Their physical detachment allowed him to position the embryos and fix the lighting to get the clarity he desired. But it was too late; the issue sold out in days and the public absorbed the images as advertised. The carnivalesque display of a fetus launched the medical obsession into a new public light: one visually aligned with the scientific prowess of the Space Race permeating American culture just a decade earlier. On the issue's twenty-fifth anniversary, *Life* published another of Nilsson's photographs of an embryo on the cover, with similar caption describing a look at "How Life Begins." Again, the embryo floated in a transparent sac adrift on an abstract black background. By *Life*'s second publication of Nilsson's photographs, the transparent body had become the norm for viewing a growing fetus.

It is the notion of the transparent body that Rei Kawakubo rejects in *Body Meets Dress—Dress Meets Body*. The collection is widely written about in its relation to the maternal body for its use of soft, padded protrusions, but its true innovation is the way in which it thwarts the audience's need to understand what is underneath, much like medicine's obsession with the pregnant body. While Kawakubo used many see-through and semi-opaque fabrics for this line, the majority of the pregnancy-referencing lumps and bumps are covered by fully opaque fabric, rejecting the gaze that would seek to penetrate the interior of the most distinct aspect of this collection. The collection's name itself refutes our ability to ease our discomfort by searching to understand what is happening inside the dresses. *Vogue* described the collection as "tubelike gingham dresses stuffed with lumpen filler" ("Spring 1997" 2015), while MoMA describes the works in their collection as "pads placed on the abdomen, the hips, the back as well as the shoulder region" ("Items" 2017). Through her naming of the line, Kawakubo simply states that the body meets the dress and the dress meets the body, not acknowledging the existence of another structural entity, refuting the notion that there is an interior happening in the garments, between body and fabric. By placing her transparent fabrics directly next to the covered protrusions, Kawakubo exaggerates what parts of the body are blocked from the viewer's gaze—which parts we can see (primarily skin)—and binds the maternal references as part of the body's presented interior. Following this line of thinking, Caroline Evans notes that by "blurring" the "boundaries between body and dress... subject and object, or self and other," Kawakubo negates the ability to think of the wearer or the dress in any sort of "mutually exclusive terms" (Evans 2003: 269). *Body Meets Dress—Dress Meets Body*, then, recreates the historical discomfort at the inability to define the pregnant body as either decisively one or two, self or other. The same discomfort is legible in its critical reception.

Kawakubo's work came as contemporary technology advanced beyond the basic sonogram; a commercial market has opened outside of obstetrics offering new 3D and 4D sonograms as a type of take-home souvenir. This new market for for-profit, commercial, non-diagnostic ultrasounds has accelerated the technology's capabilities and most expectant parents are able to get clear images of their fetus' face well before it is born. These appointments have an end goal of a "take-home shot," or a clear image of the fetus without any obstruction from any maternal material. This technology is used as an enforcer of body borders, and creates a false narrative of a singular, autonomous other. This allows fetal features and newfound "personalities" to form an individual identity well before fetuses are viable on their own. These projections are just one way in which the understanding of the beginning of life is being pushed to before birth, shifting the narrative from one of a growing fetus into that of an individual subject with autonomy at a point when it is not yet viable outside the womb. This shifting timeline has created a call for "fetal rights," a still undeclared set of rights that rivals that of the pregnant person's, of which this fetus still exists as a part. The arguments for fetal rights have moved to define personhood for a fetus as beginning earlier and earlier on the fetal timeline, encroaching into pregnancy timelines and negating the autonomy of pregnant persons.

As previously established, Rei Kawakubo rejects the notion of the transparent womb through her use of opaque fabrics. Therefore, she also rejects the notion of "fetal rights" by preventing an allowance of early onset subjecthood. In fact, Kawakubo uses her padding to lengthen the timeline of maternity. By placing padding under ruching reminiscent of a wrapped and tied fabric, Kawakubo invokes imagery of a traditional wrap sling baby carrier, continuing maternity into the postpartum. In direct opposition to technology moving the individual fetal identity earlier and earlier, Kawakubo binds the postpartum body and baby into one, carrying weight and shape under one skin and as one body. Instead of simply rejecting an earlier timeline for identity, she actually delays the separation of identity and comments on the reproductive labor and babies' dependency postpartum. Reflecting this notion, and again exposing negative societal perspectives on maternity, *Style Journo* described the silhouette of a *Body Meets Dress—Dress Meets Body* model as a woman who is "physically attached to her burdens" and who implicates the encumbrances of reproductive labor (Hall 2013). By the use of gingham print throughout, Kawakubo further aligns this burden of reproductive labor with the burdens of domestic labor reminiscent of a 1950s housewife.

The reference to sling-style baby wraps also allows Rei Kawakubo to contend the maternal body as private—as opposed to public—in this collection. In ongoing research, my interviews with postpartum moms about their experience with sling-type baby wraps echo this sentiment. Interview subjects have described the sling as a "single body barrier" for themselves, but it is also apparently read as such by others.[2] They have commented that while wearing the baby in a wrap, as opposed to a front pack or a stroller, fewer people dare to reach out and touch the baby uninvited, perhaps because within one layer of fabric skin, the carrier declares the baby to still be in internal space. In a corporeal argument made by phenomenologist Paul Ferdinand Schilder, "the body schema does not end with the human skin as a limiting boundary, it extends far beyond it" (quoted in Sampson 2017: 345). Following this argument, French ethnologist Jean-Pierre Warnier uses the example of a blind person's walking stick (2006: 187). He argues that a walking stick is used as an extension of the body and that an outer, other environment is perceived to start only at the end of the walking stick, not in the space between the body and the stick. This is true for both the user and those interacting with the user. Following this same logic, if a woman wearing a baby wrap navigates the world with it as an extension of the bodily self—for example not running into objects by extending the understanding of where her body ends as a point beyond the wrap—the wrap itself is acting as a new skin and body schema. And if the bodily self can extend beyond the skin, Kawakubo is using her *Body Meets Dress—Dress Meets Body* line as an alternative skin, one which by encompassing the postpartum baby and body is extending maternity. It is claiming the baby as still internal and forbidding public interaction.

By using larger pieces of padding to reference a growing baby and by presenting a single skin for the baby and mother to exist inside of postpartum, she is not only rejecting the public gaze but also public touch, which is a huge point of contention around the perceived-to-be-public pregnant belly. Like in pregnancy, the postpartum body is in a state of transformation. While society views the postpartum as a time for the body to return to its "normal" state, many postpartum people find that the return to a pre-pregnancy body is not and will never be the reality for them. By including the postpartum body into her timeline of the maternal body, Rei Kawakubo problematizes a largely incorrect cultural understanding of what it is, what it does, and how it exists. In a period when cultural regulations constrain the body and attempt to shrink it to its original shape, Kawakubo allows for a further expansion of the body as the baby continues to grow. *Body Meets Dress— Dress Meets Body* presents clothing without sizing, similar to a one-size-fits-all sling wrap. Unlike clothing that seeks to contain the body, e.g., the corsets of the previous chapters in this section, Kawakubo allows for a flexible container, upending the tradition of wrapping as female-body containment and shrinking.

Moving with a postpartum understanding of an extended body schema may be best displayed in Kawakubo's costume collaboration with dance choreographer Merce Cunningham. In their Brooklyn Academy of Music production *Scenario* (1997), dancers wore designs padded similarly to those of *Body Meets Dress— Dress Meets Body*. Suzy Menkes recalls feeling "rather uncomfortable" about the designed costumes and referred to them as a "disfigurement" that resembled "cancerous cells" that were protruding in an oddly "upbeat, even jolly" way (quoted in Ahmed 2016). Cunningham himself was intrigued by the grotesque unfamiliarity of his own dancers, saying, "if you saw the person from the front, you expect a certain familiar image. But when the person turns around, you see a totally different image, which is quite unexpected" thanks to "the shape of the costume" (ibid.). Both Menkes and Cunningham display a level of discomfort with unknown body boundaries, unexpected bodily shapes, and a new body schema.

Conclusion

More than twenty years after this line emerged, society is still grappling with preconceived notions about pregnancy, maternity, and the postpartum that Rei Kawakubo challenged in *Body Meets Dress—Dress Meets Body*. It appears as though fashion critics, curators, and academics are as well. Although pieces from the line have appeared in many exhibitions including Kawakubo's retrospective at the Metropolitan Museum of Art, the maternal silhouette and references are generally avoided or skirted around (Figure 10.1).

Figure 10.1 The "Body Meets Dress, Dress Meets Body" collection exhibited as part of the 2017 Rei Kawakubo retrospective at the Metropolitan Museum of Art, New York. Rei Kawakubo / Comme des Garçons: Art of the In-Between (2017) installation / The Metropolitan Museum of Art / Image courtesy of the author.

The catalog for the aforementioned retrospective, *Rei Kawakubo Comme des Garçons: Art of the In-Between,* features two images of *Body Meets Dress—Dress Meets Body* pieces. One might take this to mean that curator Andrew Bolton gave the line a fair amount of consideration and (re)visitation, and perhaps he did; however, it yielded little insight. Early in the catalog's introduction, Bolton introduces the line by saying it "was and remains one of Kawakubo's most challenging and provocative collections" (Bolton 2017: 13). The catalog and accompanying exhibition sectioned Kawakubo's work into thematic sections based on word "dualisms" that Bolton explains are not meant to be thought of as binaries, but as an "opportunity to challenge conventional interpretations of such dichotomies, uncovering the limitations of our understanding" (ibid.). *Body Meets Dress—Dress Meets Body* appears briefly in the "Then/Now" section but joins Kawakubo's aforementioned *Scenario* costumes to dominate the "Object/Subject" section. If we are to take Bolton at his word and consider the implications of the space between our cultural understanding of a subject and an object, particularly as it pertains to the pregnant body, one can immediately summon a history of public spectacle and medical grandstanding. More disturbingly, one can see the direct consequence from an obscurity between objecthood and subjecthood in the ongoing political regulation of the pregnant body.

Notes

1   This descriptive term was used by many outlets, including *Vogue*'s digital archive of the runway, ("Spring 1997 Ready-to-Wear Comme des Garçons" 2015). The nickname may be a nod to Georgina Godley's 1986 line entitled "Bump and Lump," which also featured inserted padding to create an atypical and maternal silhouette. It has become the common term of reference for this collection.

2   Here, I am referencing my own and ongoing research, a series of interviews regarding fashions and products for carrying babies with recent new moms. Quoted is Carly Ruby.

References

Ahmed, O. (2016), "Lumps and Bumps at Comme des Garçons S/S97," *AnOther*, January 5. Available online: https://www.anothermag.com/fashion-beauty/8174/lumps-and-bumps-at-comme-des-garcons-s-s97 (accessed October 29, 2019).

Betterton, R. (2014), *Maternal Bodies in the Visual Arts*. Manchester: Manchester University Press.

Bolton, A. (2017), *Rei Kawakubo Comme des Garçons: Art of the In-Between*. New York: Metropolitan Museum of Art.

Cosgrove, B. (2013), "'Drama of Life before Birth': Lennart Nilsson's Landmark 1965 Photo Essay," *Time*, March 4, 2013. Available online: https://time.com/38746085/drama-of-life-before-birth-landmark-work-five-decades-later/ (accessed May 21, 2022).

"Drama of Life before Birth" (n.d.), *Lennart Nilsson Photography*. Available online: https://www.lennartnilsson.com/ec/the-drama-of-life-before-birth/ (accessed May 21, 2022).

Evans, C. (2003), *Fashion at the Edge: Spectacle, Modernity, and Deathliness*. New Haven, CT: Yale University Press.

Granata, F. (2017), *Experimental Fashion: Performance Art, Carnival and the Grotesque Body*. New York: I.B. Tauris & Co Ltd.

Hall, J. (2013), "Body Meets Dress, Dress Meets Body," *Style Journo*, July 18. Available online: http://stylejourno.blogspot.com/2013/07/body-meets-dress-dress-meets-body.html (accessed October 29, 2019).

"Items: Is Fashion Modern?" MoMA. October 1, 2017–January 28, 2018. Available online: https://www.moma.org/audio/playlist/43/702 (accessed November 4, 2019).

Matthew, S. and L. Wexler (2000), *Pregnant Pictures*. New York: Routledge.

Russo, M. (1994), *The Female Grotesque: Risk, Excess, and Modernity*. New York: Routledge.

Sampson, E. (2017), "The Cleaved Garment: The Maker, The Wearer and the 'Me and Not Me' of Fashion Practice," *Fashion Theory: The Journal of Dress, Body and Culture*, 22 (3): 341–360. Doi: 10.1080/1362704X.2017.1366187.

"Spring 1997 Ready-to-Wear Comme des Garçons" (2015), *Vogue*, August 20. Available online: https://www.vogue.com/fashion-shows/spring-1997-ready-to-wear/comme-des-garcons (accessed November 7, 2019).

Warnier, J.-P. (2006), "Inside and Outside: Surfaces and Containers," in C. Tille, W. Keane, S. Küchler, M. Rowlands, and P. Spyer (eds.), *Handbook of Material Culture*, 186–96. London: Sage Publications Ltd.

Section 3

Identity

"Mother is the name for God in the lips and hearts of little children," wrote Victorian novelist William Makepeace Thackeray in his 1848 social satire *Vanity Fair*, emphasizing the then relatively new conception of mothers as omnipresent and all-powerful in the lives of their offspring (1909: 363, quoted in Thurer 1994: 183). Given the previous section's discussion of the Victorian era's complicated attribution of saintliness to mothers, I hesitate to reinforce a false holiness, but an enduring truth of Thackeray's statement lies in the power of naming to create a mother's identity. If "motherhood" is a state, and "mothering" an act, "Mother" is the self. However, I know no mother today whose children call them "Mother"— something in the de-formalization of our present culture generally prevents it— so I have come to think of this aspect of motherhood as "Mama," as I've previously mentioned. This is what my own children call me, and it's how I frequently refer to myself—with my kids, yes, but also to others in contexts where the kids have a presence-absence. "It's Mama's night out," I might say to friends, if I'm lucky. "Mama" is the private space we've created between us but also one of the screens through which I interface with the world. It is not the only identity I wear, but it is nonetheless with me all the time.

As Joanne Entwistle succinctly explains, "Dress is [...] the means by which identities are marked out and sustained" (2000: 117). When, as in the transition to parenthood, a person's identity changes, it follows that dress will do so as well. There may be an awkward phase while one sorts out one's relationship to those changes; the genre of mama-fashion advice literature that Holly M. Kent's chapter takes as its subject, for instance, claims to assist in smoothing over that awkwardness, to help mothers use dress to "speak" their new identities in ways that can be understood by society. But, as Kent shows, too often they serve as what Finkelstein calls "bonds that link individuals in a mutual act of conformity to social conventions"—sanding down the edges of an individual person's identity to fit into a prescribed range of appearances that won't necessarily serve their emancipation (1991: 122, quoted in Entwistle 2000: 114).

Throughout this volume, I hope there has been an adequate emphasis on the fact that, while maternity wear may be the first thing that comes to mind when pairing "fashion" and "motherhood" together, it is only the beginning of the way the two interrelate.

As opposed to what it means to "father" a child (essentially, to beget one), Rich knowingly states that: "To 'mother' a child implies a continuing presence [...] often for years" ([1976] 1995: 12). That continuing presence means continual evolution of the mother as a subject and as a dressed body, one who is acted upon by multiple countervailing forces. Identity generally is understood in the social sciences to be flexible, impermanent, shaped over time and in interaction with others. As communications scholars Heisler and Butler Ellis described in a study of motherhood's effect on the individual's public "face" (per Irving Goffman), "being labeled and treated as a mother by others may produce 'mothering' behaviors on the part of women as well as alterations to the way women see themselves" (2008). I love the use of "alterations" in this statement, evoking the tailoring of clothing to the body as it changes over time.

This section sees the themes of the previous ones—the consumption of constructed narratives and the haptic experience of reproducing and/or caregiving—come together to play out in the lives of individuals. If the institution of motherhood alienates the physical from the psychic, perhaps the examination of identity offers a path to reintegration. The methods in these chapters therefore focus much more on subjectivity as lived, particularly those by Sarah Garland and Liza Betts that utilize oral history and auto-ethnography, to draw out the ways that clothing carries profound meanings regarding motherhood as a continuous element of one's life.

Garland and Betts' chapters use first-person narratives in ways that, per Imogen Tyler, "bear witness to the 'unique temporality' and transient subjectivity" of motherhood "from an embodied perspective" in a way she claims is "largely absent from Western culture" and that I have already identified as entirely appropriate to further studies incorporating fashion and motherhood, as both fields have encouraged inclusion of such narratives in scholarship (Young 1990: 160, in Tyler 2000: 292; see also Jenss 2018; and Kawash 2011). Themes of mother-daughterhood reappear (after rearing their heads in previous chapters by Lisby, Jalli, Lamm, and Case) and remind us that every mother is also a child, working to reconcile the image(s) of "mother" they inherited with who they themselves have turned out to be.

Published in 1976, the same year as *Of Woman Born*, Jane Lazarre's memoir of early motherhood *The Mother Knot* includes my favorite ever description of dressing for the "continuing presence" of parenthood. She recalls those "sloppy days" as representing "a kind of freedom which was based on a strong, realistic understanding of what it means to be a parent of young children": she and the others she was parenting alongside would, she says, "see beyond the soiled clothing and rumpled hair to the naked, open, still youthful bodies underneath the cloak of parenthood" (1976: 57). The cloak of parenthood is a perfect metaphor of self-fashioning and one I have not gotten out of my head since reading that passage. There is truth and beauty to be found in collective recognition that while much about us changes when we undertake parenting, there is so much that remains true to who we are and always were.

References

Entwistle, J. (2000), *The Fashioned Body: Fashion, Dress and Modern Social Theory*. London: Polity.

Heisler, J. M. and J. Butler Ellis (2008), "Motherhood and the Construction of 'Mommy Identity': Messages about Motherhood and Face Negotiation," *Communication Quarterly*, 56 (4): 445–67.

Jenss, H. (2016), *Fashion Studies: Research Methods, Sites and Practices*. London: Bloomsbury.

Kawash, S. (2011), "New Directions in Motherhood Studies," *Signs*, 36 (4): 969–1003.

Lazarre, J. ([1976] 1997), *The Mother Knot*. Durham, NC: Duke University Press.

Rich, A. ([1976] 1995), *Of Woman Born: Motherhood as Experience and Institution*. New York and London: W. W. Norton & Co.

Thackeray, W. M. (1909), *Vanity Fair*. New York: Cassell and Company.

Thurer, S. L. (1994), *The Myths of Motherhood: How Culture Reinvents the Good Mother*. New York: Penguin.

Tyler, I. (2000), "Reframing Pregnant Embodiment," in S. Ahmen, J. Kilby, C. Lury, M. McNeil, and B. Skeggs (eds.), *Transformations: Thinking Through Feminism*, 288–302. London: Taylor & Francis Group.

11

"Mommy Fashion is Still Fashion"

US Style Guides for Pregnant Women and Mothers in the Twenty-First Century

Holly M. Kent

There is a fundamental tension at the heart of all prescriptive literature. As a genre, advice guides at once promise hope and empowerment to their readers and also play on their fears, anxieties, and insecurities. Fashion advice literature is no exception to this rule. In print, on television, and online, counsel about fashion is often deeply contradictory: at once promising to help audiences unlock their unique and distinctive senses of style (though doing so by following pre-set lists of fashion "dos" and "don'ts") and encouraging audiences to express themselves in how they dress yet also encouraging them to distrust their sartorial instincts and shaming them for their stylistic choices.

The genre of maternal fashion guides is a relatively new one within the US literary marketplace. While prescriptive literature intended for women about how to dress and prescriptive literature focused on how to be a "good" mother has abounded since the nation was established, until recently there have not been many guidebooks devoted specifically to instructing pregnant women and new mothers about how they ought to dress.[1] This chapter examines such prescriptive literature (specifically, books focused on fashion and style intended for pregnant women and new mothers) in the twenty-first-century United States, considering the nature of the counsel these authors offer to their readers. While these guides present themselves as breaking away from a conservative sartorial past in which pregnant women were forced into desexualized styles and encouraged to forego an interest in fashion in the service of selfless maternity, the advice presented in this literature in many ways echoes and reinforces long-standing fatphobic and conservative ideas about pregnant women's and mothers' proper self-presentation, and their overall roles, in US society.

Fashion Advice in Print in the Twenty-First-Century United States

In the digital age, anyone with a cell phone and internet access can readily find numerous websites, blogs, and social media accounts providing style inspiration and advice. While a great deal of twenty-first-century fashion discourse takes place online, print guides about style have also remained popular (suggesting the American public's ongoing appetite for receiving advice about what to wear, and what not to wear, from a range of different mediums).

Overwhelmingly addressed to a female readership, twenty-first-century fashion guides frequently focus on providing a clear sense of fashion rules designed to help take any sense of stress about dress away from their readers. These fashion guides promise to make dressing easy and fuss-free, offering counsel about how to create the perfect capsule wardrobe, organize one's closet for maximum efficiency, and dress correctly for different types of occasions. These guides frequently frame these concerns as a problem unique to modern women, who are called on to dress for a wide variety of scenarios (both personal and professional) and are constantly walking the tightrope (particularly in professional contexts) of dressing either "too" conventionally femininely, or not conventionally femininely enough. Twenty-first-century fashion guides promise to help their female readers successfully thread this seemingly impossible needle of looking both attractive and appropriate at all times.[2]

Many fashion guides come from sources readers might be expected to know, trust, and desire to emulate: a fashion periodical or TV show, or a fashionable celebrity. During the early twenty-first century, fashion guides have appeared from popular fashion periodicals such as *Elle*, *InStyle*, and *Lucky*, fashion experts from TV shows such as *What Not to Wear* and *Project Runway*, and celebrity stylists and celebrities such as Lauren Conrad, Eric Daman, and Rachel Zoe. The success of these guides indicated that readers are eager to learn the behind-the-scenes secrets of how to dress from those deeply embedded in the fashion world.[3]

Although some maternal fashion guides are written by well-known names in the fashion industry, the majority of them are not. Instead of a wealthy, famous stylist or celebrity instructing an "ordinary" woman about how to dress, these guides often take on a more intimate tone, of a woman who has herself experienced (and learned how to dress during) pregnancy, offering sisterly fashion advice to other women. As Sofie Valkiers puts it in her 2019 book *Little Black Book for Moms*, she wrote her book since she wanted to share "one of the most precious parts of your life with the rest of the world, because you hope that it can at least make other mamas feel: you're not alone :)" (2019: 150).

Maternity Fashion Guides: The Authors

This chapter considers fashion guides written by nine different authors between 2003 and 2018. Of these nine authors, eight are American and one is Belgian (the Belgian author, Sofie Valkiers, is included as she is a high-profile fashion blogger in the United States as well as Belgium, and her books are readily accessible on the US literary marketplace). In the twenty-first century, the US continues to play a significant role in global fashion media, with American fashion editors, authors, and publications being influential voices in shaping global fashion discourse. These writers' works also help to illuminate uniquely American cultural expectations (Adrienne Rich's "institution") about and lived realities ("experience") of motherhood. The US lags notably behind other Western, industrialized countries in terms of both the concrete governmental resources it provides to, and larger cultural expectations surrounding, motherhood. Unlike the majority of European countries, the US offers little (if any) guaranteed or paid parental leave, and few (if any) educational and material resources for new parents. Although the late twentieth and early twenty-first centuries have seen some shifts in expectations for fathers in the work of parenting, dominant cultural ideals still center mothers as children's primary caregivers, with mothers (rather than fathers) expected to make any needed professional and personal sacrifices for the sake of their children. It is within this larger cultural and national context that these guides have been written and marketed to their pregnant and postpartum readers.[4]

All nine authors refer to a male partner or spouse in their books. These writers range from the notably wealthy (such as prominent, successful maternity fashion designer Liz Lange; please see this book's Appendix for an interview with Lange) to the seemingly comfortably middle class (with none of these authors expressing any concern or giving explicit advice about dressing in times of economic insecurity, and all of these authors recommending brands, designers, and products that would not be accessible for less affluent readers). All of these authors are white, reflecting the ongoing lack of racial and ethnic diversity in many fashion media spaces (despite the long-standing, and ongoing, work on the part of fashion writers and influencers of color to diversify the historically white-dominated fashion industry).[5] The authors of these guides therefore represent perspectives that still tend to dominate fashion discourse: white, affluent, and (seemingly) heterosexual.[6]

These authors also do not offer considerable diversity in terms of their professional backgrounds, with most of these writers coming from the realms of advertising, fashion design, and fashion journalism. Of the nine authors discussed, two are fashion-focused journalists and bloggers (Amy Tara Koch and Sofie Valkiers), two are fashion designers (Liz Lange and Lauren Sara), two are advertising and marketing professionals (Melissa Fiendell and Betty Londergan), two are professional stylists (Erin Busbee and Katie Rice Jones), and one is a popular self-help author (Karen Salmansohn). While there is some variety in terms of their background and professional focus, the overwhelming majority of these authors are rooted in the fashion world, and draw on their expertise as designers, journalists, and fashion media professionals in crafting their advice for their readers.

The authors examined in this study uniformly disdain the maternity fashions of years past. For much of US history, dressing for pregnancy centered on concealing pregnancy for as long as possible and obscuring the pregnant body from view. It was only in the late twentieth century that these expectations began to meaningfully change and there was more overt celebration of the pregnant body in the fashion media, and form-fitting garments designed to highlight (rather than conceal) the pregnant body, such as body-conscious dresses, crop tops, and two-piece swimwear, became more widely available in the fashion marketplace.[7]

Maternal fashion advice writers of the early twenty-first century, therefore, were publishing their books during an era in which a notable shift in pregnancy fashions had happened relatively recently, and in which the notion that pregnant women could remain stylish and continue to care about fashion was still comparatively new. The association of pregnancy with dowdiness, (literal) matronliness, and a distinct lack of fashionability is still a powerful stereotype and cultural expectation that the authors of these guides challenge throughout their books.

Stylish Mama: Affirming Maternal Style

The authors in this study emphasize that while many (including, they assume, many of their own readers) persist in defining pregnancy as an innately unstylish time, it can instead be a season of vibrant, exciting sartorial experimentation. As Lauren Sara tells her readers in her 2003 book *Expecting Style*, "[y]ou think that 'maternity style' is a paradox, but you are wrong" (12). Her book, she notes, will clear up the misconception that "being pregnant means they [pregnant women] have to forgo fashion and give up their favorite clothes" (ibid., 11). Melissa Fiendell begins her 2012 work *No More Mom Jeans: A Deliciously Witty Guide for New Moms Who Want to Ditch the Sloppy Sweatpants and Embrace Mommyhood with Style* by asking, "[i]s it possible to be a new mom and still be stylish?" answering her question with a resounding "yes" (ibid., 10). In her 2014 volume *Fashion Dues and Duen'ts: A Stylist's Guide to Fashionably Embracing Your Baby Bump*, Katie Rice Jones reassures her readers that pregnancy need not be "this fashion-less place," and in her 2003 guide *Liz Lange's Maternity Style: How to Look Fabulous During the Most Fashion-Challenged Time*, Liz Lange muses (somewhat contradicting her book's subtitle) on "[p]regnancy style. To some, this idea seems baffling, but to me it's always made perfect sense" (Rice Jones 2014: 9; Lange 2003: 8).

Indeed, rather than being a fashion desert, these advice guide writers encourage their readers to think of pregnancy as a fashion opportunity. Rice Jones asserts that "maternity wear can be just as stylish as its regular-fit counterpart" and Valkiers enthuses that "mommy fashion can be really fun!" (Rice Jones 2014: 21; Valkiers 2019: 84). Readers who may have felt alienated by fashion in the past can use pregnancy as a chance to educate themselves about style, according to Amy Tara Koch, who writes in her 2010 book *Bump It Up: Transform Your Pregnancy into the Ultimate Style Statement*, "[i]f you have lived for years mystified by runway trends, pregnancy is a golden opportunity to exit your comfort zone and bring your inner glamazon to life" (2010: 99). Throughout their guides, these authors work to redefine pregnancy as a chance for fashion excitement, rather than as a time spent in unwelcome exile from a previously stylish existence.

Contrasting Past and Present in Maternity Fashion

These authors underline that modern-day pregnant women have the opportunity to dress very differently than previous generations of expecting women did, and that the mode of dress they advocate for in their books is a notable (and progressive) break from a retrograde, undesirable maternity-fashion past. Sara reflects that, unlike in previous decades, "there is no need to wear a Peter Pan-collar smock top and orange leggings. There is more out there than sack dresses and juvenile prints. You do not need to dress like a sofa just because you are pregnant" (2003: 11). Modern women, Sara argues, need to turn away from the infantilizing, unattractive pregnancy styles which long dominated the maternity market, and embrace being fashionable throughout their pregnancies. "Today's woman," Sara affirms, "has no time to slow down for pregnancy and no room to miss a beat of the fashion pulse" (ibid., 52). Sara frames pregnant women as both wanting and needing to keep up their previously fast-paced, busy lifestyles throughout their pregnancy—and this includes not letting their interest in fashion tail off. Sara's work thus echoes the "having it all" language that has dominated postfeminist discourse since the 1980s: the expectation (and pressure) that women can (and ought to) juggle professional work, domestic labor, motherhood, personal relationships, and meeting exacting standards of beauty with ease—an ideology that ignores the lack of structural support for US women who combine paid work and motherhood, ongoing expectations that women do the overwhelming majority of domestic and emotional labor in their households, and the often punishing nature of contemporary beauty standards.[8]

Lange similarly draws a binary between previous generations' definitions of maternity fashion (emphasizing how these styles infantilized and desexualized pregnant bodies), and contemporary designs meant to affirm and celebrate pregnant women, writing:

> There's absolutely no reason a woman must sacrifice her sense of style just because she's pregnant. She shouldn't have to dress like a child just because she's having a child; it's one thing to put a toddler in a sailor suit, but it's another thing completely to condemn a grown woman to such a fate. Instead, a woman should be able to dress as she would in her normal life.... More importantly, those clothes should show off—rather than hide—an expecting woman's body. Not only do more fitted clothes make you look thinner (a definite plus!), but they also assert that pregnancy is a natural, beautiful, and sensual state.
>
> 2003: 8

She argues that previous modes of dress for pregnant women unfairly stripped grown women of their adult sophistication and sexiness and sought to hide what she defines as the "natural, beautiful, and sensual" time of pregnancy. Modern-day maternity fashions, Lange emphasizes, are a valuable step forward in honoring the pregnant body (provided, she notes, that it remains thin) and highlighting pregnant women's ongoing beauty and sexuality.

Lange and author Karen Salmansohn (in her 2003 book, *Hot Mama: How to Have a Babe and Be a Babe*) advocate for modern-day pregnant women to break with past expectations about public presentation of the pregnant body, specifically, by wearing bikinis. "Dare to wear a bikini," Salmansohn tells her readers, "and show off your creation in the making" (2003: 49). Lange likewise advises "if you dare, take the plunge and go for a colorful bikini. This is the ultimate suit to show off your new shape in all its glory" (ibid., 39). In direct contrast to previous generations' ideas of concealing and desexualizing the pregnant body, Lange and Salmansohn encourage their readers to don a revealing, sexualized, public-facing garment, thus ensuring that their bodies are on display rather than hidden away. Notably, even amidst this encouragement to embrace a skin-baring, overtly sexy garment during pregnancy, both Salmanson and Lange underscore the "daring" nature of doing so, demonstrating an awareness that donning this particular type of swimwear during pregnancy is still likely to be regarded as taboo, transgressive, and presumably undesirable by some onlookers.

In their guides, authors encourage their readers to embrace being in a new era of pregnancy fashion: one in which they are not encouraged to dress in an infantilized way that suggests their pregnant bodies are shameful, undesirable, and deserve to be hidden away. However, even as they frame contemporary pregnancy fashions as liberating, their counsel nonetheless expresses more conservative ideas of who pregnant women are and ought to be, by valorizing thinness, continuing to present baring the pregnant body as "daring" and transgressive, and adding remaining stylish to the seemingly unending list of tasks that all women (pregnant or not) are expected to complete.

Fashion as Self-Care for Pregnant Women?

Like all writers who center their work on fashion, maternal style guide authors operate within a larger culture that defines caring about style as something frivolous and trivial. These authors diligently seek to counter this widespread denigration of fashion and encourage their readers to (amidst the demands of pregnancy and motherhood) take time to indulge in the pleasures of clothing. Defending her decision to continue to care about style as she entered motherhood, Fiendell states that she found contentment in "trying to maintain my stylish side, a somewhat shallow activity" (2012: 209). Reassuring her readers that taking time to think about (and take pleasure in) clothing is a positive good for pregnant women and new mothers, Betty Londergan (in her 2006 guide, *I'm Too Sexy for My Volvo: A Mom's Guide to Staying Fabulous!*) tells her readers "[i]t is possible to resist the relentless pressure to be selfless" as a pregnant woman or new mother, and that "[f]rom now on, everything is about the baby—*except* for that shallow and lovely part of you that still wants to look pretty and have nice things" (xv). Still defining fashion as "shallow," these writers nonetheless defend pregnant women's and new mothers' right to retain an interest in dress, purely for their own benefit. In a culture that still expects mothers to be unfailingly selfless, these authors assert the value of women continuing to immerse themselves in fashion culture for their own individual enjoyment.[9]

This insistence on the importance of remaining interested in style is presented in these guides not just as a self-indulgent pleasure but also as a baseline necessity. Many of these guides warn their readers against losing their conventionally attractive appearance and sense of style amidst the physical and emotional demands of pregnancy and motherhood. Rice Jones emphasizes to her readers the importance of "[m]aintain[ing] your style standard while pregnant" (2014: 1). Londergan warns her audience to "pluck out these daily temptations to look your worst," and Fiendell cautions that "this is no time to start neglecting yourself. If you do things can go downhill. Fast" (Londergan 2006: 149; Fiendell 2012: 51). Koch and Sara warn against the perils of focusing on comfort, rather than stylishness, during pregnancy, with Sara warning that "oversized Hanes T-shirts do not have to be your new nightgown, and your college sweats do not have to be your at-home staple," and (in a distinctly classist assertion), Koch cautions that not paying enough attention to dress will result in "someone in the supermarket asks if you are available to clean her house next week because her cleaning lady is on vacation" (Sara 2003: 32; Koch 2010: 17).

These writers discuss caring about fashion not just as a pleasure, but also as an obligation, arguing that any pregnant woman who fails to dress stylishly is perilously turning her back on proper standards of feminine self-presentation (and according to Koch, failing to effectively visually demonstrate her class status, as well). Alongside the encouragement to engage in self-care by continuing to take joy in clothing are stern warnings to avoid dressing purely for comfort and failing to meet mainstream expectations for feminine dress. Dismissing the reality that some pregnant women and new mothers might want or need to dress purely or primarily for comfort, these guides insist that fashionability should remain a top priority for those wishing to dress correctly during pregnancy and early motherhood.

Policing the Pregnant Body

One of the most fraught topics in pregnancy advice guides is that of the pregnant body. While some of these guides celebrate the pregnant and postpartum body, others echo and reaffirm the fatphobia and intense policing of women's bodies endemic in US culture. Several guides go out of their way to praise (specific) parts of pregnant women's bodies, particularly the curvaceousness of the pregnant form. Playing into dominant ideals of female beauty, Sara encourages women who were "[f]ormerly flat . . . to make the most of your new bust" (2003: 39). Koch similarly urges her readers to "[h]ave fun with your bodacious newfound curves. Flaunt your belly and boobs in a Lycra dress" (2010: 49). In her work, Salmansohn praises the (idealized) pregnant body for "the larger breasts, the rounder curves, the glowing skin. (Kate Moss, eat your heart out—or at least eat a brownie or something!)," and asserts that women should embrace the idea that "[v]oluptuousness is next to goddessness. Then get out and exercise" (2003: 94, 45). Even in their praise for the pregnant form, these authors reinforce dominant ideals of feminine beauty (in which large breasts and clear skin are valued, and in which thin women are both praised and judged for their thinness), and pregnant women can embrace their curvaceousness (provided they maintain an active exercise regime, presumably to limit the extent of that curvaceousness) (Figure 11.1).

Several of these books seek to strike a tone of sisterly solidarity with readers, affirming pregnant women's (potentially complex) feelings about living in (and dressing) their changing, growing bodies in a profoundly fatphobic society. Reflecting on her postpartum experiences, Erin Busbee writes in her 2019 book *Style Made Simple*:

> I would love to sit here and tell you that after having [her child], I was reveling in the miracle of life and how glorious my body is. But the truth is, I was pretty traumatized by what I saw. This new body wasn't mine! Trying to dress this version of myself was a whole new style challenge I was not prepared for. I felt like a mess.
>
> 6

Lange tells her readers that "[y]our changing body and shrinking wardrobe can be a source of some anxiety, even in the midst of such happiness and excitement. So many women I know describe themselves as feeling fat and unused to the way their new pregnant body feels" (2003: 39). Opening up space for their readers to have conflicted feelings about the ways in which their bodies are changing during pregnancy, these authors nonetheless also reinforce widespread cultural negativity surrounding being or feeling "fat."

Much of the advice on how to dress as a pregnant person in these works focuses on fixing perceived "problems" with the pregnant body (most of which centered on that body looking too large). Rice Jones writes, "[a]s your stylist, it is

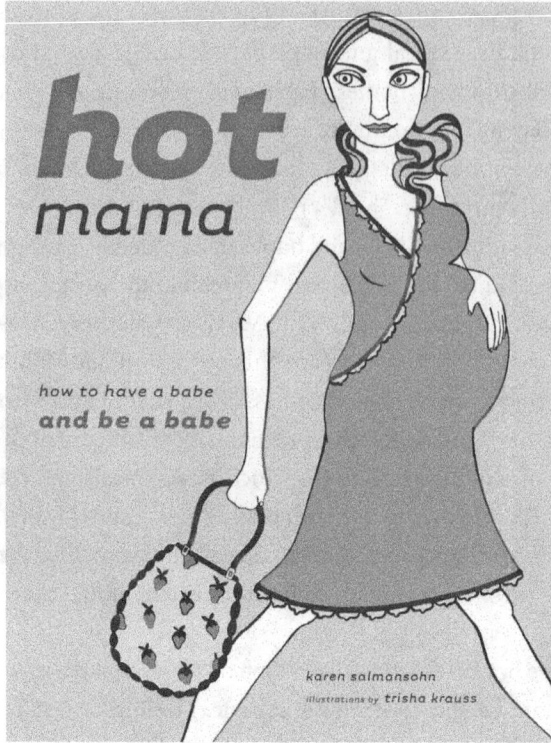

Figure 11.1 Cover of *Hot Mama: How to Have a Babe and Be a Babe* by Karen Salmansohn. HOT MAMA: HOW TO HAVE A BABE AND BE A BABE. © 2003 Karen Salmansohn. Illustrations by Trisha Krauss. Published by Chronicle Books, LLC.

not my mission to point out your figure flaws, but instead direct you to the right kind of *figure fixers* to address them" (2014: 72). Her "figure fixers" almost all center on looking smaller throughout pregnancy and postpartum. Both Lange and Sara caution against wearing any garments with extensive amounts of fabric, with Lange warning that "[t]oo much fabric and volume will only make you look bigger than you are, and as much as I stand behind celebrating your new body, that doesn't mean showing it off in unflattering ways," and Sara cautions to "[s]teer clear of sweatshirts with kangaroo pockets. They add bulk, which is the last thing you need" (Lange 2003: 84; Sara 2003: 32). In an explicitly fatphobic assertion, Londergran asks her readers to carefully select garments which make it clear that "you actually look pregnant and not like the new Plus Size prototype" (2006: 19). Postpartum, Koch advises her readers to "[w]ear pregnancy SHAPEWEAR to hold everything in," and Fiendell tells her audience that:

This is the chapter where I am supposed to tell you things like, "It took nine months to take it off" or "Embrace your delicious new mommy curves." Well, I'm not going to. Getting your body back into fighting shape is an important part of the quest to claim your most stylish, magnificent life as a new mom. After all, even the best clothes lose their fabulousness if you can't fit them over your ass.

Koch 2010: 134; Fiendell 2012: 101–2

While these guides validate the curvaceousness of the pregnant body, their primary focus remains ensuring that readers avoid dressing so as to look "fat" while pregnant and postpartum.

Pregnancy is Sexy: Romance, Sexuality, and Marriage in Maternal Fashion Guides

As previously discussed, one of the primary points underlined in twenty-first-century maternity fashion guides is previous generations' desexualization of the pregnant body. Unflattering, frumpy, or infantilizing garments, Lange affirms, unfortunately make women "forget that feeling sexy and sensual is what pregnancy is all about" (2003: 83). Salmansohn echoes this point, asserting that "[t]here's nothing sexier than a pregnant woman who boldly and enthusiastically shows off her belly" (2003: 60). Londergan likewise encourages pregnant women to continue to dress in a way that makes them feel beautiful and sexy, affirming they should make this a priority for themselves, rather than their "husband or random construction workers" (2006: xv).

While Lange, Salmansohn, and Londergan advocate for dressing in a way that affirms women's sexuality for their own benefit, others emphasize the need to continue to dress sexily throughout pregnancy and early motherhood for the sake of their male partners. Fiendell cautions her readers against "parading around in your husband's t-shirts and old boxer shorts," instructing them to instead "[r]eplace old gear with a few classic sexy pieces for date nights with your husband" (2012: 20). Recounting her efforts to construct a sexy outfit to wear to go out with her own spouse soon after the birth of their child, Fiendell recalls, "I'll never forget the look of, I think *relief* is the best word for it, on my husband's face on our first post-baby date … I think in his (and maybe all men's) minds there was worry that motherhood would transform his wife into the kind of woman that would rock high-waisted pants and a scrunchie" (ibid., 33–4). In her work, Fiendell thus defines dressing sexily, not as something pregnant women and new mothers do for themselves, but rather as something they do to ensure that their male partners will still view them as desirable. This advice is notably being given to mothers who are recently postpartum, likely experiencing physical, hormonal, emotional, and psychological challenges, who might not have cultivating and maintaining a sexy appearance rated high on their list of priorities.

Taking the issue of romance, sexuality, and maternity from a different angle, several guidebook authors affirm that male partners "owe" pregnant women expensive jewelry for having endured the physical challenges of pregnancy. Listing the types of outfits that every pregnant woman needs, Salmansohn encourages her readers to buy "the hot mama seduce-your-partner-into-buying-you-some-nice-jewelry outfit" (2003: 67).[10] In her section on desirable "bling" for pregnant women to wear, Fiendell tells her readers to "leave this page open on daddy's pillow tonight as a subtle hint" (2012: 49). Koch bluntly advises her readers to:

> [s]tart hunting down your push present... Get hubby or partner used to the idea that he may have to sacrifice his weekly poker nights (to pool his cash) to honor this age-old tradition. Fancy jewelry or a fur may seem excessive. But when you add dollar signs for each hideous detail of the pregnancy—nausea, bad skin, cellulite, huge rump, exhaustion—you rapidly reach the diamond zone.
>
> 2010: 121

In their guides, these authors thus frame pregnancy in part as a material exchange, contending that the bearing of a child deserves financial reward. Pregnant women have done the literal labor of carrying and bearing the couple's children (and in doing so, have endangered their own physical attractiveness, according to Koch), and as such, deserve a direct material benefit. On the one hand, these overt calls for material recognition of the all-too-often unrecognized and undervalued work of pregnancy and mothering seem to carry an empowering element—honoring the unpaid (and often physically taxing and dangerous) work of pregnancy with immediate material gain.

On the other hand, the dynamic suggested by these authors (to subtly cajole a male partner into buying expensive jewelry for them as a reward for childbearing) plays into conservative notions of heterosexual partnership, which assumes (and accepts) a distinct power imbalance between male and female romantic partners. These authors' ideas about "push presents" echo traditional notions defining male partners' primary role as economic, and female partners' central roles as sexual, emotional, and domestic. According to this framework, women are expected to maintain heteronormative ideals of sexual desirability and availability, take responsibility for their household's domestic labor, and undertake care work for their male partners and children, in exchange for their male partner's economic support. These writers' discussions of push presents are reminiscent of the notion that "diamonds are a girl's best friend": that women can expect generous financial gifts from male romantic partners, provided they successfully embody traditional female roles (whether those be as sexual partners, wives, and/or mothers). Recognizing women's fundamental economic precarity in a heteronormative, patriarchal financial system, this ideology contends that women's best chance of achieving economic stability is to work within that system, by seeking to live up to heteronormative, patriarchal feminine ideals. These authors' advocacy for push presents troublingly suggests that one lavish gift is sufficient economic reward for women's mothering work (ignoring the reality that no single gift, no matter how expensive, could financially equal the true volume of women's reproductive, emotional, parental, and domestic labor over the course of pregnancy, let alone over all of motherhood).

Conclusion

As this chapter has explored, the fashion advice literature written for pregnant women and new mothers in the twenty-first century is deeply complex and often contradictory. Affirming the fundamental need to celebrate and affirm the beauty of the pregnant body, authors also castigate their female readers for failing to rigorously maintain dominant standards of stylishness and thinness during pregnancy and new motherhood. Asserting the need for pregnant women and new mothers to maintain and assert their ongoing identity as sexual beings, these guides also put pressure on women to dress sexily, less for themselves and more for their male partners. Condemning past ideas about fashions for pregnant women as limiting and retrograde, these guides themselves construct their own rigid rules about how pregnant women should (and should not) dress. As the twenty-first century moves forward, the print marketplace will hopefully offer a more diverse range of voices, with a wider array of perspectives about what it means to live in (and dress) a pregnant body.

Notes

1   Please note that throughout this chapter, when discussing pregnant people and pregnant fashion, I refer to "women" and use "she/her" pronouns. This is not to

negate or erase the experiences of pregnant people who do not identify as female, but rather to reflect the audiences to whom the guides I examine are explicitly addressed: cisgender pregnant people who identify as women. For discussions of US prescriptive literature targeting female readers, see Leavitt (2003).

2   For examples of this type of twenty-first-century fashion guide, please see Freer (2015); Karen (2020); Lumbatis (2021); Mak (2017); Messiah (2021); Murphy (2019); Rees (2016); and Roth (2013).

3   For examples of this genre of style guide, please see Conrad (2010); Daman (2009); Editors of *InStyle* Magazine (2009); France and Linett (2008); Garcia (2010); Gunn (2012); Kelly and London (2005); Siriano (2009); Weber (2019); Woodall and Constantine (2003); Zee (2015); and Zoe (2008).

4   For more studies of differences in social policies and cultural attitudes towards motherhood in twentieth-century and twenty-first-century Europe and the United States, see Collins (2018); Cooke (2014); Gangl and Ziefle (2009); Gash (2009); and Morgan (2006).

5   For more on recent controversies about racism and lack of inclusion on online fashion communities, see Cochrane (2020); Graham (2019); Hargrove (2018); Magsaysay (2020); and Schiffer (2020).

6   While none of the authors explicitly identify as heterosexual, they refer exclusively to having male partners and spouses, and to romantic and sexual relationships with men.

7   For more on changing ideals of pregnancy fashions, see Lindig and Chilton (2021); Lois (2011); and Mannering (2017); for more on Liz Lange's role in and perspective on this change, see the Appendix in this volume.

8   For more on late-twentieth- and early-twenty-first-century post- and antifeminist ideologies, see Faludi (1991); Negra and Tasker (2007); and Tarrant and Howard (2001).

9   For more on cultural conceptions of motherhood in US history and culture, see Apple and Golden (1997); Clements and Thompson (2011); Demo, Borda, and Kroløkke (2015); Vandenberg-Daves (2014); and Wilson and Yochim (2017).

10 While Salmansohn is one of the few authors to refer to a "partner" rather than explicitly to a "husband," she does consistently gender this partner as male.

References

Apple, R. D. and J. Golden, eds. (1997), *Mothers and Motherhood: Readings in American History*. Columbus, OH: Ohio State University Press.
Busbee, E. (2019), *Busbee Style: Style Made Simple*. Monee, IL: Independently published.
Clements, M. and T. L. Thompson (2011), *Tuning into Mom: Understanding America's Most Powerful Consumer*. West Lafayette, IN: Purdue University Press.

Cochrane, L. (2020), "'I Cannot Be Silent': Exposing the Racial Pay Gap Among Influencers," *The Guardian,* last modified July 24, 2020. Available online: https://www.theguardian.com/fashion/2020/jul/24/i-cannot-be-silent-exposing-the-racial-pay-gap-among-influencers (accessed December 11, 2021).

Collins, C. (2018), *Making Motherhood Work: How Women Manage Careers and Caregiving.* Princeton, NJ: Princeton University Press.

Conrad, L. (2010), *Lauren Conrad Style.* New York: HarperCollins.

Cooke, L. P. (2014), "Gendered Parenthood Penalties and Premiums aross the Earnings Distribution in Australia, the United Kingdom, and the United States," *European Sociological Review*, 30 (3): 360–72.

Daman, E. (2009), *You Know You Want It.* New York: Penguin Random House.

Demo, A. T., J. L. Borda, and C. Kroløkke, eds. (2015), *The Motherhood Business: Consumption, Communication, and Privilege.* Tuscaloosa, AL: University of Alabama Press.

Editors of InStyle Magazine (2009), *The New Secrets of Style: Your Complete Guide to Dressing Your Best Every Day.* New York: InStyle Press.

Faludi, S. (1991), *Backlash: The Undeclared War Against American Women,.* New York: Three Rivers Press.

Fiendell, M. (2012), *No Mom Jeans: A Deliciously Witty Guide for New Moms that Want to Ditch the Sloppy Sweatpants and Embrace Mommyhood with Style.* Cincinnati, OH: Next Chapter.

France, K. and A. Linett (2008), *The Lucky Guide to Mastering Any Style: How to Wear Iconic Looks and Make Them Your Own.* New York: Gotham Books

Freer, A. (2015), *How to Get Dressed: A Costume Designer's Secrets for Making Your Clothes Look, Fit, and Feel Amazing.* Berkeley, CA: Ten Speed Press;

Gangl, M. and A. Ziefle (2009), "Motherhood, Labor Force Behavior, and Women's Careers: An Empirical Assessment of the Wage Penalty for Motherhood in Britain, Germany, and the U.S.," *Demography*, 46 (2): 341–69.

Garcia, N. (2010), *The Little Black Book of Style.* New York: Harper Collins.

Gash, V. (2009), "Sacrificing Their Careers for Their Families? An Analysis of the Penalty to Motherhood in Europe," *Social Indicators Research*, 93 (3): 569–86.

Graham, M. (2019), "Instagram Influencers are Often White, and Now the Brands that Pay Them are Getting Pushback," *CNBC*, last modified August 29, 2019. Available online: https://www.cnbc.com/2019/08/29/instagram-influencers-are-often-white-leading-to-brand-criticism.html (accessed December 11, 2021).

Gunn, T. (2012), *Tim Gunn's Fashion Bible.* New York: Gallery Books.

Hargrove, C. (2018), "How #RevolveSoWhite Sparked a Diversity in Fashion Movements on Instagram," *Refinery29*, last modified January 11, 2018. Available online: https://www.refinery29.com/en-us/2018/01/187586/valerie-eguavoen-you-belong-now-instagram (accessed December 11, 2021).

Karen, D. (2020), *Dress Your Best Life.* New York: Little, Brown Spark.

Kelly, C. and S. London (2005), *Dress Your Best: The Complete Guide to Finding the Style That's Right for Your Body*. New York: Random House.

Koch, A. T. (2010), *Bump It Up: Transform Your Pregnancy into the Ultimate Style Statement*. New York: Ballantine Books.

Lange, L. (2003), *Liz Lange's Maternity Style: How to Look Fabulous during the Most Fashion-Challenged Time*. New York: Clarkson Potter.

Leavitt, S. A. (2003), *From Catharine Beecher to Martha Stewart: A Cultural History of Domestic Advice*. Chapel Hill, NC: University of North Carolina Press.

Lindig, S. and C. Chilton (2021), "The Evolution of Maternity Style," *Elle Magazine*, last modified February 27, 2021. Available online: https://www.elle.com/fashion/personal-style/g28423/maternity-style-evolution/ (accessed November 28, 2021).

Lois, G. (2011), "Flashback: Demi Moore," *Vanity Fair*, last modified June 22, 201. Available online: https://www.vanityfair.com/news/2011/08/demi-moore-201108 (accessed December 1, 2021).

Londergan, B. (2006), *I'm too Sexy for My Volvo: A Mom's Guide to Staying Fabulous!* Avon, MA: Adams Media.

Lumbatis, A. (2021), *The Ultimate Book of Outfit Formulas: A Stylish Solution to What Should I Wear?* Portland, OR: Ten Peaks Press.

Magsaysay, M. (2020), "The Watchdogs Making Sure Fashion does More than Talk about Being Inclusive," *Los Angeles Times*, last modified December 11, 2020. Available online: https://www.latimes.com/lifestyle/story/2020-12-11/commentary-black-lives-matter-messages-and-fashion-brands-what-now (accessed December 10, 2021).

Mak, W. (2017), *The Capsule Wardrobe: 1,000 Outfits from 30 Pieces*. New York: Skyhorse Publishing.

Mannering, L. (2017), "A Brief History of Maternity Clothes," *HuffPost*, last modified December 6, 2017. Available online: https://www.huffpost.com/entry/a-brief-history-of-matern_b_156618 (accessed December 1, 2021).

Messiah, L. (2021), *Style Therapy: 30 Days to Your Signature Style*. New York: Harry N. Abrams.

Morgan, K. J. (2006), *Working Mothers and the Welfare State: Religion and the Politics of Work-Family Policies in Western Europe and the United States*. Redwood City, CA: Stanford University Press.

Murphy, A. (2019), *How to Not Wear Black: Find Your Style and Create Your Forever Wardrobe*. New York: Penguin Random House.

Negra, D. and Y. Tasker, eds. (2007), *Interrogating Postfeminism: Gender and the Politics of Popular Culture*. Durham, NC: Duke University Press.

Rees, A. (2016), *The Curated Closet: A Simple System for Discovering Your Personal Style and Building Your Dream Wardrobe*. Berkeley, CA: Ten Speed Press.

Rice Jones, K. (2014), *Fashion Dues and Duen'ts: A Stylist's Guide to Fashionably Embracing Your Baby Bump*. San Anselmo, CA: Know Act Be Books.

Roth, L. A. (2013), *Style Bible: What to Wear to Work*. New York: Routledge.

Salmansohn, K. (2003), *Hot Mama: How to Have a Babe and Be a Babe*. San Francisco, CA: Chronicle.

Sara, L. (2003), *Expecting Style*. New York: Bulfinch Press.

Schiffer, J. (2020), "Influencer Marketing, Long Lacking Diversity, Faces a Reckoning," *Vogue Business*, last modified June 19, 2020. Available online: https://www.voguebusiness.com/companies/influencer-marketing-long-lacking-diversity-faces-a-reckoning (accessed November 27, 2021).

Siriano, C. (2009), *Fierce Style: How to Be Your Most Fabulous Self*. New York: Grand Central Publishing.

Tarrant, S. and A. Howard, eds. (2001), *Antifeminism in America: A Historical Reader*. New York: Routledge.

Valkiers, S. (2019), *Little Black Book for Moms*. Tielt: Lannoo Publishers.

Vandenberg-Daves, J. (2014), *Modern Motherhood: An American History*. New Brunswick, NJ: Rutgers University Press.

Weber, B. R. (2019), *Makeover TV: Selfhood, Citizenship, and Celebrity*. Durham, NC: Duke University Press.

Wilson, J. A. and E. C. Yochim (2017), *Mothering through Precarity: Women's Work and Digital Media*. Durham, NC: Duke University Press.

Woodall, T. and S. Constantine (2003), *What Not to Wear*. New York: Riverhead Trade Press.

Zee, J. (2015), *That's What Fashion Is: Lessons and Stories from My Nonstop, Mostly Glamorous Life in Style*. New York: St. Martin's Press.

Zoe, R. (2008), *Style A to Zoe: The Art of Fashion, Beauty, & Everything Glamour*. New York: Grand Central Publishing.

12

Out of Time

Constant Change, Maternity Dressing, and Pregnancy in Lockdown

Sarah Garland

Pandemic Time

When I think back to spring and summer 2020, and to my pregnancy and encounters with maternity wear, it is difficult to separate which of my responses were part of having a baby and which were part of the new circumstances and dangers of the Covid-19 pandemic. Pregnant against a backdrop of life as usual, I might assume that my sense of suspension and uncertainty came from adjusting to the idea of motherhood. But my pregnancy ran alongside a period of globalized change and risk, and my memories of maternity blend with those of the first months of the pandemic. The way that I characterized my own variety of unease drew from wider cultural conversations about time. Alongside the global traumas of illness and death, pandemic time prompted exclamations such as, in one meme, "what a year this week has been," describing an edgy blend of newly available hours and disturbed routines.[1]

Pregnancy time, too, it felt to me, was a strange adjustment. My early-pandemic sense of suspended motion was perhaps less than that reported by non-pregnant people; for me each week was punctuated by the ritual of consulting websites and apps that showed me other people's increasingly baby-like ultrasounds labelled by week and that told me my baby was now the size of a walnut, plum, or grapefruit. (By "watermelon" I didn't need an app to tell me there was a substantial being in my belly). The disappearance of novelty felt by many in the pandemic caused a sense of temporal unmarkedness, which, for me, intensified the sense that pregnancy was an in-between time, a time of trying to tell what has happening inside me, all the while coming to terms with a perilous

Figure 12.1 The author while pregnant, 2020. Courtesy of Sarah Garland.

world which had pressed pause on many normal aspects of the social and industrial. I wanted to hold still and capture this moment before we became a family and our lives changed some more, but I was also impatient to meet our daughter and to have passed through the twinned worries of carrying her and of coronavirus. In England, where I was, periods of beautiful weather and the changing and flowering of our back garden went alongside news reports of wild nature returning to emptied-out towns. Some days it was easy to settle into the feeling that there might be truth in old conceptions of pregnancy as part of the larger temporal cycles of plant and animal life (Figure 12.1).

On other days, though, the waiting was interminable, particularly when we were waiting for news from doctors and consultants, and this waiting meshed with the interminability of lockdown. By the time of my first ultrasound, England was moving into a partial, then full, social lockdown. The timescale of lockdown and easing and then locking down again ran alongside the timeline of my own growing baby. Even when the strictures lifted a little in the summer of 2020, I remained deeply cautious about the safety of travelling, eating out, and socializing. I'll not know what it is like to be pregnant without the deep somberness of the national and international situation rumbling on alongside this new life—only that, like the locked-down streets, my own pregnancy often felt very quiet and deeply serious.[2]

In the pages that follow I'd like to repurpose this inward turn to attempt some pandemic-era reflections on the mental and corporeal challenges of clothing a growing body in a manner that felt almost satisfying, and, in some small way, ethical. Under the influence of lockdown those challenges felt temporal—like running into a sense of time that was malfunctioning, or that I couldn't negotiate properly—and I'd like to expand that perspective into some larger meditations on the ways in which clothing a pregnant body disrupts everyday notions of dress and time. Dressing our body with a mind to the future might slow down the speed with which garments are worn and then outgrown, but it might also create a situation where the pregnant person is wearing clothes that don't yet fit them, or where a nursing bra, for example, is out of joint with a not-yet or not nursing mother. And if dressing is a negotiation between mind, body, and social context, this becomes even more complex when all three are changing swiftly and unpredictably. Maternity's untimeliness is also a sticking point if we are looking to reduce the speed and impact of our consumption. Ideas of investment buying, slow fashion, and reduced consumption aren't easily compatible with the changeable nature of the pregnant body.

I mention my own historical circumstances because my account of maternity dress is colored by the double uncertainty of pandemic and pregnancy, as well as by a peculiar absence of many of the more usual discourses of, and audiences for, the antenatal body. The pandemic removed me from the touch of non-pregnant or non-medical others, and I remember wondering whether my pregnancy and postpartum period were anachronistic, unexpectedly like the inherited image of the Victorian mother-to-be, "confined" to the private sphere.[3] Because of coronavirus, the casual narration of my pregnant visibility I was mentally preparing for never materialized.[4] I spent much of that year or so meeting only medical professionals, immediate family, and the other couple in our official "bubble," all of whom knew I was pregnant relatively early on. I was never in a position to be offered a seat on a bus, or to have strangers in the supermarket casually comment on my "bump" or on how parenthood might be. Before coronavirus I had projected forward my life at work in the university, imagining speaking with colleagues and classes about the baby or their own pregnancies. I had felt in other pregnant people a beautiful gravity and arresting fascination that seemed to cut through the staidness of campus life, and I wondered whether my own pregnant body would disrupt, too. I had imagined the strange newness of lecturing from within a body that was more exuberant in its secondary sexual characteristics and the clothing I might choose to carry me through this period. My imagined responses were very much in the tradition Eileen Green outlines in "Suiting Ourselves," where female professors' accounts characterized their professional visibility as of "a mixture of pleasurable performance and of embodied vulnerability" where they were expected to "physically embody the authority of professor or senior academic" (2001: 100).

Instead, though, my encounters with maternity clothing were by necessity very inward, very tied to the space of my home, my private body, and to the new, hurriedly navigated space of virtual meetings. In three-dimensional life, my bump was long past anything as subtle as "showing," but from the shoulders up on screen my past self continued, visually uninterrupted. Virtual meetings and work-from-home protocol removed me from public situations, and almost from the pregnant gaze in general. The unwritten and nuanced codes of business-casual, creative semi-formal, and smart-ish leisure wear that are still in evidence in the university moved upwards on the body and I, like others, retained a fairly covered-up look, plus the gendered theatricality of jewelry and make-up, to pull myself back from thinking about our baby into the kinds of externally directed modes of attention I needed for on-screen meetings. I bought a couple of tailored under-bump trousers on eBay in those first pre-pandemic weeks with the intention of wearing them at work with large button-up shirts, but I didn't use the trousers at all because by the time they fitted we were in full lockdown and I, like many non-pregnant people working remotely, was able to choose more comfortable garments. As novel as the "novel coronavirus" was, I now see the challenges of maternity dressing as less unique than I did at the time, and it's this kind of perspective I'd like to bring to the reflections that follow. As Laura Snelgrove, editor of this volume, wrote in an issue of *Fashion Studies Journal* dedicated to fashion and motherhood: "We've heard a lot about the work-from-home uniform and the reign of sweatpants. Well, if Covid has seen you joining the ranks of the forever-sweatpants people, welcome! Parents of young children have been here for a while" (2021).

Past Strategies, Future Uncertainty

During pregnancy your body is frequently uncomfortable and adding a layer of uncomfortable clothing on top of that was something I, like many pregnant people, resisted. I usually create a temporary sort of "capsule wardrobe" every few months; I choose items from my storage that coordinate and fit the varied conditions of the British climate, add a few pieces to it that reflect things I've seen that have excited me in color, cut, or fabric, and put the rest back in two large wooden coffers. This time, after my 20-week ultrasound, I undertook that ritual weeding-out of clothing that might dig, chafe, or not move with my belly for the next six months or so. This still felt risky because as an older mother—I got pregnant at 42—I had been socialized to see my pregnancy as precarious, but it also felt like a small act of faith, too. I hadn't realized that this time packing away my out-of-season clothes would also feel like divestment because I wasn't able to say with certainty what kinds of in-person social situations I might encounter.[5]

Clothing was always a tool for me to navigate the future, but that tool had become unreliable because the future was now unreliable. As I looked at my wardrobe and imagined my second trimester working from home under lockdown, and my third, which would be the summer vacation for university, and then my maternity leave, I came to packing away my work shirts, my work trousers, my heeled boots, my formal coats, anything that needed to be laundered on delicate, couldn't be worn unfastened, or that didn't stretch. My wardrobe isn't expensive or old enough to be classed as vintage but it is carefully considered—I shop to bring into being an outfit that already exists in my mind's eye, I dye things that don't feel right color-wise, I buy in any size or gender as long as I like it, I adjust the fit of garments, I re-thrift garments that don't feel right—and to be putting so much of it away amplified the feeling of being cut adrift that had begun when lockdown sent us all home to work, childmind, or wait.

The sense about which Beth Beverly writes wherein dressing a postpartum body feels like dressing "a moving target"—a frequently exasperating challenge requiring "equal parts patience, creativity, and psychic vision"—began for me when I lost the ability to feel secure in the imagination of my future body and its dressed encounters (2021). I didn't know what size I would become, when that might be, what shape might come with that, or whether I'd have a postpartum body that was less healthy. I also didn't know whether I'd switch to part-time working or would return to a job that was mostly online, mostly formal, or mostly informal. I didn't know whether having a baby might prompt a total re-evaluation of my work and my values. I didn't know whether I'd feel the same about my body after our daughter was born, whether the kinds of clothes I owned would still suit my new roles, or how I looked and felt, and I didn't know whether I would return to ironing and hanging clothes. In another era perhaps clothing designed with built-in adjustability would have eased this; Rebecca Lou Bailey writes of how designated clothing for the period of maternity really only took off in the early twentieth century, before which gowns were temporarily modified, or were voluminous enough to be accommodating (1981: 38). But both that history of capacious tea-gowns (still present in the maternity dominance of maxi dresses and "buffet" dresses) and the imagined future of transformable and modular maternity clothing are much less in daily evidence in the West than our pregnancy-unfriendly fitted-at-the-waist trousers and fitted-at-the-bust-and-hips tops.

Before pregnancy I had come to a set of dressing strategies that I felt generally worked for me. This turned out not to be the case with my pregnant body. As Michael Carter points out in *Being Prepared*, there is a bias towards the future in dressing, an anticipatory dimension to the ways we think about clothing (2017). Fashion is notoriously present- and future-oriented, but we don't need to follow trends to know dress to be an accommodation of an imagined future. Even the kinds of storied garments laid out in Emily Spivack's *Worn Stories*, in which the narratives and past encounters of individual items hold together "miniature memoirs" for their wearers, are put on the body to structure emotions in the present (2014). Dressing for the day sees us "getting ready"; it depends on weather forecasts, forecasts about the tenor of occasions and social encounters, a sense of the kinds of movement required of our bodies, and, for some of us, a sense of how we might like our clothes to help us feel today. In Alison Guy and Maura Banim's still-useful model, women's dressing mediates between "the woman I want to be," "the woman I fear I could be," and "the woman I am most of the time" (2000: 316). Of these thoughts, "wanting" and "fearing" are present- and future-oriented, and maternity dressing left me disconnected from those two dimensions of time. Having my first child during a pandemic felt like being caught between the existing patterns of my life. I didn't know the woman I wanted to be and didn't have access to the woman I am most of the time. Temporarily rootless, my main guide to maternity dressing was paying attention to my increasingly visceral encounters with pregnancy garments.

Shopping for Maternity Wear

Despite the excitement that can accompany pregnancy, shopping for maternity clothing can be more of a challenge than a celebration. Maternity sizing is strange, either based on trimesters or on inconsistent non-maternity sizing, and even outwardly rational systems don't take into account the fact that part of the anxiety of pregnancy is often that you don't know where on your body you might carry pregnancy weight, how much of this extra energy store there might be from week to week, and how long you might be pregnant for. There is always also the pressingly real concern with revealing a pregnancy and then having to go through a very public loss. It's difficult to try on maternity clothing, too. In my city of 200,000 there are no stores solely selling maternity wear, very few brick-and-mortar department or thrift stores left stocking maternity clothing, and only one selling maternity wear alongside children's clothing and equipment. None of these were open during lockdown. Many women (myself included) shy away from buying significant amounts of maternity wear, instead buying loose or larger non-maternity clothes.[6]

The untimeliness of maternity clothing thus manifests in problems with bodily fit and fit to life circumstances. The fashion industry's attempts to solve this include (and indeed, perhaps rest on) the normalization of stretch garments—in the process normalizing the wearer's moves into the domestic and private spaces implied by these more casual and closely fitting clothes. Looking through mothers' online forums and in online department stores confirms that maternity clothing shopping is generally a matter of looking for cheap, multi-tasking, and temporary "basics" in the form of nursing-friendly camisoles, T-shirts, jeans, leggings, longline sweaters, and sleepwear. The dominance of leggings in the archetypal pregnancy wardrobe symbolizes many of these ambiguities. Forums, social media, and blogs insist that leggings are *the* pregnancy and mum uniform because of the stretch, the versatility, and the ways in which a pair made of fabric with good recovery might be wearable beyond pregnancy. These mirror the last decade's rise of leggings as casual-wear, sped up by their ability to show off a striking body—often a worked-upon body, of which more is said in the introduction to this book's section on Material—but also perhaps by the fact that factory seamstresses are usually paid by the seam and so leggings offer lower production costs, and by the fact that selling stretch garments online is less risky in terms of sizing. These items of leisurewear are sold as part of the recent boom in fashions that promote wellness and health, a trope that is even more paramount in the discourses of motherhood and pregnancy. Drawing on the idea of yoga, they encapsulate an odd paradox, a new iteration of the old stereotype of mothers as both yielding and strong. The leisure and self-care connotations of fitness activities, and of this type of form-fitting soft Lycra-jersey sportswear, form part of the iconography of a Westernized version of yoga and meditation. These images and outfits appear across social and print media as part of the package of idealized motherhood, constructing a maternal femininity which draws calmness and strength from a healthy body and mind. And yet, the reasons leggings appear as part of a ubiquitous "mom uniform" (which Entwistle and Wissinger acknowledge as amounting to a "technique of the self," per

Foucault) is because they enable what is often exactly the opposite of a meditative leisure lifestyle (2021). Leggings make dealing with parenthood's significant domestic labor a little less difficult because they allow a greater ease of movement (and dressing) than jeans or pants, because they can physically support the body in the tough everyday demands of moving around a pregnant and changing body, and because they make easier the extensive range of activity that comprises the substantial bodily labor of parenting.

During pregnancy I also felt uprooted in terms of the temporalities of age. Fashion is a kind of call and response between the social and the personal—albeit negotiated, adapted, sometimes resistant—and even if one's response isn't to take an interest in the fast-moving cycles of couture or high-street trends it's still hard for many, myself included, to give up the preparedness and social creativity of dressing with others at least a little in mind. The internalization of my new situation as a vulnerable person (two vulnerable people, by the end) who no longer went into a shared workplace felt like a kinship with the elderly and retired, and the medical protocols that stressed my age at every point compounded this.[7] In another way, it felt disorientatingly like youth again. This was not just part of the obvious newness of the situation to my partner and me, but also the newness of working from home by decree, and the suspicion that the new post-pandemic, post-baby future might be resistant to these small practical ways I was trying to manage it. I also realized I was feeling the loss of my more formal work wardrobe that allowed me to feel active in a professional world I enjoyed, and it was hard to not feel this as symbolic as I psychically stepped back from work each month to think more and more about the arrival of our daughter.

Even without the gaze of the public eye, though, dressing for pregnancy sometimes recalled the frustrations and body-consciousnesses of those young adult years. Jennifer P. Ogle, Keila E. Tyner, and Sherry Schofield-Tomschin write about pregnancy as a "liminal" period in a manner similar to adolescence, with a series of concomitant disruptions in identity (2013). They write of a series of interventions pregnant people make in the presentations of their identities that are centered around maternity dressing. They also use Guy and Banim's schema and find patterns of change or disruption in each category. It is the impediments to clothing used as identity signifiers they isolate that resonate most strongly with me: "disruption owing to the desire to be thrifty [for me, sustainable], disruption owing to the offerings of the contemporary maternity wear market, and disruption owing to shifts in body shape" (Ogle, Tyner, and Schofield-Tomschin 2013: 125). I should have respected that feeling of being a teenager again and should have asked my teenage self how to manage this next transition (she would have immediately suggested the small wins in trying out new looks, sewing things, dyeing things, going to thrift stores, using makeup and accessories to match your outside look with your inside mood), but instead, perhaps because of being locked down at home, I went straight to the virtual high street. Many of the maternity stockists have brand identities aimed at women much younger than myself, and here my biological age surfaced not as a resource but as a frustration; I found myself virtual-window-shopping in a world where hundreds of glossy young women with neat basketball bellies were depicted in form-fitting Lycra garments.[8] My own sense of body, of the 40-something season of life I was in, wasn't that of the imaginary carefree young mother with the neat bump, and both medical and internet accounts of the risks of motherhood over 40 primed me to notice age still more. Whatever was in my future, I felt fairly sure it wasn't the body, or even the emotional and mental style, of a 25-year-old. I wasn't even unusual in being older; the average age of a mother in England and Wales in 2019 was 30.7 years (Office for National Statistics). Despite this, the imaginary time of maternity clothing is still an idealized youth, and the models I saw seemed to me to be coyly tugging hemlines of ditsy floral dresses or playful pyjama sets in a manner that echoed the toddlers they would soon be raising. It was as if with the loss of their waists women became equated with the equally waistless shapes of babies and it was only logical to designers and marketers that we both might feel at ease in jaunty rompers, dungarees, and frills.[9]

This, too, is strangely out of time. Writing in 1980, Rebecca Lou Bailey suggested that the youthfulness of pregnancy clothing was compensatory, affirming the "innocent naivety of its wearer" in the face of visible evidence of sexuality, and, after the pronounced turn even more towards youthfulness in the 1940s, seeking to ward off the suggestion of maternity as a passage from young woman into wife, and into physical "matronliness" (1981: 36, 276). Taking Bailey's approach and reading against the styling, the body-conscious and health-inspired maternity fast fashion of our own time also offers testimony to its own opposites—a worry that motherhood will remove the pregnant person from desirable sexuality and from the public acknowledgement of that, a worry that motherhood will be harassed and unhealthy rather than yoga-calmed, and a worry that birthing a brand new human will emphasize the socially stigmatized aging of the mother's own female body and role. Maxi dresses and buffet dresses offer a world of vacation florals and prints in a time where any leisure is hard-won, and structured workwear offers reassurance that nothing will really change at a time where everything is often in flux. In this, our own time continues directly from the post-Second World War situation in which, Bailey writes, "a constant and lasting tug-of-war" developed between opposing symbolic values, as maternity garments tried both "to reveal and cover; provide an impenetrable barrier around the wearer, a safe fabric barrel, and yet convey fluffy juvenile insouciance; cater to a physically active lifestyle but one existing in a vacuum where nothing ever becomes disarranged" and "to be as stylish as ever, and at the same time totally inconspicuous" (1981: 276). The intolerable ambiguities of the pregnant body in the 2020s are contiguous with those of the eighty years previous.

The outsider status of the pregnant body did sometimes occur to me as one whose rebellion I might enjoy, and I remember a moment of defiance as the summer approached where I excitedly bought yardage of some exuberant prints, 1970s vintage style with rich colors, large patterns, and repeats. My style inspiration was to be Margot Leadbetter from the BBC 1970s sitcom *The Good Life* and I was, wonderfully, pregnant and excited, and I would wear lipstick even if I wasn't going out, damn it! I hurriedly made some wide gathered skirts to sit over my bump, seizing the opportunity to add more color and swirl to my everyday. Pregnant people on the internet, however, tend to cup their arms around their bellies, pulling in the fabric of these maxi garments and giving a misleading sense of ease. The summer of 2020 was so hot that these expanses of material actually just became hot and sticky; they didn't offer my body any protection from chafing or sweating and having to gather them in my hands as I moved didn't really help with my (equally compensatory) tidying, decluttering, and nesting. I've still got those fabrics—the gathered skirt didn't require cutting into it much—and I eye them guiltily, wondering whether mothering in the less conspicuous easy-care clothing that fits into busy days is still somehow a defeat.

Secondhand Maternity

The usual fashion cycles stopped and reformulated themselves during the pandemic, fashion weeks were paused or virtual, seasons and collections collapsed, but maternity wear is often out-of-time in other senses, too. A wardrobe of "basics" changes slowly because it takes a few years for the fashion silhouette to radically shift, but it's also striking how normal it is to keep an uncharacteristically minimal maternity wardrobe. Pregnant people claim to wear an item of clothing "to death," or to love an item of clothing so much for its comfort they "live in it" for a couple of months and rotate through very few items that fit for those few months. In one sense, this repeat wearing and distancing from the micro-trends of the fashion system is a much more sustainable way to dress. It's closer to the "slow" approach to clothing that suggests that long term use of a smaller number of items in a loved and well-worn wardrobe is a much more ethical mode of consumption. Maternity dressing might show us how it is possible to dress creatively with less. On the other hand, maternity clothing currently passes through the wardrobe very fast because of the emphasis on returning to past garments and roles. The pressure to "bounce back" to a pre-pregnancy body is often expressed as a pressure to discipline and reverse the body (hence the well-worn trope of zipping up pre-pregnancy jeans), or to return to an identity encapsulated by a pre-pregnancy wardrobe (giving up the "mom uniform"), again creating a disjunction between a past self, believed to be captured in existing clothing, and an unpredictable, perhaps still lactating or bleeding, present-time body.

As Nicky Gregson and Vikki Beale point out, maternity wear is positioned as "the other" to "ordinary clothing," and there is emotional significance to getting rid of it in a way that doesn't apply to other garments (2004: 697). The rituals they document of passing on a bin-bag of maternity clothes to friends and family lead to months of wearing colors and shapes one might not have chosen at any other time, and improvised maternity capsule wardrobes are instead records of gifts, fortuitous finds, making do, and guesses about the future self. This is more sustainable on an ecological level but doesn't have the emotional durability of long-treasured objects.[10] Secondhand maternity garments live a strange disjunctive parallel flow alongside pregnant people—they persist beyond the choices of their first wearers, their utility troubling the conventional association between identity and clothing. Pre-pregnancy clothing also has a second life in maternity as shirts are worn open, trousers extended with elastics, and dresses lifted at the waist or hem to accommodate the loss of waistline. (One of my favorite tips for adapting clothes for late pregnancy comfort came from my sister, whose midwife recommended satin pyjama bottoms so that you can slide around in bed more easily.) Unless it can easily make these transitions between eras or people, "slow" fashion, in the sense of carefully made, grown, and designed, enters a collision course here with a period of rapid psychic and bodily change, short-term wear, and competing financial demands. Although the perception of time during pregnancy is often the extended time of waiting and of anxiety, maternity itself is very fast.

My own encounter with buying maternity clothing was also complicated by trying to keep a pledge I had made a couple of years earlier to buy as little new clothing as possible for sustainability reasons. I still buy occasional new knitwear or accessories, but by and large I restrict my shopping to secondhand or remaindered sources, or to fabric for sewing. These aren't without environmental impact—there is still impact upstream of the garment, somebody else has to consume for me to re-consume secondhand, and my sewing projects use virgin yardage—but I did feel like I was doing something to withdraw my support from some of the exploitation and damage of the fashion system. Slower fashion, though, often uses the kind of tailoring and fabrics that assume a body that doesn't change through time. There's a wicked design challenge in the fact that the kinds of natural fibers that are easier to recycle, compost, or re-sew don't easily lend themselves to clothing a changing body without the extra fabric and labor costs of folds, pleats, and gathers. (Maternity clothing that does market itself as future-conscious, in the form of being ecologically conscious, often resolves this through the use of bamboo fibers. However, gendered "green guilt" and greenwashing are often bound up with these products sold as part of an imperative that mothers consume differently.) Indeed, maternity dressing, and pregnancy advice in general, felt to me as if a raft of cultural and medical forces were forcibly directing me unthinkingly towards disposability, towards considering only the present few months. There were suggestions to buy a nightgown for labor that you would throw out afterwards, to buy underwear for the postpartum period that you would throw out, and to buy cheap T-shirts and leggings for the maternity period that had just enough wear in them for the second half of pregnancy and a few weeks after giving birth. These went alongside disposable underwear, disposable sanitary pads, disposable breast pads, disposable teats, nappies, wipes, and tiny-baby clothing cheap enough to throw out if the stains did not lift. The message here is that early parenthood is too exhausting for laundry (which is true, especially if you are alone for that period) but also that the bodily stuff of labor and birth, and by extension, maternity, are irredeemably outside the usual order of things; uncleanable, unsafe, and taboo.

Despite the evenings I spent window-shopping on the internet, I decided to keep my sustainability pledge. I discovered maternity and baby clothing rental very late in my pregnancy, so my maternity wardrobe was a palimpsest of compromises, makes, and exciting finds. In this way, I also reflect Ogle, Tyner, and Schofield-Tomschin's analysis as they use Kevina Cody and Katrina Lawlor's theory of liminal consumption, derived from "tween" shoppers, to suggest "the possibility of both vexing and empowering outcomes for liminal consumers" (Ogle, Tyner, and Schofield-Tomschin 2013: 121) Being between clear social categories can result in "frustration, confusion, and invisibility within the marketplace," but it can also inspire "'fruitful' consumption activities that reflect agency and ambition" (ibid.). I had my nursing tops, some gifted by a generous friend, others secondhand from a Swedish brand that another friend had recommended for their soft fabric and innovative cut, and after trial and error I found a pair of thrifted jeans that didn't hurt in my second trimester. I realized that my usual secondhand brand of T-shirts would serve if I bought two sizes bigger, and that many of my button-up shirts could be worn open. My most exciting moments were as a sewist, when finally things fitted, and finally it felt like there was a passable congruence between what I felt inside and what I looked like outside. This is in keeping with the conclusions of Addie Martindale and Ellen McKinney, who note that for dressmakers, wardrobe satisfaction often grows with the number of self-made garments (2020). I was able to adapt a non-maternity sewing pattern for elasticated trousers to give me two pairs of trousers in colors and fabrics that mirrored the ones I chose pre-pregnancy, and I made a ruched maternity T-shirt and a new set of underwear. I also sewed plain pyjama bottoms in black and navy to wear in the heat of the summer daytime, by which time I had reached "watermelon" stage; by the end of maternity these me-made garments were the only ones that fit. I also bought large men's lambswool and merino jumpers in five or six rich colors to keep me warm through the winter when our daughter was born. For nursing I turned camisoles around back-to-front and used the information another friend pointed me to on the website "Can I Breastfeed in It?" to return postpartum to "normal" tops with camisoles to shield my stomach.

Conclusion

Some of these maternity clothes I still wear, some I've given back to charity shops, but looking back on it now, I'm struck by how similar my solutions were to the ways I tried to manage the monumental changes of adolescence, and how at odds this is with a linear sense of time, age, and propriety. There was a substantial amount of refusing clothes too, as there was in my teen years. In Guy and Banim's terms, I had quite a strong sense of the woman I didn't want to be, and that was one who was tired, anxious, uncomfortable, and self-conscious. (Of course, these fears are all markers of shadow-feelings; perhaps one only fights being tired or anxious or uncomfortable this hard when they are ever-present threats.) When I started meditating on writing this essay while I was pregnant, I thought it might perhaps be about a "liminal" in-between period, as Ogle, Tyner, and Schofield-Tomschin's work surmises, but now, working from home with a one-year-old daughter in daycare, it seems more like a transitional one. The navigation of uncertainty through attention to dress and the turn away from more formal shapes and woven fabrics towards casualwear and stretch, knit fabrics all continue as part of new hybrid working environments and work-from-home days. What I thought of as the throughgoing physicality of pregnancy continues into the present with the bodily demands of being mum to an energetic and assertive toddler. Some of my maternity wardrobe is also my new-mum wardrobe, and although some garments have lasted for over a year (and many will last much longer in the sense of not wearing out) I'm still feeling a little sense of lag here, as my body has changed again but those men's jumpers have not caught up with my smaller post-baby body. My formal trousers fit differently than they used to, and I'm still trying to work out whether I can feel comfortable again in them. Maternity clothing points to a transient time, but it's hard to determine the nature and duration of that transience when you are living through it, and it's hard to find mental space from which to evaluate that transience once you are responsible for another person.

The first piece of clothing I bought as a new mother after my daughter was born was a waterproof anorak with a hood, a garment I had ignored pre-parenthood in favor of umbrellas and more tailored winter coats. On our very first walk in the winter drizzle, though, when my daughter was about a month old, I realized quickly I couldn't hold an umbrella and push the pram safely. I also realized that because motion reliably sent my little one to sleep there were enough bad-weather walks in my future to need a mac for the first time in years. I wasn't sure exactly what my own version of "dressing as a mum" or dressing to mother might be, but as I got more and more rained upon it became clear that it was linked to clothing that required less maintenance but was also more in tune with my new unexpectedly and relentlessly physical job as parent. My coat needed to be one tolerant of water and movement and coffee or milk splashes, that was swift to take on and off and to bundle under the buggy if weather improved or if I needed to nurse in a cafe, that freed up my hands, and that took me firmly into the active and outdoors world. My coat also needed, I decided, to be a bright color—a yellow, red, or orange—to give me a visual lift out of the sleeplessness and relentlessness of new motherhood and to remind me a little more of the fun and the play.

Nowadays, I don't always notice this to-and-fro because since my daughter was born my attention has become even more outer-directed—the time of mothering is a constant present—but I still feel it during the cracks between work and parenting. At these times, there's still much in the theatre of femininity

I feel temporarily divested from as a new mother and as a person living through a pandemic. I remember the day I put on large hoop earrings and lipstick as a kind of celebration of going out for coffee after lockdown had ended: the mask smudged my lipstick and my earrings got caught in its straps. I'm still estranged from scarves and large jewelry because my daughter will pull on them, and although I would like to dress with a little more everyday drama again, her bossy tugs win out. I now also realize, again through estrangement, the extent to which I like my clothes to be a little resistant, or to rustle a little as I move, or to prop my body with a firm fabric, or to act on my proprioception with seams and panels to nudge my posture into more upright forms. I'm even more aware now that these kinds of shapes and fabrics are more costly, that they are the ones that require me to choose to spend valuable non-work time ironing, and that these clothes are ones that don't move aside easily to nurse, or to carry a baby on my hip or in a sling. Nevertheless, I still miss them, and am wondering whether it's possible for me to broker a compromise between personal decoration and utility. Despite all the signals that the near future is a casual one, there is still a sense of excitement and hope for me in dressing for encounter.

Notes

1 There is a significant amount of scholarship emerging on the altered perception of time in the Global North during the pandemic. See, for example, Grondin, Mendoza-Duran, and Rioux (2020).

2 My own situation was and is a privileged one. I had a full-time permanent job as an academic that paid me through the pandemic and through a good proportion of my maternity leave, and I benefit from the UK's free-to-access National Health Service. The meditations in this essay are those which depend on a base of safety in healthcare, and in the social and financial realms, and these are unfortunately not even close to being representative of the wider pandemic experience. Still, I hope that the focus on dress I can bring here, albeit from my place of relative safety, may be of use when thinking through the role of clothing in a personal and national period of uncertainty.

3 See Lauren Downing Peters' chapter elsewhere in this volume for a reconsideration of the Victorian maternal image.

4 For an in-depth exploration of the ways in which pregnant people feel, negotiate, and respond to the social gaze at their growing and changing bodies, see Nash (2012). The sense of surveillance of motherhood continues with the domination of Instagram- and Pinterest-hosted models of ideal parenting and femininity.

5 Sophie Woodward's classic *Why Women Wear What They Wear* (2007) is excellent on the ways in which dress choice is made with a mind to anticipating future social situations.

6 See Abnett (2015).

7 For a welcome intervention in the taken-for-granted invisibility of elder dressing strategies, see Julia Twigg's work, particularly *Fashion and Age: Dress, the Body and Later Life* (2013).

8 *Business of Fashion* reports that many women "downgrade their clothes shopping from higher-end brands during pregnancy," and that "mainly married women over 35 shop predominantly at Topshop and H&M during pregnancy, despite not being in these retailers' usual younger, value-led demographic." In recent years, this mainstream market has stretched to include online value retailer ASOS, again, aimed at a much younger market than the average 30-something new mother (Abnett 2015).

9 Looking back on it now, I realize that there were other people, and other non-corporate blogs, magazines, and social media accounts, offering other versions of motherhood, but I didn't think of this during lockdown. I also wonder whether the background seriousness of the pandemic was feeding my frustration with the mandatory cheerfulness of much maternity wear.

10 See Chapman (2005).

References

Abnett, K. (2015), "Could Rental Businesses Fix the Maternity Fashion Market?," *Business of Fashion*, December 7. Available online: https://www.businessoffashion.com/articles/retail/could-rental-businesses-fix-the-maternity-fashion-market/ (accessed December 1, 2021).

Bailey, R. L. (1981), "Fashions in Pregnancy: An Analysis of Selected Cultural Influences, 1850–1980," PhD diss., Michigan State University.

Beverly, B. (2021), "How to Dress a Moving Target," *Fashion Studies Journal*, 7. Available online: https://www.fashionstudiesjournal.org/fashion-motherhood-3 (accessed December 1, 2021).

"Can I Breastfeed in It?" Available online: https://cibii.co.uk/ (accessed December 1, 2021).

Carter, M. (2017), *Being Prepared: Aspects of Dress and Dressing*. Sydney: Puncher and Wattman.

Chapman, J. (2005), *Emotionally Durable Design: Objects, Experiences and Empathy*. London: Earthscan.

Entwistle, J. and E. Wissinger (2021), "Dress Like a Mum/Mom: Instagram Style Mums and the Fashionable Ideal," *Fashion Theory* 27 (1): 5–42. Doi: 10.1080/1362704X.2021.1934326.

Green, E. (2001), "Suiting Ourselves: Women Professors Using Clothes to Signal Authority," in A. Guy, E. Green, and M. Banim (eds.), *Through the Wardrobe: Women's Relationships with Their Clothes*. Oxford: Berg. Doi: 10.2752/9781847888921?locatt=l abel:secondary_bloomsburyFashionCentral.

Gregson, N. and V. Beale (2004), "Wardrobe Matter: The Sorting, Displacement and Circulation Of Women's Clothing," *Geoforum*, 35 (6): 689–700.

Grondin, S., E. Mendoza-Duran, and P.-A. Rioux (2020), "Pandemic, Quarantine, and Psychological Time," *Frontiers in Psychology*, 11:581036. Doi: 10.3389/ fpsyg.2020.581036.

Guy, A. and M. Banim (2000), "Personal Collections: Women's Clothing Use and Identity," *Journal of Gender Studies*, 9 (3): 313–27. Doi: 10.1080/713678000.

Guy, A., E. Green, and M. Banim, eds. (2001), *Through The Wardrobe: Women's Relationships with Their Clothes*. Oxford: Berg. Doi: 10.2752/9781847888921?locatt=l abel:secondary_bloomsburyFashionCentral.

Martindale, A. and E. McKinney (2020), "Self-Sewn Identity: How Female Home Sewers Use Garment Sewing to Control Self-Presentation," *Journal of Consumer Culture*, 20 (4): 563–77. Doi: 10.1177/1469540518764238.

Nash, M. (2012), *Making "Postmodern" Mothers: Pregnant Embodiment, Baby Bumps and Body Image*. Houndmills and New York: Palgrave Macmillan. http://site.ebrary.com/ id/10621888 (accessed December 18, 2021).

Office for National Statistics (2019), "Birth Characteristics for England and Wales: 2019." Available online: https://www.ons.gov.uk/peoplepopulationandcommunity/ birthsdeathsandmarriages/livebirths/bulletins/ birthcharacteristicsinenglandandwales/2019 (accessed December 10, 2021).

Ogle, J. P., K. E. Tyner, and S. Schofield-Tomschin (2013), "The Role of Maternity Dress Consumption in Shaping the Self and Identity during the Liminal Transition of Pregnancy," *Journal of Consumer Culture*, 13 (2): 119–39. Available online: Doi: 10.1177/1469540513480161.

Snelgrove, L. (2021), "Fashion & Motherhood: A Letter from the Editor," *Fashion Studies Journal*, 7. Available online: https://www.fashionstudiesjournal.org/fashion-motherhood-3 (accessed December 1, 2021).

Spivack, E. (2014), *Worn Stories*. New York: Princeton Architectural Press.

Twigg, J. (2013), *Fashion and Age: Dress, the Body and Later Life*. London: Bloomsbury.

Woodward, S. (2007), *Why Women Wear What They Wear*. New York: Berg.

13

"Ole Rag 'n' Lumber"

Intergenerational, Gendered, and Classed Relationships with Clothing from Rag 'n' Bone to Depop

Liza Betts

This essay explores intergenerational, gendered, and classed relationships with dress, clothing, and dressing practices through a combination of anecdotal narrative, material culture analysis, oral history, and critical analysis. It presents a journey through four generations of women in the same family from East London, from a twentieth-century "rag-and-bone" merchant to a contemporary teen using virtual resale clothing platforms such as Depop.

The narratives are deeply personal; they contextualize individual items of clothing while revealing wider histories of gendered class formations, lived experience, and the fluid manifestations of class consciousness. Audre Lorde comments on the transformative power of exploring the self and the experiences we have been subjected to:

> As they become known to and accepted by us, our feelings, and the honest exploration of them, become sanctuaries and spawning grounds for the most radical and daring of ideas. They become a safe house for that difference so necessary to change and the conceptualization of any meaningful action.
>
> [1984] 2007: 26

Through explicit subject positioning, it is hoped that this writing may give voice to the invisible and will therefore change the perception and understanding of a particular set of lived class experiences. Importantly, the narratives make visible implicit moments of contestation (Lefebvre 1968) that exist in engagement with dress and fashion, as well as the practices of dressing politicized bodies and how such moments, often imperceptible, can and often do take place against the backdrop of the mother–daughter relationship, an idea that has been explored in previous chapters of this book, including those by Darnell Jamal-Lisby and Kimberly Lamm.

The work is written as an example of a "patchwork text" (Scoggins and Winter 1999); it incorporates anecdotal narrative as well as critical analysis of class experiences. Each of the four narratives can be read as a separate essay but when patched together the sections form a personally informed and poignant overview of the development of class experience in London for women (in particular, mothers) across the latter part of the twentieth century and the early part of the twenty-first. This approach "brings to the fore the political issues embedded in writing styles" and is seen "as a tool for the study of those that are multiply marginalized" (Ilmonen 2019: 13).

The four generations examined are the author's paternal grandmother, Eliza, the author's mother, Sheila, the author, Liza, and the author's daughter, Maia. The narratives begin in the poverty-stricken immediate post-war period in the UK and end with contemporary teenage engagement with reuse and online recycled clothing platforms. They contain analysis of transient identity formations that emerge as a result of engagement with material culture and are embedded in an imagined past, saturated in a sensory "present," but simultaneously speak to an idealized future.

A mixed-method approach is used, combining oral histories that document the direct experiences of three of the four narratives. Ethnographic research has been employed in the form of extended qualitative interviews. It is suggested that the type of narrative and lived experience under examination rarely features in academic writing in the way presented here, via the lens of acknowledged subjective forces and informed by interwoven lived experience. As Nathan Connolly comments,

> the closer you get to the bottom the more likely you will find marginalized communities and social exclusion and the less likely you are to find writing that speaks of these lives written by the writers who live it.
>
> 2017: 64

Eliza

Eliza Betts was my paternal grandmother—a woman who died before I was born but who has been a constant presence throughout my life. Eliza was born in 1915 into poverty in East London; she married young and had had eight children before she was 31.

In the mid-to-late 1940s, one of Eliza's jobs was rag-and-bone merchant. Rag-and-bone merchants were collectors of old clothes or textiles, and historically, old bones, which were resold to make glue.

Against the backdrop of post-war shortages and clothing rationing in the UK Eliza would walk an area of around 40 streets, collecting used clothing and pieces of cloth or textiles in an old pram. She would return home with the "rags" and would divide them; some would be identified as good enough for resale, and these would be washed and ironed or pressed, predominantly by her children. Some would be identified as useful to clothe the children or herself and they too would be washed and pressed. The items that had been marked out for resale were taken to local, more affluent residential locations and resold. She was well known in the areas in which she resold the textiles as having a good eye for "quality" items that would satisfy the complex sartorial taste systems at play within this particular context of consumption (systems that have always extracted more than just function from the garments circulated). Brooks employs a poignant quote from Adam Smith dated from 1776 in his 2015 book *Clothing Poverty*: "the old clothes which another bestows on him he exchanges for other old clothes that suit him better" (Smith 1776, quoted in Brooks 2015: 77), which speaks to the often-ignored selection practices and concept of sartorial choice or formations of taste employed by consumers of discarded items.

The saying "ole rag 'n' lumber" (meaning old clothes or textiles and lumber, a term encompassing any or all other types of items that might be discarded) is what she would call out as she walked the streets collecting the textiles, and my father has a vivid memory of hearing her call, her voice, traveling, meandering, and winding its way into his school building through open windows while he sat with his friends in class. There was no shame attached to the recognition of her voice and the purpose and meaning it conveyed; all the children in the class were in the same social position and suffering poverty at similar levels. They were experiencing what Paul Dave explains as a "consolidated collective identity" (Dave, quoted in Ashby and Higson 2000: 349), embodying resistance in the form of ambivalence, refusing to entertain middle-class narratives of embarrassment or shame but rather gaining strength and identity through subtle defiance. As Baudrillard comments, "their strength is actual, in the present, it exists in their silence, in the ability to absorb and neutralise, they are superior to any power acting on them" ([1981] 1994: 3).

Eliza's narrative is simultaneously poignant and empowering and can be explored in a number of important ways that speak to the tension that exists within and throughout writing on social class in the UK. The laboring body that

Eliza inhabited has not often been represented in the same way as the heroic industrial working-class male was and still is. Often, constructed histories present female manual or physical work as occurring at unique social, cultural, or political moments—for example, the use of female labor during the First and Second World Wars. Alternatively, they present much broader theoretical discourses such as feminist perspectives on the developing role of women in society or the exploitative feminized labor of historical and contemporary fashion production; however, the broad nature of these areas of study means individual narratives are often omitted.

With the focus on the heroic male laboring body and its relationship to traditional industrial heritage in the UK, the work of women has been reduced to a supporting role that was/is often confined to the domestic sphere, as Williamson, Beynon, and Rowbotham comment: "only a particular kind of labour is usually focused on. Millions of different jobs that people do all over the place never seem to feature" (2001:101).

In reality, women from the lower classes have always had to engage with hard physical labor—and still do, alongside the men and children. The labor engaged with, despite familiar narratives to the contrary, is diverse, requires a myriad of skills and knowledge, and, importantly, exists in a space beyond the reductive ternary of sex worker, cleaner/servant, or factory worker. The social knowledge employed by Eliza in order to both buy and sell successfully exists within a system outside legitimized or valued knowledge systems, particularly within the context of the late 1940s, a period that predates the fashion for shopping "vintage," a practice much more familiar within contemporary fashion consumption.

After the Second World War the feminizing of the laboring body became problematic within mainstream society and was viewed as a dangerous ingredient in the breakdown of traditional family structures and hierarchies identified by sociological functionalists as imperative for society to operate successfully (Bynder 1969; Murdock 1949; Parsons 1959). Clearly the concern here was for the middle-class female laboring body. There was a conscious desire to re-position that type of female body back within the domestic sphere and identify those types of women once more as inactive, rather than productive, members of society with a decorative function or as embodied evidence of a successful man via conspicuous consumption (Veblen [1899] 1994). Christian Dior's New Look is often pointed to as an example of this dynamic in fashion history.

Eliza's body was not marked out as fashionable, valuable, desirable, or subject to regulation in the same way as other female bodies because of the class position she occupied. As Walkerdine, Lucey, and Melody write, the painful recognition of otherness marked on the body, felt by working class women, a feeling of less or lacking that had to be managed or whether concealed or revealed demonstrates that working class subjects know exactly how they are positioned.

2001: 42

Eliza and many other women like her were, and continue to be, subject to narratives of disgust (Lawler 2005a, 2008; Skeggs 2004, 2005) or produced as socially deficient (Haylett 2001). The work Eliza did and the way she used her body to do it is subject to continuing prejudices that deal not least with the notion of hygiene. Her body occupies two distinct realms of physicality often attributed to the working class. In the first realm, working-class bodies are seen as the repositories of middle-class fears; they are often labeled as socially deficient, lacking value, undisciplined, and unhygienic (Lawler 2005a; Skeggs 2004; Walkerdine, Lucey, and Melody 2001). A parallel realm exists, wherein in order to receive any form of acknowledgment or limited forms of respect, experiences such as Eliza's must embody the pain, struggle, and suffering of the authentic and heroic (male) laborer (Lawler 2005b, 2008). To exist in both spaces, as Eliza and many other women did and still do, requires the skill of absorbing the affect associated with the explicit and implicit injuries of class (Sennett and Cobb 1972) and the devaluing of women's role in society.

As a result of Eliza's gender and circumstances, she can be thought of as an example of an individualized working-class self that is denied a visible existence (Casey 2010). Identity, as Skeggs (2005) argues, is not a concept we all have equal access to; for some within society, identity is something imposed upon them by others in order to maintain boundaries and privilege. Those who do not have access to the means by which identity is managed become subject to the power relationships embedded within social knowledge and the implosive violence it produces.

Eliza's identity is inextricably linked to the work she had to do. She was defined and categorized by it; her voice literally spoke to and of it. The gap between who Eliza was and who she was allowed to be is where understandings about the working classes are formed, maintained, and have managed to preserve oppressions that privilege experiential distance. As Skeggs comments, "struggles with personhood have a long history tied to classifications" (2005: 121). Here the struggle exists both internally via common negotiations with the self and externally as social, cultural, political, and economic factors conspire to construct identities on behalf of those denied a self: "self-narration is linked to the idea of character or personhood where only the bourgeoisie are capable of being an individual" (ibid., 124). The middle-class voyeuristic lens through which working class identities are often constructed or articulated routinely misinterprets, misrepresents, or omits altogether great swathes of nuanced class experience, including that of motherhood. Maintaining the self as we negotiate motherhood is a complex and difficult process; individual roles, priorities, and interests will inevitably change as part of an unavoidable morphing from "I" to "we." When this process is experienced by the marginalized, who are part of a system of hierarchy that prohibits some from fully expressing or developing the self, the notion of a compromised narrated self is rendered simultaneously both more meaningful from a middle-class perspective and meaningless from the point of view of the marginalized.

Sheila

Sheila was born in East London in 1939; she was the eldest of three children born to LMF—Little Maggie Frappell—and "Alf," or Alfred. The family were not well off but there was work and a regular income for Alfred in the docks of the East End and Margaret (Maggs) bore and raised her children stoically to understand that family was a concept to be respected, preserved, and maintained against external forces, above all else.

Sheila was/is an intelligent girl/woman; she had ambitions of becoming a police officer. Unfortunately, her family, and her father in particular, forbade this career choice and so Sheila settled for various low-skilled roles in retail, light industry, and admin before becoming a dental nurse. Work, for those of the working classes, often circumnavigates the concepts of "career" or "choice" and becomes much more about what is available, offering a fair salary for a fair day's work, and for women, particularly within the context of the 1960s and 1970s in the UK, what is manageable in relation to whatever domestic responsibilities or children they may have.

Sheila is my mother. We have a very difficult relationship.

The relationship is difficult because we are so very different and yet so very similar. We are born of different times; we have different understandings of what it is to be a woman and a mother, yet in many ways we are one. My mother became a woman against the backdrop of shifting class and gender formations in the UK in the post-war period; the shifts left a residue of internalized conflict to complement the conflicts produced socially and culturally. She exists on the theoretical periphery of feminism but her lived experience is evidence of feminism in action. She has a strong voice that will not be quieted, and she lives life according to her own individual boundaries and moral codes—a feminist, surely! Yet, in many ways she is anti-woman, always a critical commentator, offering judgements, not necessarily support, and holding women to a higher standard than male counterparts, often apportioning blame and shame. She has taught me many things—how to be a woman and why I will not be a woman like her. Yet, I love my mother.

The discussion here focuses on a particular item of clothing that was important to her as a young woman. In the mid-1950s, when she was 17, she and her friend designed and made her a skirt. What is interesting about this object is that it was intended to very clearly mark my mother out as different. The skirt was full, in line with Dior's aesthetic introduced as the previous decade had drawn to a close. It was of a navy-blue, mid-weight wool and had a "grown-on," higher than was usual waistband, with shoulder straps that were attached to the front and back of the skirt—a pinafore of sorts. She wore the skirt a lot, and she holds familiar and warm memories of it still.

The mid-to-late 1940s and early 1950s were a time of change within the class systems and structures of the United Kingdom as a result of the development and increasing popularity of post-war socialism. The working classes had begun to feel valued and legitimized. However, the conservative governments from 1951 to 1964 had reimposed ideas of privilege and hierarchy and subjected the population to them once more; these ideas distorted the evolution of working-class consciousness and became layered upon and within class experience.

The class divisions reinforced in the UK at this time were clear and continued to be focused on a narrow, prescriptive, and easily managed set of markers, such as money, education, or employment. As Savage remarks, "boundaries could be clearly marked through salary and wages in the 50s and 60s, so it was easier to know who you and others were" (2015: 211).

Interestingly, this point in history, in which class markers were being reinforced politically and culturally, is also viewed as a moment where in some contexts, economic symbolism and the obvious display of wealth was becoming less desirable, while the value of authentic "working class-ness" was gaining value and traction. This is often seen through a shift in the focus of representations (Williamson, Beynon and Rowbotham 2001) within theater, popular cinema, and literature that drew on the narratives and interior tragedy of class struggles; for example, *Saturday Night and Sunday Morning* (Allan Sillitoe 1958), *Look Back in Anger* (John Osborne 1956), and *A Taste of Honey* (Shelagh Delaney

1958). Class struggle may have been fashionable at this time but clearly, for many
still experiencing the daily privations of a harsh working-class existence, those
representations were visible articulations of a struggle they were not given the
tools to either articulate, embrace, or resist (commissioning and publishing were
managed by the middle classes, as remains the case today). As such, they
reinforced the experience of class etched into the psyche (Raey 2017) that carried
with it the endemic heavy burden of shame (Connolly 2017; Sayer 2005).

My mother's experiences of the self and her awareness of her position and
value sit atop the tension described. At a time when the working classes were
being told to embrace their experiences, she was eager to step aside from them.
For her, bespoke clothing choices were deliberately sought out to position her as
respectable and aspirational and to generate the possibility of achievements that
would practically, if not theoretically, move her away from the confines of the
social class that she felt restricted her.

In order to do this, she needed to mark herself as sartorially different and set
a boundary of distinction between herself and others like her. She was attempting
to transition from "difference" to "distinction." Difference here is understood via
the work of the Marxist scholar Henri Lefebvre as a concept that organizes and
categorizes (within groups) and creates hierarchies. Distinction is a stage further
than difference; it separates, marks boundaries, and produces a distance that is
impossible to traverse (Lefebvre 2005).

Sheila was aware of the power woven into the value system of clothing. She
was simultaneously expressing a different type of taste, one that is part of the
working-class system of value and cannot be separated from her subjective
positioning, and one that was renouncing that same position. She was defying
her own existence through sartorial difference; as Baudrillard explains, "defiance
comes from that with no name or meaning, it is defiance of existence" ([1981]
1994: 70).

For groups that are often understood through the broad strokes of collective
categorization, the right to difference, let alone distinction, is not always available.
Lefebvre states that,

> it is not easy to grasp the paradox, which eludes all reductionist thinking,
> whereby the homogenous covers and contains the fragmented, making room for
> a strict hierarchization.

2005: 84

My mother desired and attempted to claim the right to difference through her
choice of the skirt. For her, the desire to mark a separation from other members

of the working classes was key to her identity. She would not and still will not consider shopping from the vintage/resale/charity/secondhand market; to do so would be to admit a lack of achievement, success, or improvement in social position. Buying new and not relying on others' "castoffs" was a sign of progress and respectability. The desire and ability to buy new, often expensive, bespoke, or rigorously sourced items made the precarious nature of her position or experiences opaque, or so she believed.

Culturally, socially, and financially my mother remains working class. Ironically, her inability to transcend the negative associations she has inscribed to particular forms of consumption re-positions her firmly back in the realm of the working class. As Sartre states,

> by projecting ourselves towards the possibility to escape the contradictions of our existence, we reveal who we are and enter another realm of contradictions, thus at the same time that we surpass our class, our class identity is made manifest.
>
> 1968: 100

It is her awareness of the fine line that balances existence or experiences, how potent certain actions, behaviors, or symbols are or can be within the realms of hierarchized difference, and how easily one can slip and fall to the wrong side of the line—the precarious nature of "being" or owning identity when experienced through working-class experience—that fixes her position and prohibits any form of conceptual if not practical social mobility. The anxiety around such precarity that Sheila feels and how she understands fashion, dress, or clothing to play such a key role in our position on the right or wrong side of the line of difference is a familiar aspect of class experience. My mother, in her uniquely blunt way, educated me about this through her own anxiety and inadvertently opened my eyes to the sartorial or identity-forming oppressions faced by girls like me and women like her. For her, there was no viable alternative; for me, there was resistance. Hopefully, as my daughter develops into a woman, resistance evolves into a defiant refusal to accept.

Liza

I was born in East London in 1971, the third child of Bill and Sheila. For as long as I can remember there has been both a disconnect and a connection to my family, my siblings, and my mother. This was the result of a tangible sense of acceptance, belonging and togetherness, and difference, of being "apart" and also "a part" of a group, a family. The notion of family as a means of support and protection was instilled in us by our parents for whom the family unit must/should be preserved and maintained at all costs. This is a necessity for survival and a reflection of the precarity of everyday working-class lived experience.

My connection and disconnection with my mother has a long, and at times painful, history. We are connected through the concept of care; as a younger child I endured a number of years of invasive medical treatment, and my mother steered me and supported me through this. She championed my achievements and fought for me at every turn. But she never understood me. She still does not understand me. Now, I find myself caring for my mother as she ages, and her body begins to yield; I steer her through the days and fight for her to have the retirement she desires and deserves.

My politics and my mother's general rejection of politics separate us, and yet our experiences of being working-class women and mothers ultimately bind us together. I feel as though my class consciousness has developed in part because of what she is and what she is not, what she has taught me and what I have had to teach myself so that I can understand who I am, and how I am understood and positioned in the society of which I am a part.

The anecdotal narratives drawn upon here speak to both the connection and the separations that exist between us in relation to clothing and fashion, but they exist as a result of the conflict and tension that defines our mother-daughter relationship—a tension that sits at the intersection of identity politics and being.

In my last year of primary school, aged 11, I needed a new coat. The year 1981 was a period of political, cultural, and social conflict within the UK; the country was three years into the first term of the divisive and problematic political reign of Margaret Thatcher. Inflation was at 9 percent and unemployment at 10 percent—the highest it had been for over fifty years. The country was about to go to war with Argentina over the remote Falkland Islands and there were civil and race riots in many major UK cities. In the area of East London where I grew up and within the milieu of youth styles, a particular fashion object became very popular—the oxblood leather box blazer: single breasted with one button fastening, a straight hem, and narrow lapels. This clothing object could be/was employed in a chameleon style by many of the youth cultures of the time. It spoke to a dangerous, subversive aesthetic with a value system different to the mainstream. It was confrontational, rock-and-roll cool, and gender neutral. I wanted one of my own.

My mum refused to buy me one of the jackets.

Instead, she bought me a powder blue, soft leather "safari"-style jacket. It had a zip front, elasticized waist, stand collar, and four slanted zipped pockets. It was different in every stylistic element. The motivation for this decision that was communicated to me was the importance of difference, of standing out, not following the crowd. Why, she asked, did I want to be like everyone else? No, she said, I needed something that would make me visible and mark me as different. Of course, as a shy 11-year-old, I didn't want to stand out or be visible. I wanted to fit in, maintain my invisible status, gain access to the fluid and transient world of "cool" and, importantly, feel as though I belonged. It was only when I reflected on this episode recently that I saw the congruence between my mother's actions, her own sartorial experiences as a teen, and the motivations and the social politics of Thatcher, the mawkish individualism and anti-collectivism of the evolving neoliberal agenda.

Later in the mid-1980s, as a 15-year-old, my sense of self and my confidence had developed. I had embraced the notion of difference, I no longer wanted to be just like everyone else, my interests were developing and evolving away from the local and national mainstream ideas, and I used clothing as a way to communicate this. On one occasion, my friend and I went on a Saturday shopping trip to London's Covent Garden and, as you do with teenage friends, we bought matching pairs of used Levi's jeans from the shop American Classics. There was a nostalgic nod to the 1950s and Americana within popular fashion and music at the time in London, and my friend and I wanted to reference this.

We returned home excited and victorious and planned, as teenagers often do, to wear our matching Levi's to a local club that evening.

My mother was having none of it.

In fact, when I showed my mum what I had bought, her rage and frustration were incandescent. She was so angered she decided to march me back up to the shop in Covent Garden—a 50-minute journey on the London tube. Completely misunderstanding the concept, purpose, and appeal of the shop, she complained that the staff had knowingly deceived a child and sold them used goods and she (to my horror) demanded a refund from the cool and amused cashier.

Within this moment of embarrassment my relationship with my mother fractured. This was at a time where the cultural turn towards individual experience and expression was gaining traction (Byrne 2005), but I was denied my own individual sartorial expression by a woman who had not only told me this was important a few years earlier but who I later came to learn had claimed her own through her style choices. The difference between us, as well as my mother's concept of individuality, was embodied in the threads of the jeans and my mother's working-class shame. I understood, as an angry and disillusioned teen, that style distinctions are not simply a product of class difference (Ashby and Higson 2000) but that within class experience individual aesthetic choices are made that conceptually transcend social position. As Casey comments, there is "no straightforward relationship between consumption and social position" (2010: 231).

What I have come to understand is that, as Forrest explains, "class has an interactive relationship with space" (2017: 39). We all have a relationship with historical space; my mother's relationship with social class is different to mine because the relationships emerged during different historical periods. During the mid-1950s class was seen as a possession to be discarded or rejected in order to achieve the idealized social mobility and distance from the hidden injuries and suffering experienced by many of the working class, including my grandmother. In the mid-1980s, class distinctions were being redrawn as the gap between the haves and the have-nots widened, while propaganda reframed the fable of mobility to convince some it had been achieved—for example, the "right to buy" social housing scheme in the UK. At the same time, particularly in the industrial heartlands of the UK, entire communities and generations were cast adrift. The historical space within which we emerge as social beings, as women, defines us in ways it can take a lifetime to process or understand.

In addition to the relationship with historical time, class has an interactive relationship to the conceptual space of the mind where identities are formed. Henri Lefebvre claims that contestation begins from negation (1968); to contest class position conceptually one has to understand and experience class as a negation. Growing up in Thatcher's Britain of the 1980s and during my time in the film and television industries in the 1990s, I was made well aware of the problematic ways the working class was produced through representations that had little or nothing to do with my own experiences of class, gender, and dressing.

My experience of social class and the conceptual formation of my constantly evolving class identity is the space where my ideas about fashion and dress have emerged. These ideas own my grandmother's struggle, understand yet reject my mother's motivations, and claim a space to empower and value different ways of being (Skeggs 2004) outside legitimized and reductive systems of discrimination and control. This is the experience of being working class that I hope to pass onto my daughters.

Maia

Maia is my daughter. Born fifteen years ago, she changed my life forever. We are close, I think, I hope. In my mind I understand her; we discuss her hopes and dreams for the future, her fears, her anxieties. I support and love her unconditionally. I try to stand in her shoes and understand what life is like now for girls who are growing into women in the digital age. The world has changed significantly and I'm approaching the point where the shifts occur too fast for me to process, but Maia teaches me. I also have another daughter, Mirielle, and I marvel constantly at how the girls can be so different in character and temperament. I have an equally powerful connection and conversations with Miri, but her interests are very different to her sister's.

Maia loves clothes. She asked for a subscription to *Vogue* as a Christmas present aged 12; she understands form, design, and color. She is astute and informed in relation to historical references and contemporary discourses around dress, fashion, and identity. She is developing her own sense of style and refuses to blindly follow the crowd; she is happy to mark herself as different and stand by her convictions.

She has a determined and single-minded streak and from a very early age knew what she did and did not want to wear. She defiantly refused to wear the uniform shoes when she started nursery school—it took the nursery staff more than a week to gently coax her out of the colorful Wellington boots she preferred and into the black Mary Janes. She has at times driven me to distraction as she wrangles with the sensory relationship she has with materials; seams and fabrics had to feel right and be positioned correctly for her body and if they were not, she would refuse to wear the item, often leaving an exasperated and panicked me thinking, "what do I do?"

As she grew older, and her body began to develop, our conflicts centered around what was "appropriate" or not to wear. I found myself face-to-face with the embodied third- and fourth-wave feminist mantra of *choice*. Part of me supported this. I wanted to be able to champion her choices and encourage her desire to express herself in whatever way she wanted to, but I was also terrified. I had to help her understand the rules of the game women are still expected to play—a game we did not choose with rules not of our making. We mourned together the curbs to her expressive freedom that women across the globe find themselves powerless to control.

Maia also wrangles with her class position. She is aware of her own privileges and also of the oppressions she continues to encounter. She understands that both her and my experiences speak to the idea of class in transition (Williamson, Beynon, and Rowbotham 2001) and that working-class identities can be and often are confusing as boundaries become continually blurred (Casey 2010; Connolly 2017). She knows her family history, the stories of the women who preceded her and the spaces they occupied within society, the work they did, and the experiences they were subject to. She understands that familial history plays a part in how class consciousness and class identity develop and evolve. Despite the economic or social advances that have been made, the histories that live within us still play a part in determining where we think we belong. Her mother may be an academic, but she is a working-class academic. She is also very aware of how class inequality is constantly re-made (Haylett 2001) and reframed via the symbolic notion of taste that is frequently applied to fashion, clothing, and dressing practices.

My daughter's relationship with clothes has distilled down into a conscious form of consumption. As Palmer and Clark comment, "Second-hand clothing industries exist worldwide, predicated on excess production of clothing and a market for reusing worn clothes" (Palmer and Clark 2005: 3). A large part of what Maia consumes comes from the resale market: charity shops, "retro" boutiques, and online resale platforms such as Depop and Vinted. Her relationship with secondhand or used clothing is unapologetic. There is no shame, disgust, or denial. She uses the relationship to claim her right to difference (Lefebvre 2005)—a difference formed from the patchwork of experiences that made those who made her who she is. Maia's past, and the pasts of her mother, grandmother, and great-grandmother, are present in her engagement with the items of clothing she purchases. Additionally, the items also hold their own histories of past use, and it is the combination of those histories and her experiential present where she is marked and marks herself as different. Lefebvre states that difference "exists socially only as something perceived, and yet is perceived as such only in relations that are at once reciprocal and extensive. It situates differential elements, derived from particularities and history" (2005: 115). Maia perceives her own difference through an evolving identity formed from the histories of the women outlined in this essay and the histories of the objects she buys.

The jacket to be discussed was purchased online via the Depop app. It is a heavy, dark brown, lightly padded, worn leather bomber jacket. The style resembles an American aviator G-1 jacket, previously known as the M-422A jacket, available to American fighter pilots since the 1940s and popularized in cinematic representations such as 1986's *Top Gun* (directed by Tony Scott).

When asked why she chose to purchase the jacket my daughter explained that it looked practical and warm; she also understood the popular culture references, but for her, it communicated something meaningful about an imagined past of the 1980s or 1990s, a form of anemoia, or nostalgia for a time outside direct experience. She was very pleased with the purchase and when it arrived, she carried out a meticulous process of familiarizing herself with the object, moving it about through her hands and fingers, trying it on, and, importantly for her, smelling it. Macindoe explains that,

> smell is a complex entanglement of the personal and the social. Whilst sensed by an individual body, it is inevitably social: communicated, negotiated, and invested with meaning through social relationships.

> 2018: 387

The smell of the jacket and my daughter's embodied response to it became a part of her constantly evolving identity formation. She formulated or breathed in a fictional memory of an-other (Sartre 2007: 230), fabricating an environment and significance from her sensory response to the object and creating a model of a real without an origin. In Baudrillard's terms, she manufactured the hyper-real for her own purposes and satisfaction (Baudrillard [1970] 1998).

This process opened up possibilities of who she might choose or grow to be, and how she would communicate this to others through dress. Sartre claims that the concept of what might be possible allows us to escape the contradictions of our existence (1968). Maia's existence is a contradiction, a tension of aggressive consciousness and oppression played out across her class and gender identity. Within such a fractious context, Lefebvre reasons: how can we not have recourse to the imaginary, the resurgence of the historical past, the evocative fiction of other lives and different things? (2005: 82, 83). In my role as mother, which has developed in response to my identity as daughter and imagined granddaughter, I hope that I might have at least crafted a space or place for her, where to challenge or transgress expected boundaries is normalized so that the privilege of creativity I hoped to impart can emerge (Lefebvre 2005). Hopefully she can feel free to create an identity of her own making, not fixed to rigid class and gender classification, to contest that which is imposed upon her and consciously and strategically claim the right to an empowered difference.

Conclusion

This piece of writing has attempted to draw together four intergenerational narratives to explore the experiences and identities of working-class women in relation to clothing, consumption, and dressing practices. The purpose has been to try and make visible the types of engagement with dress that sit at the margins of what is considered fashionable. Such engagement is explored through a lens that offers a personal connection to each of the narratives and claims an unapologetic position with regard to the subjective understandings and analysis presented.

The experiences and evolution of the working-class women in East London examined here demonstrate a familiar trajectory of social progress yet reinforce the continued oppressive presence and experience of social class as a factor for many within the UK. This work has attempted to present an account of the extremes and nuance of class position and how the systems of class speak to different generations.

The primary research undertaken here is personal and grounded by ethnographic interviews (although Eliza's thoughts and feelings are conspicuous in their absence). The writing speaks to the powerful connections between mothers and daughters and the notion of a utopia often omitted when discussing marginalized or classed experiences. Here, the utopian ideal refers to the threads that connect acceptance through difference, support through struggle, and understanding through sharing; I certainly understand my own mother's positions and motivations much more by sharing and articulating her experiences and negotiations with the internal injuries of both her class and her gender. Each of these utopian threads or concepts speak to the notion of "care" and are critical, now more than ever, as we find ourselves at a time of political, social, and cultural fracture. Perhaps an appropriate conclusion would be for us to look toward marginalized and oppressed groups, familial or not, for solutions, rather than continuing to offer a picture where such groups are presented as the problem to be solved.

References

Ashby, J. and A. Higson (2000), *British Cinema Past & Present*. London: Routledge.

Baudrillard, J. ([1970] 1998), *The Consumer Society: Myths and Structure*. London: Sage.

Baudrillard, J. ([1981] 1994), *Simulacra and Simulation*. Ann Arbor, MI: University of Michigan Press.

Brooks, A. (2015), *Clothing Poverty: The Hidden World of Fast Fashion & Second Hand Clothes*. London: Zed Books.

Bynder, H. (1969), "Emile Durkheim and the Sociology of the Family," *Journal of Marriage and Family*, 31 (3): 527–33.

Byrne, D. (2005), "Class, Culture and Identity: A Reflection on Absences Against Presences," *Sociology*, 39 (5): 807–16.

Casey, E. (2010), "Struggle and Protest or Passivity and Control? The Formation of Class Identity in Two Contemporary Cultural Practices," *European Journal of Cultural Studies* 13 (2): 225–41.

Connolly, N., eds. (2017), *Know Your Place: Essays on the Working Class by the Working Class*. Manchester: Dead Ink.

Forrest, D. (2017), "*Jimmy McGovern's The Street* and the Politics of Everyday Life," in D. Forrest and B. Johnson (eds.), *Social Class & Television Drama in Contemporary Britain*, 29–44. London: Palgrave Macmillan.

Haylett, C. (2001), "Illegitimate Subjects?: Abject Whites, Neoliberal Modernisation, and Middle Class Multiculturalism," *Environment and Planning D: Society and Space*, 19: 351–70.

Ilmonen, K. (2019), "Identity Politics Revisited: On Audrey Lorde, Intersectionality and Mobilising Writing Styles," *European Journal of Women's Studies*, 26 (1): 7–22.

Lawler, S. (2005a), "Disgusted Subjects: The Making of Middle Class Identities," *Sociological Review*, 53 (3): 429–46.

Lawler, S. (2005b), "Introduction: Class, Culture and Identity," *Sociology*, 39 (5): 797–806.

Lawler, S. (2008), *Identity: Sociological Perspectives*. Cambridge: Polity Press.

Lefebvre, H. ([1968] 2009), *The Explosion: Marxism and the French Upheaval*. New Delhi: Aakar Books.

Lefebvre, H. and G. Elliott, trans. (2005), *Critique of Everyday Life, Volume 3: From Modernity to Modernism: Towards a Metaphilosophy of Daily Life*. London: Verso.

Lorde, A. ([1984] 2007), *Sister Outsider*. London: Penguin.

Macindoe, J. (2018). "A Sense of Forgetting and Remembering: A Sense of Smell & Clothing," *Clothing Cultures*, 5 (3): 377–89.

Murdock, G. P. (1949), *Social Structure*.New York: Macmillan.

Palmer, A. and H. Clark (2005), *Old Clothes, New Looks: Second Hand Fashion*. Oxford and New York: Berg.

Parsons, T. (1959), "The Social Structure of the Family," in R. N. Anshen (ed.), *The Family: Its Functions and Destiny*. New York: Harper.

Reay, D. (2017), *Miseducation: Inequality, Education and the Working Classes*. Bristol: Policy Press.

Sartre, J. P. (1968), *Search for a Method*. London: Vintage.

Savage, J. (2015), *Social Class in the 21st Century*. London: Penguin.

Sayer, A. (2005), "Class, Moral Worth and Recognition," *Sociology*, 39 (5): 947–63.

Scoggins, J. and R. Winter (1999), "The Patchwork Text: A Coursework Format for Education as Critical Understanding," *Teaching in Higher Education: Critical Perspectives*, 4 (4): 485–99.

Sennett, R. and J. Cobb (1972), *The Hidden Injuries of Class*. New York: Norton & Co.

Skeggs, B. (2004), *Class, Self, Culture*. London: Routledge.

Skeggs, B. (2005), "The Making of Class and Gender through Visualizing Moral Subject Formation," *Sociology*, 39 (5): 965–82.

Veblen, T. ([1899] 1994), *The Theory of the Leisure Class*. New York: Dover.

Walkerdine, V., H. Lucey, and J. Melody (2001), *Growing Up Girl: Psychosocial Explorations of Gender and Class*. London: Palgrave.

Williamson, J., H. Beynon, and S. Rowbotham (2001), "Changing Images," in S. Rowbotham and H. Beynon (eds.), *Looking at Class: Film, Television, and the Working Class in Britain*, 99–115. London and New York: Rivers Oram Press; and New York: New York University Press.

APPENDIX

Sexy Mamas

Liz Lange and the Golden Age of Designing for Pregnancy

Pamela Roskin

In the 1990s, a paradigm shift occurred in maternity dressing, at the helm of which was fashion designer Liz Lange. Under her leadership, clothing for pregnancy changed both in silhouette and in concept. Lange's tenure as a maternity fashion designer provides evidence of Caroline Evans and Minna Thornton's claim that the "cultural conception of the feminine is capable of being both reproduced and changed through dress" (1991).

It can be hard to imagine now, but before Lange emerged in the late 1990s, maternity fashion was considered a "contradiction in terms" (Gault 1998), meaning that the designation "fashion" barely applied to this category of dress. Lange turned maternity wear from "frumpy to chic," in Gault's words. Gone were the Princess Diana ruffles, replaced with "clingier, bulge-hugging" items that became bestsellers, such as the tube top (Stapinski 1999). But it wasn't just the clothing that changed: the very notion of pregnancy, and ultimately motherhood, had changed. It was during this period that sociologists Susan Douglas and Meredith Michaels coined the term "the new momism"—a notion of motherhood as equal parts romantic, sexy, devoted, and vaguely feminist (2004). The "new momism" was aspirational and had a veneer of celebrity cachet—the perfect fodder for glossy magazines. As style writer Helene Stapinski noted at the time, "Pregnant is sexy. Pregnant is hot" (1999).

Lange launched her New York City fashion brand in 1998 for expectant women with an understanding of the American cultural zeitgeist—this was after the Annie Leibovitz-Demi Moore pregnancy photos, the Dan Quayle "Murphy Brown" speech, and heated discussions nationwide about paid maternity leave. She saw a shift in not only how women dressed while pregnant but also how they were perceived and, perhaps more importantly, how they specifically *chose* to be perceived.

Below are extracts from an interview with Liz Lange that took place on February 5, 2020 in New York City about the launch of her line:

A lot of people think I created my line because I was pregnant. I wasn't pregnant. In 1997, maternity clothing was 1,000 percent oversized, juvenile looking. It blurred the line between the baby you were delivering and you. It was full of babyish details like Peter Pan collars and bows. You didn't feel like yourself when you were pregnant.

Clothing is a statement. It is awful to be wearing something you don't feel comfortable in. And I asked myself, "why can't maternity clothing look like the clothing you wear all the time?"

When I launched, I got a crazy amount of press. It was at the time that mothers became a focus. *Mommyhood* became a focus. When a celebrity is seen wearing something, it'll sell out. I saw that as an opportunity. I would read *Page Six* to see which celebrity was pregnant and I would reach out to their publicist. I had my pick of the litter. It shouldn't have been that easy.

My clothes were different because they were tight, they were sexy. I don't have an archive but if you saw what I was designing, by today's standards the clothes would be considered loose and not sexy but from where we were before, the pieces were seen as really form fitting.

I wasn't looking for an idea. I started very small. Everything was made to order. I used the fashion index, local factories.[1] I called them up: "If I fax you an order will you make them for me?" There was a two-week turnaround time. Women would just call me with their order and I'd have it made for them. It made sense to me not to keep any inventory. I couldn't believe the response. A princess in Saudi Arabia ordered from me! I was so surprised by how desperate women were for clothes that they *liked* while pregnant.

I don't have a political ax to grind. I'm not a feminist. I am pro-fashion. I just saw an opening. I knew women were meant to look good while pregnant. Today it's gone too far—the sexy pregnancy. Women feel scared of social media pressure for perfect motherhood. That doesn't exist.

I wasn't going to advertise in baby magazines. Only in fashion magazines. Mothers second, women first.

I invest in other companies now but I don't mind that this is what I'm known for, what I'll always be known for: the queen of maternity wear.

Notes

1 Lange is referring to an index of local manufacturers provided to her by New York City's Garment District Business Improvement District.

References

Douglas, S. J. and M. W. Michaels (2004), *The Mommy Myth: The Idealization of Motherhood and How it Has Undermined Women.* New York: Free Press.

Evans, C. and M. Thornton (1991), "Fashion, Representation, Femininity," *Feminist Review*, 38 (1): 48–66. Doi: 10.1057/fr.1991.19.

Gault, Y. (1998), "Not Frumpy but Chic: Retailers Cater to Stylish Expectant Set," *Crain's New York Business*, June 22.

Stapinski, H. (1999), "Pregnant Women Turn Me's Heads: Feeling Big, Ugly and Decidedly Unsexy? Don't. Guys Dig Expecting Gals," *Hamilton Spectator*, October 26.

Contributors

Liza Betts is Lecturer and Researcher in the Cultural & Historical Studies Department of the London College of Fashion at the University of the Arts London, UK. She also works at Kingston University, is an external examiner at the University for the Creative Arts, Farnham, Surrey, UK, a member of the Performing Dress Lab, and co-creator of a creative arts "Solidarity Space," an online space for working-class academics. Liza is a continuing PhD candidate whose research integrates both theory and ethnographic research around creative practice. In 2022, she published "HBO's Euphoria and the Complexities at Play in the Costumed Representations of Contemporary Masculinities," in *Film, Fashion & Consumption*.

Karen Case is one of the founders of the Doctoral Program in Educational Leadership at the University of Hartford, West Hartford, Connecticut, USA. She has been a librarian, middle school teacher, and Peace Corps volunteer. Karen lives in the woods, 2.3 miles from her two adored grandchildren. Among her publications are: "Almira and Me: Remembering the Maternalist Roots of Almira Lincoln Phelps," in Olivia Ungar, Rebecca Jaremko Bromwich, Noemia Richards, Melanie Younger, and Maryellen Symons (eds.), *Environmental Activism and the Maternal: Mothers and Mother Earth in Activism and Discourse* (2020); and co-authored with Julie Sochacki, "Compassionate Pedagogy: A Narrative Based Curriculum for Undergraduates Who are Refugees," in Thomas DeVere Wolsey and Ibrahim Karkouti (eds.), *Teaching Refugees and Displaced Students: What Every Educator Should Know* (forthcoming).

Morolake Dairo is a researcher at the School of Media and Communication, Pan-Atlantic University, Lagos, Nigeria, by night. By day, Morolake works as a marketing communication professional in the Nigerian FINTECH space. Her doctoral thesis explores the concept of city branding and how it relates to fashion cities. Morolake has published, "User-Generated Content (UGC) and Fashion Media: A Study of *Asoebibella* in Nigeria," in *Fashion Studies* (2022).

Lauren Downing Peters is Assistant Professor of Fashion Studies and Director of the Fashion Study Collection at Columbia College Chicago, Illinois, USA. She is the author of *Fashion Before Plus-Size: Bodies, Bias and the Birth of an Industry* (2023) and the co-editor with Hazel Clark of *Fashion in American Life* (2024).

Sarah Garland is Associate Professor of Writing and Visual Culture at the University of East Anglia, Norwich, UK. Her research works at the intersection of word and image across twentieth-century experimental and popular forms. Her research also takes in the everyday arts—dress, interiors, food, non-professional writing, and painting—and asks about the role of aesthetic practice in everyday life.

Holly M. Kent is Associate Professor of History at the University of Illinois Springfield, Illinois, USA. She is the author of *Her Voice Will Be on the Side of Right: Gender and Power in Antebellum Antislavery Fiction* (2017) and the editor of *Teaching Fashion Studies* (2018). She teaches courses on US women's history.

Kimberly Lamm is Associate Professor of Gender, Sexuality, and Feminist Studies at Duke University, North Carolina, USA. She is the author of *Addressing the Other Woman: Textual Correspondences in Feminist Art and Writing* (2018). Her research, which has appeared in journals such as *Women's Studies Quarterly*, *Feminist Theory*, and *Oxford Art Journal*, brings psychoanalytic feminism to bear on the study of US and Anglophone literature, film, and visual culture.

Maureen Lehto Brewster is a PhD candidate in International Merchandising at the University of Georgia, Athens, Georgia, USA. She previously obtained an MA in Fashion Studies at Parsons School of Design, The New School, New York, USA. Her research focuses on fashion history and theory, celebrity culture, social media, race, and gender. Among Maureen's publications is, "Making Lemonade? Beyoncé's Pregnancies and the Postfeminist Media Gaze," in Morna Laing and Jacki Willson (eds.), *Revisiting the Gaze: The Fashioned Body and the Politics of Looking* (2020). You can follow her on TikTok and Twitter at @culturescholar, and on Instagram at @soldbycelebs.

Pui-sze Leung obtained her MA from the Department of Sociology, Goldsmiths, University of London, UK. She is particularly interested in cities, fashions, and visual culture. She has experience in the fashion industry and publishing sector. This is Pui-sze's first publication.

Darnell-Jamal Lisby is the Assistant Curator of Fashion for the Cleveland Museum of Art, Cleveland, Ohio, USA, and the institution's first fashion curator, encompassing a mandate linking the institution's collections through fashion. His career comprises writing for various mainstream and academic publications, teaching, and consulting fashion curatorial and academic efforts at various institutions worldwide. He has published, "Jay Jaxon: An Unsung Couturier," in Elizabeth Way (ed.), *Black Designers in American Fashion* (2021).

Indira Jalli teaches Cultural Studies at the Indian Institute of Technology in Hyderabad, South India. Her fields of interest include film and gender. Indira published, "Caste[ing] Gender: Caste and Gender in Ancient Indian Jurisprudence," in Julius O Adekunle, and Hattie V Williams (eds.), *Color Struck: Essays on Race and Ethnicity in Global Perspective* (2010) and "Body and its Fringes: Beauty as a Genre in Arcitecting the Nation," in Martin Doll and Oliver Khons (eds.), *Figurationen des Politischen 1 und 11* (2016).

Christina Moon is an anthropologist by training and Assistant Professor of Fashion Studies in the School of Art and Design History and Theory at Parsons School of Design, The New School, New York, USA. Among Christina's publications are *Labor and Creativity in New York's Global Fashion Industry* (2020) and "Fashion City: Diasporic Connections and Garment Industrial Histories between the US and Asia," in *Critical Sociology* (2018).

Katrina Orsini is the programs associate at the George Washington University Museum and the Textile Museum, Washington, DC, USA. She was a Smithsonian Fellow at the Cooper Hewitt, Smithsonian Design Museum, New York, where she split her time between the Textile and Education departments. Her research focuses on the connection between pregnancy, obstetric and gynecological design and reproductive justice, and "sustainable" fashion and biotextiles. Among Katrina's publications are "Turning Viability on its Head," *DAMN Magazine* (2022) and "Speculative Design for a Better Pregnancy," *OBJECTIVE* (2021).

Pamela Roskin is part-time Assistant Professor at Parsons School of Design, The New School, New York, USA. She has an MA in fashion and textile studies.

Among her publications is, "Alex Katz and American Fashion," in *Fashion Studies Journal* (2016).

Claire Salmon is a fashion historian whose studies focus on women, lingerie, and their historical relationship. She completed her BFA at Parsons School of Design , The New School, New York, USA, and her MA at the Royal College of Art in London, UK. She has worked at the Victoria & Albert Museum, Christie's, and Kerry Taylor Auctions. This is Claire's first publicatioin.

Laura Snelgrove is the Editor in Chief of the *Fashion Studies Journal* and an independent fashion scholar. She has taught at Parsons School of Design, The New School, New York, USA, and the Université du Québec à Montréal, Canada, contributed to academic and popular journals and books, and presented research across North America and the UK. Among Laura's publications is, "Experiencing the Clothed Body in Public Space," in Holly M. Kent (ed.), *Teaching Fashion Studies* (2018). This is her first edited volume.

Kin-long Tong is a PhD student at the Department of Information Studies, University College London, UK. His research has been published in academic journals, such as *International Journal of Heritage Studies* and *Sociological Forum*. He is interested in information politics, such as publishing and archival culture in authoritarian and (post)colonial contexts.

Index